THE SOUTH WEST COAST PATH

About the Author

Paddy Dillon is a prolific outdoor writer with a score and more books to his name, as well as a dozen booklets and brochures. He writes for a number of outdoor magazines and other publications, as well as producing materials for tourism groups and other organisations. He lives on the fringe of the Lake District, and has walked, and written about walking, in every county in England, Scotland, Ireland and Wales. He generally leads at least one guided walking holiday overseas every year and has walked in many parts of Europe, as well as Nepal, Tibet and the Canadian Rockies.

While walking his routes, Paddy inputs his notes directly into a palm-top computer every few steps. His descriptions are therefore precise, having been written at the very point at which the reader uses them. He takes all his own photographs and often draws his own maps to illustrate his routes. He has appeared on television, and is a member of the Outdoor Writers' Guild.

Cicerone guides by Paddy Dillon:

Irish Coastal Walks
The Irish Coast to Coast
The Mountains of Ireland
Channel Island Walks
Walking in the Isles of Scilly
Walking in the Isle of Arran

Walking the Galloway Hills
Walking in County Durham
Walking the North Pennines
GR20 Corsica: High Level Route
Walking in the Canaries Vol. 1 West
Walking in the Canaries Vol. 2 East

THE SOUTH WEST COAST PATH

by
Paddy Dillon

2 POLICE SQUARE, MILNTHORPE, CUMBRIA, LA7 7PY
www.cicerone.co.uk

© Paddy Dillon 2003
A catalogue record for this book is available from the British Library.
ISBN 1 85284 379 9

Advice to Readers

Readers are advised that while every effort is taken by the author to ensure the accuracy of this guidebook, changes can occur which may affect the contents. It is advisable to check locally on transport, accommodation, shops, etc, but even right of way can be altered.

The publisher would welcome notes of any such changes.

Front cover: View across Pendour Cove near Zennor to distant Gurnard's Head on Day 18

CONTENTS

INTRODUCTION

The South West Coast Path is Britain's longest waymarked trail, measuring a staggering 1015km (630.5 miles). It is not just a long walk, but an astounding and varied experience. This remarkable and continuous coastal trail is based on the paths trodden around the cliffs and coves by generations of coastguards. The route starts in Minehead on the Somerset coast and quickly moves along the North Devon coast. After completely encircling the coast of Cornwall, it continues along the South Devon coast. A final stretch along the Dorset coast leads to a conclusion at South Haven Point on Poole Harbour. No other stretch of British coastline compares for scenic splendour, interest, history, heritage, accessibility

A view back along the roller-coaster route close to Port Gaverne on Day 11

and provision of facilities all rolled into one.

It would take a fit and dedicated long-distance walker a month to walk the South West Coast Path, while others would be happy to enjoy the experience, savour the delights of the trail, and take anything up to two months or more to cover the distance. Hardy backpackers will happily carry a tent, sleeping bag and cooking equipment, while others prefer to mix youth hostels with bed-and-breakfast establishments. Some walkers prefer a luxurious approach, spending their nights in splendid hotels and sampling seafood menus. The South West Coast Path can accommodate all types, but bear in mind that many of the facilities are only open through the summer season.

Individual approaches are bound to vary. Some walkers crave to cover the whole trail in a single expedition, while others take a weekend here and there, and make an occasional week-long trip, to complete the distance over a year or two. You must walk within your limitations; covering distances that are comfortable for you; choosing accommodation that suits your tastes and pocket. Allow time to visit museums and heritage centres, if you have a passion for local history, or to observe birds along the cliff coasts if you are interested in wildlife. Given the nature and complexity of the coast, it makes sense not to rush, but to enjoy the experience to the full.

While some might be daunted at the prospect of walking for weeks on end, staying somewhere different every night, and keeping themselves fed and watered, it is simply a matter of careful planning. Almost every town and village along the way offers some kind of accommodation and refreshment, and you just need to know what is available in advance.

This guidebook describes the

Looking back at rocky stacks and islets on the way to Hell's Mouth on Day 17

whole of the waymarked trail from Minehead to Poole, and indicates the level of services along the way. The route is well marked with 'Coast Path' signposts and standard National Trail 'acorn' symbols. Read about each section before setting out; you may, for example, need to ensure that ferries are running across awkward tidal rivers, or secure accommodation in advance in summer, or you might like to know if the next sandy cove has a beach café. You should be able to break the route into manageable portions to suit your own ability. There is no need to stick slavishly to the daily breakdown given here, as there are plenty of intermediate places where you could break the journey.

A little cove beside the Helford River on the way to the Helford Ferry on Day 24

COASTAL WALKING THROUGH HISTORY

Man has been active along Britain's coasts since Neolithic times. The earliest settlers were basically hunter-gatherers who lived in the valleys and on the coastal margins, most of the inland country being heavily forested wilderness. These early people may have initiated a network of vague paths along the coast; maybe, just maybe, you will walk partly in their footsteps. Bronze Age fortifications and Iron Age cliff castles along the coasts of the South West signify a certain level of social unrest and warfare as waves of settlers made their way to these shores from Europe. In more peaceful inter-ludes, settlers would surely have trodden the cliff paths.

Fishing and seafaring have always been important activities around the coast. There are dozens of natural sheltered harbours with deep-water channels; villages and towns grew up around these, and fortifications were built to afford them protection from raiders. A lookout for unfamiliar and dangerous vessels would have been kept from the clifftops. Some fisher-men also manned clifftop lookouts to spot shoals of pilchards, mackerel or herrings, and would raise a 'hue' to let their comrades know where to make a good catch.

Fishermen and sailors were ideally positioned for wheeler-dealing with foreign vessels, and when heavy duties were slapped onto imported goods early in the 18th century, they used their intimate knowledge of the coastline to land all manner of goods at remote spots. The government responded by administering harsh penalties and punishments for smuggling; smugglers simply became more devious, resulting in the establishment of the Coastguard Service in 1822.

Coastguards were stationed at intervals along the coast to patrol the cliffs and coves, keep an eye on any suspicious activities, and clamp down on the smuggling trade. They tramped back and forth along their coastal beats, treading out clear paths with unrivalled views of the rugged coast. The continuous coastal path largely came into being from that time.

As the coastguards were suppressing an illegal activity that local people felt was important to

The Devil's Frying Pan is a deep hole passed on the way to Cadgwith on Day 23

their survival, they were most unwelcome. It was almost impossible to procure accommodation for them, so they were obliged to live in specially constructed coastguard cottages, many of which were well away from towns and villages. Even after renovation into holiday homes, some coastguard cottages still resemble military barracks. Over the years, coastguards became less involved in tracking down smugglers, and switched to scanning the seas to ensure the safety of passing ships. Often they were stationed in lonely lookouts on prominent headlands, with binoculars, telescope and notepad. Eventually the Coastguard Service became administered centrally, using radio, radar and computers.

The old coastguard lookouts are beginning to be reopened by the National Coastwatch Institution, a charity made up of volunteers who are taking on the role of the former coastguards. They keep an eye on shipping, and also on Coast Path walkers, and are recognised as an important part of the emergency cover network along the coast.

Today use of the Coast Path is rather different. Almost everyone who walks on the path today does so for exercise and enjoyment. Ramblers may walk from one town or village to the next, while long-distance walkers simply keep plodding day after day while the infinite variety of the route unfolds before them: beaches and bays; cliffs and coves; sea stacks and sand dunes; fishing villages and holiday resorts. With all its ups and downs and ins and outs, the route is often like a monstrous roller-coaster and leads walkers through history and heritage, scenic splendour and the wonders of the natural world. It has been estimated that anyone completing the whole trail will climb three times the height of Mount Everest!

Many towns and villages along the South West Coast Path have fine little museums or heritage centres, with fishing and smuggling being oft-repeated themes. Visit them to obtain a clearer picture of local history.

Walkers turn around a rock ledge cut into the flanks of Sharp Tor on Day 33

Name that beast on the way to the National Marine Aquarium!

A PROTECTED COASTLINE

The South West Coast may have been spoiled in a few places by industry and inappropriate development, but for the most part it is cherished and protected. The Exmoor National Park covers the early stages, and much of the coast of North Devon, Cornwall, South Devon, East Devon and Dorset is designated as Areas of Outstanding Natural Beauty. The last long stretch of coast has been designated as England's first Natural World Heritage Site: the 'Jurassic Coast'. Long stretches of coast are Heritage Coasts, while smaller areas may be protected as National Nature Reserves, Local Nature Reserves or Sites of Special Scientific Interest. The National Trust own and manage considerable stretches of the coast, some of it acquired during the 'Operation Neptune' campaign, which enabled some significant sections to be purchased.

TRAVEL TO THE SOUTH WEST

By Air: The main regional airports are Bristol and Exeter; although a fair distance from the start of the Coast Path, these may suit those who have to travel from the furthest reaches of Britain, or who are coming from overseas. There are also direct daily flights to Newquay in Cornwall from London Gatwick and London Stanstead airports.

By Train: Virgin Trains travel from Scotland, through Northern England and the Midlands to feed into the South West of England. The celebrated Cornish Scot service can be used to reach Taunton, from where there are regular buses to Minehead. If you are walking the Coast Path in stages, the same train can get you to all points down the main line to Penzance. Change onto local Wessex Trains to travel the branch lines and reach the coastal railway stations at Barnstaple, Newquay, St Ives, Falmouth, Looe, Torquay and Exmouth. Virgin Trains Wessex Scot runs from Poole and Bournemouth to Scotland. Other main line services include Great Western trains from London Paddington to Penzance, also with the option of changing onto local trains to reach the coast. South West Trains run from Weymouth, Poole and Bournemouth back to London Waterloo at the end of the walk. Rail services can be checked by phoning 08457-484950.

By Bus: Most towns have National Express offices or agents, and most

Tourist Information Centres have details of services. National Express buses serve a number of towns, including Taunton, Barnstaple, Bideford, Westward Ho!, Newquay, Perranporth, Hayle, St Ives, Penzance, Falmouth, St Austell, Plymouth, Brixton, Paignton, Torquay, Teignmouth, Dawlish, Bridport, Weymouth, Swanage, Poole and Bournemouth. While you may have to

The power of nature and the forces that shape the landscape are evident

change two or three times en route, there are some useful long-haul services to the South West. These include Edinburgh/Glasgow to Penzance, Newcastle to Plymouth, Grimsby to Westward Ho!, Liverpool to Weymouth, Eastbourne to Falmouth, and services from London to places such as Swanage, Plymouth, Newquay and Penzance. Bear in mind that there are seasonal variations on some services. Details can be checked by phoning 08705-808080.

GETTING AROUND THE SOUTH WEST

By Train: Rail services in the South West consist of branch lines from the main line, with Wessex Trains being the main operator. The West Somerset Railway offers seasonal steam-hauled services to Minehead, but doesn't connect with main line services at Taunton, though there are bus links. The only coastal railway station in North Devon is at Barnstaple. Coastal stations around Cornwall include Newquay, Hayle, St Ives, Penzance, Falmouth, Par and Looe. Stations on the South Devon Coast include Plymouth, the steam-hauled Paignton & Dartmouth Railway, Torquay, Teignmouth, Dawlish, Dawlish Warren, Starcross and Exmouth. Stations on the Dorset Coast include Weymouth, Poole and Bournemouth. Steam-hauled services at Swanage do not connect with the rest of the rail network.

Looking back along Kenneggy Sands after passing Prussia Cove on Day 21

Looking along the Coast Path from Zone Point to Porthmellin Head on Day 25

By Bus: Walkers who plan to break their journey and cover the South West Coast Path in several stages may need to use local bus services. With careful reference to timetables, walkers could choose a handy base and 'commute' to and from sections of the Coast Path. Most bus services in the South West are operated by the big bus company called 'First', though there are areas with other operators.

It's a good idea to get hold of the *Public Transport Map & Guides* produced by Devon County Council, Cornwall County Council and Dorset County Council. These are widely available in Tourist Information Centres. When you need to check a specific service, full contact details are available in these publications, or you can phone Traveline, whose details are below.

The two most important services are the regular buses from Taunton station to Minehead when you start the walk, and from Sandbanks to Poole or Bournemouth when you finish. Throughout this guidebook, places with bus services are mentioned, with some indication of onward or backward connections along the coast, but do enquire further if you need specific timetable information; this is often subject to change, and some areas are only served by buses during the peak summer season.

Ferries: Although the South West Coast Path is presented as a continuous walk, it is actually broken into a number of stretches by several long, narrow, tidal rivers, especially on the southern stages. You need to use ferries, and since these are part of the South West Coast Path experience shouldn't be seen as 'cheating'. If the urge seizes you, you can walk around the estuaries, but this will take you away from the coast, and it may take

15

The view from the rugged slopes at Freathy to distant Rame Head on Day 30

anything from several hours to a few days to reach a point that can be reached by ferry in a matter of minutes.

Be warned that while some ferry services operate all year round, others are seasonal or irregular, being subject to tidal and weather conditions. In the peak summer months of June, July and August, all ferries will be operational. Others may run from May to September, or Easter to October. Anyone walking during the winter months will find some ferries absent. In this guidebook, contact numbers are given for the ferries, with some indication of the level of service

you can expect. For regular, all-year-round ferries, it is sufficient to turn up and catch one on a whim. A few ferries should be checked in advance or your walk may grind to a halt on a lonely shore.

Traveline & Taxis: The easiest way to check the current availability of any train, bus or ferry is to phone Traveline on 0870-6082608. Give them your requirements and they will find the right services and connections. If you need a taxi at any point, phone the National Taxi Hotline free on 0800-654321. This will put you in touch with the nearest taxi operator in the scheme and you can negotiate your trip and check the price straight away.

TIME & TIDE

The old proverb states that 'time and tide wait for no man', and this is true on the South West Coast Path. Carry a copy of the tide tables (widely available in shops and Tourist Information Centres) or check the tide times at regular intervals and keep a note of high and low water. You are warned against walking along beaches at the foot of cliffs when there is a danger of being cut off by the rising tide, and against wading across tidal channels, which are often dangerous and unpredictable. However, you will have to wade across the tidal River Erme (or face a long walk around in search of a bridge). The South West Coast Path is rarely routed along beaches, but it is always a good idea to be aware of the tides and not be caught unawares. High tides backed by gale-force winds can lead to some lower coastal paths being overwhelmed and even sea defences can be breached.

ACCOMMODATION

There is abundant accommodation around the South West Coast Path, but you need to think carefully a day or two in advance to be sure you aren't left without a roof over your head. There are long and difficult stretches of coast that seem remote from habitation, and some places where lodgings are restricted to only one or two addresses. Even in the big towns and resorts, it can be difficult to obtain a bed for the night in the peak season. If you are persistent, however, you will always be able to find something.

Nare Head seen in the distance from a point before Pendower Beach on Day 25

Splendid and rugged scenery unfolds along the Coast Path day after day

Backpacking: If you are prepared to carry all your gear, backpacking is a great option. You can walk with a high degree of freedom: setting off at dawn, walking until dusk, generally pleasing yourself. If you want to use campsites, there are several marked on OS maps, and a few more besides. However, some sites are geared for long stays, or for large family tents. The Camping & Caravanning Club produces *Your Big Sites Book*, designed to be used with OS maps, and crammed with grid references and full details of every site. Although you should always ask permission to pitch your tent, some

walkers do camp wild, unobtrusively, leaving no evidence of their overnight stay. It is better to ask politely for permission to camp, and offer to pay, rather than find yourself thrown off a property for not asking!

Youth hostelling: There are around 20 youth hostels on or within easy walking distance of the Coast Path, not enough to walk from one to the other without falling back on other types of accommodation. Hostellers will either need to carry a tent (if they wish to walk within a low budget) or seek bed-and-breakfast accommodation. Youth hostels are marked on OS maps, and full details can be checked with the latest *Youth Hostel Association Handbook*. There are also a couple of independent backpacker's hostels that might also prove useful.

Bed-and-Breakfast: Walkers who want to travel lightweight and enjoy a bit of luxury can consider using B&Bs, guest houses and even hotels. These are available at regular intervals, though in irregular concentrations. Be aware that not every establishment wants someone staying for one night only; many of them prefer weekend or week-long bookings. Some accommodation providers are well used to dealing with walkers, and may be prepared to collect you, drop you off, or even move your luggage on to the next place you have booked. There is usually a charge for these useful extra services.

Block bookings: If you book all your accommodation for the duration of your long trek in advance, you may regret it later. Bad weather, fatigue or injury can prevent you covering the distance to your next lodging, and trying to unwind arrangements can become a nightmare. Outside the peak summer season you should be able to book two or three days ahead, then book another night or two in advance, based around your performance on the trail. The South West Coast Path Association, whose contact details are noted below, produces a good accommodation list. Walkers

recommend many of the addresses, so there is a good chance that you will be very well looked after.

Book a Bed Ahead: You can save yourself time and frustration by visiting a Tourist Information Centre and asking them make a booking for you, even for two or three days ahead. Let them have your requirements, then retire for a cream tea and pop back after half an hour to see how they fared. They typically charge you 10 per cent of the cost of your overnight, but that will be deducted from your bill by the proprietor. In effect the service is free, and it saves you time and money. The 'Book a Bed Ahead' system is known as 'BABA' in the trade.

Warning: If for any reason you fail to reach a place you have booked, please contact them and cancel. This may seem like a mere courtesy detail, but when you make a booking you are also entering into a contract with the accommodation provider. If they hold your booking and you fail to show, they may turn away other prospective clients, thereby losing money. They are entitled to make a claim against

Accommodation, food and drink are generally easy to find in the summer

Cosy fishing harbours abound, though many have switched to tourism

you. Worse than that, they might alert the rescue services, who could spend a long time looking for you when you are safely tucked up in bed elsewhere!

FOOD & DRINK

In the peak summer season there is no shortage of food and drink along the South West Coast Path. In fact, many backpackers begin to regret packing all their cooking equipment as they walk past frequent offers of pasty and chips and cream teas. All the towns have an abundance of pubs and restaurants, and many small villages may have a couple of pubs and cafés. However, it is always well to know which villages don't have these services, as well as which beaches are likely to have a café. Throughout this guidebook, pubs, restaurants, cafés and shops are noted in passing. Bear in mind that in the

winter months many places close. Refreshments can seem grossly over-priced at some beach cafés, but remember that you are paying for the convenience – and taking your custom elsewhere can result in half a day's walk!

MONEY

If you are going to be away from home for weeks you either need to carry lots of money or have access to funds along the way. Most upmarket accommodation providers and restaurants will take a credit card, but most run-of-the-mill places will want cash. There are banks at irregular intervals, and most of them have ATMs. Banks in towns along the way are noted in this guidebook. Post offices are also mentioned, which could be useful if you have a Girobank account. A few supermarkets may have cash dispensers in-store, or offer a 'cash back' service. A seven-week backpacking tour might just be completed on a budget of a couple of hundred pounds, while seven weeks of staying in hotels and eating splendid meals might easily run to several thousand pounds!

Cliffs and coastlines have inherent dangers, whether obvious or not...

TOURIST INFORMATION CENTRES

There are nearly 30 Tourist Information Offices either on the Coast Path or a short distance from it. They contain a wealth of local information and the staff are usually very knowledgeable. Best of all, you can use their offices to book accommodation. They always have a good idea who will have accommodation available in town. Full contact details are given for Tourist Information Centres on the Coast Path.

RESCUE SERVICES

Rescue services can be alerted by dialling 999 from any telephone. On some popular beaches there may be a phone dedicated as an emergency line. The police, ambulance and fire service can all be contacted, as well as the coastguard and lifeboat service if necessary. You cannot call for a helicopter to effect a rescue, but based on the information you provide, one of the emergency services may request a helicopter to assist. Always give as much information as possible, espe-

cially as to the location and nature of an accident, then await further instructions. Walkers don't often suffer accidents on the Coast Path, but it makes sense to walk with care near cliff edges and always be on the lookout for unstable edges, landslips and rockfalls. Tread carefully on steep and uneven paths. Walkers who want to go swimming should read the warning notices posted at most popular beaches. In out-of-the-way places don't go swimming without a good understanding of the nature of the sea. Always check the weather forecast and be on the lookout for heavy rain or strong winds, which can make walking difficult and even dangerous.

WHEN TO WALK

For most people, the biggest hurdle can be finding the time to complete the whole of the South West Coast Path in a single trek. You need to be able to put your home life on hold for several weeks, maybe taking leave of absence from work, or wait until you retire! Ask yourself how serious you are about completing the whole trail, and whether you are equal to the task. Maybe it would be better to spread the journey over three or four trips of a fortnight or so, judiciously planned to give you a taste of all four seasons along the Coast Path. At the end of the day, it is your walk to be completed in the way you see fit.

All the services along the South West Coast Path are in full swing during July and August, but that can be a stressful time to walk. Days can be hot and humid; crowds of people mill around towns and villages; while accommodation for one night can prove difficult to obtain. Walking in May and June or September and October can be cooler without being too cold and wet. The crowds will be much reduced, though some areas will still be busy. Accommodation is easier to obtain for the night, while most places offering food and drink are still open. However, not everything will be open, and some beach cafés may be closed early or late in the season. Keep a careful check on the smaller seasonal ferries, as one or two may not be operating.

Walkers who attempt the South West Coast Path from late October to early April must expect many places to be closed, and some ferries to be absent. Winter weather can be milder than in other parts of Britain, with snowfall very rare, but it can still be cold and wet. Winter gales can be ferocious! Some places may flare into life over the Easter period, but close for a spell immediately afterwards. Winter walkers will need their wits

about them to be able to complete the trail successfully.

ONE MAN AND HIS DOG

Maybe you were inspired by *500 Mile Walkies,* by Mark Wallington, who took his dog Boogie around the South West Coast Path, or maybe your dog always goes with you on long walks. Please bear in mind that many beaches have a 'dog ban' during the summer months, and there are many fields near cliff edges where sheep and cattle graze, where a dog may cause them to run into danger. Local people will walk their dogs along daily beats, and some dogs can become aggressively territorial and resent the approach of another dog. Walkers with dogs may find that some accommodation providers won't accept them, and some pubs and restaurants won't allow dogs on the

Some stretches of the South West Coast Path seem remote from habitation

Remember that this is not an extended beach walk, but a long, long trail

premises. Think carefully before committing yourself to such a long walk with man's best friend.

DAILY SCHEDULE

It is entirely up to you how far you want to walk each day. The daily breakdown given in this book is based on a 45-day trek, but you can allow more days by splitting some of the longer stages into two days, or you can double up a couple of stages, though at the risk of wearing yourself out. The daily average is 22.5km (14 miles), generally in the range from 18 to 28km (11.5 to 17.5 miles). The longest day is 38km (23.5 miles) but this is also mostly easy and level, and can still be split into two if desired. The shortest day is 12km (7.5 miles), which happens to be the last one. Alter and adapt the schedule to suit

your own needs and preferences, aiming for something that doesn't leave you wrecked!

Note that the daily stages are not only of uneven length, but some days are fairly easy and others may be very difficult. Be sure to read each day's description carefully before committing yourself, taking note of steep ascents or descents, seasonal ferries, absence of food, drink and accommodation, or anything that might affect your rate of progress. Keep an eye on the weather forecast and tide tables. Sometimes you might be walking into driving rain, which can be debilitating. Strong winds on clifftops can be very dangerous. Prolonged wet weather makes paths muddy and slippery, while long, wet vegetation leaves legs completely sodden.

Despite all your planning, you may find yourself running out of time

The view along the chalk-cliff coast from Bat's Head to Lulworth on Day 43

towards the end. This isn't too bad if you are only short of one or two days. You could skip the one-day circuit around the Isle of Portland, (regrettably, because it is an excellent walk) but still feel that you were staying faithful to the coast. There is also an 'Inland Coast Path' across the Dorset downs, enabling you to keep an eye on the sea while omitting Weymouth and the Isle of Portland altogether. It might just give you the time you need to reach the end of the Coast Path on schedule. Other types of short-cutting may smack of 'cheating', but at the end of the day it is your walk and your walk alone!

MAPS OF THE ROUTE

The maps included in this guidebook are extracted from the 1:50,000 Ordnance Survey Landranger Series. They run from page to page to cover the whole of the South West Coast Path in strip form. If you wish to see the greater picture – more of the Coast Path at a glance, as well as more of the inland terrain – then a dozen Landranger sheets cover the entire route: 180, 181, 190, 192, 193, 194, 195, 200, 201, 202, 203 & 204. If you are in the habit of posting completed maps home at intervals, please note that you will need to refer to sheet 200 twice as its coverage runs from coast to coast!

For more detail, use the 1:25,000 Outdoor Leisure and Explorer Series. For full coverage of the South West Coast Path you need 13 Explorer sheets and three Outdoor Leisure sheets. The Explorers are: 102, 103, 104, 105, 106, 107, 108, 110, 111, 115, 116, 126 & 139. The Outdoor Leisure sheets are: 9, 15 & 20. The appropriate Landranger, Explorer and Outdoor Leisure sheets are quoted for each of the daily stages in this guidebook.

The South West Coast Path is waymarked, but route-finding is still important

Golden Cap is the highest point on the south coast at 191m (627ft) on Day 39

To see practically the whole of the South West Coast Path on a single map, refer to the Ordnance Survey Road Map sheet 7. This could be a very useful overall planning map, especially if you are walking the whole trail at once.

SOUTH WEST COAST PATH ASSOCIATION

The South West Coast Path Association has been in existence since 1973. It was formed by people with a passion for this long trail, and originally devoted itself to promoting the route and lobbying for immediate improvements. Over the years, the membership has grown and their lobbying skills have become formidable; these days the opinions of the Association are actively sought and considered by the various authorities involved with the route. As keen coastal walkers, Association members are best placed to report back to those in authority, so there is now a real sense of partnership and co-operation in maintaining and improving the trail. The Association produces promotional items and the invaluable annual *South West Coast Path Guide,* which includes a good accommodation list largely recommended by walkers. The Association also maintains a website that is useful for the latest news about path improvements, diversions, landslips, or just to see the lovely pictures: www.swcp.org.uk. Anyone can join the Association by contacting:

Eric Wallis, Secretary
South West Coast Path Association
Windlestraw Penquit Ermington
Devon
PL21 0LU
Tel: 01752-896237
email: wallispenquit@beeb.net

THE SOUTH WEST COAST PATH ROUTE

DAY 1
Minehead to Porlock Weir

After months of planning, you arrive in Minehead to start what may be the longest walk you have ever attempted. Take it one step at a time, setting your sights no further than Porlock or Lynmouth in the first instance. Oddly enough, the South West Coast Path climbs high above the coast, drifts well inland on Exmoor and loses sight of the sea. It is often a moorland walk rather than a coastal walk, but proves to be pleasant and not too demanding. There is an 'Alternative Rugged Coastpath' for anyone wanting a tougher beginning.

Map sculpture at the start of the South West Coast Path at Minehead

MINEHEAD

In the 18th century Minehead had a thriving harbour with ships sailing as far away as America. Inland from Quay Town are Lower Town and Higher Town. As shipping dwindled to little more than a small fishing fleet,

26

nineteenth-century Minehead became a holiday resort and remains so today. Although the seaside pier has gone, the old harbour wall survives. There are no longer direct rail services, but the branch line has been preserved as the West Somerset Railway, tel: 01643-707650. The modern town is centred on Wellington Square and St Andrew's Church; the old church of St Michael's high above town dates from the 14th century. Try and spend a night in town before embarking on the Coast Path.

Facilities include: abundant accommodation of all types, including a nearby youth hostel and campsite; banks with ATMs; post office; shops; toilets; pubs and restaurants. Transport links include regular buses to and from the railway station at Taunton. Places including Taunton, Porlock, Lynmouth, Combe Martin, Ilfracombe, Braunton and Barnstaple are all linked by the Exmoor Coastlink service. Tourist Information Centre, 17 Friday Street, Minehead, Somerset TA24 5UB, tel: 01643-702624, email: mineheadtic@visit.org.uk

An imaginative monument marks the beginning of the South West Coast Path at **Minehead.** The way to the start

Start:	South West Coast Path Monument, Minehead (971468)
Finish:	Porlock Weir (863479)
Distance:	15km (9.5 miles)
Cumulative Distance:	15km (9.5 miles)
Maps:	OS Landranger 181, OS Outdoor Leisure 9
Terrain:	A steep and wooded ascent, followed by gentle open moorlands and a steep descent. Field paths and woodland paths are linked by short road walks. A breach in the pebbly Porlock Ridge cannot be negotiated at high water.
Refreshments:	Plenty of places offer food and drink around Minehead. There is a tea garden at Bossington, as well as pubs and restaurants at Porlock and Porlock Weir.

is signposted along the promenade, and it is worth pausing for a moment of reflection at the monument. It takes the form of gigantic hands holding a map, based on a design by local art student Sarah Ward, executed in bronze by Owen Cunningham. The short tarmac path behind it unrolls like a red carpet. All who walk it must experience a sense of stepping out on a formidable journey, perhaps with lingering doubts, but certainly with anticipation and a sense of adventure.

If you wish to start by following the *'Alternative Rugged Coastpath'* it is signposted beyond the harbour. To follow the main route, cross the road from the **monument** and walk between two cottages. A tarmac path is signposted as the South West Coast Path, with destinations including North Hill, Porlock and even Poole. Climb a few steps, then turn right and follow a tarmac path up a wooded slope. Zigzag as indicated by markers

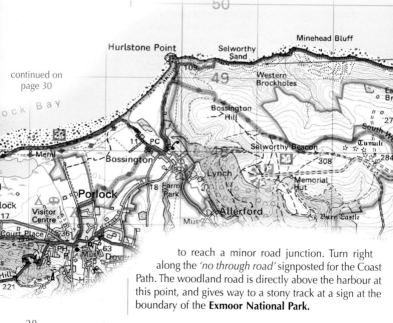

continued on page 30

to reach a minor road junction. Turn right along the *'no through road'* signposted for the Coast Path. The woodland road is directly above the harbour at this point, and gives way to a stony track at a sign at the boundary of the **Exmoor National Park.**

Follow the track gently uphill through mixed woods. Bear left at a junction signposted for the Coast Path and North Hill. The track rises and goes through a gate; the trees begin to thin out and there is a view down to a small lagoon behind a shingle beach at **Greenaleigh Point.** The path rises across a slope of gorse scrub, bilberry and heather, reaching a patch of tree scrub at a path junction. The ruins of the Burgundy Chapel are downhill, and the *'Alternative Rugged Coastpath'* passes it on its way up to meet the main route. The Coast Path leads up to a signpost and bench just short of a small car park on **North Hill** at 250m (820ft). There are good views across the Bristol Channel to South Wales and the tiny islands of Steep Holm and Flat Holm can be seen.

Turn right as signposted for Selworthy and Bossington. The path is stony but easy, flanked by gorse scrub. The *'Alternative Rugged Coastpath'* is signposted down to the right; keep left for the main path and go through a gate further along. Sheep and cattle graze a broad area of grassland to the right. The path narrows amid gorse bushes and passes through another gate,

then becomes broader again. Cross a road-end serving the grazing area and continue along a track, eventually reaching 290m (950ft) on **Selworthy Beacon.** The summit (to the left) rises to 308m (1013ft) and has fine views over Exmoor. Turn right as signposted around a corner of the grazing area and you can enjoy good views inland anyway.

The descent starts gradually. Take a right fork for Bossington, rather than a clearer track dropping to Lynch. The track becomes grassy and there are other signs pointing the way. A steep path drops down through a little valley towards the coast near **Hurlstone Point,** where the *'Alternative Rugged Coastpath'* runs in from the right. There are wonderful views along the shingle embankment of the Porlock Ridge. The ridge was heaped up 8000 years ago, but was breached by a storm in 1996, converting a freshwater marsh into a tidal salt-marsh. This affects the route of the South West Coast Path; note that you cannot safely cross the breach at high water.

Follow the path down to a gate then continue along a narrow woodland track that drifts towards a small river. Turn right to cross a footbridge over the river and enter the lovely little village of **Bossington** by way of a car park and toilets. The village is mostly owned by the National Trust, who maintain the cosy cottages using traditional skills and materials. There are a couple of B&Bs and a tea garden. Keep right to follow a road out of the village, signposted for Bossington Beach, then consider a choice of routes.

If the tide is out, walk down the road and track leading to **Bossington Beach,** where old limekilns can be seen. Turn left to follow the shingle embankment of **Porlock Ridge.** It can be hard work walking on the pebbles. Beyond the breach, the ridge leads to a road and a right turn leads into the little village of **Porlock Weir.** When the tide is fully out, the stumps of ancient trees – a **submarine forest** – are exposed on the beach.

If the tide is in, so preventing the use of the Porlock Ridge, turn left at the end of the tarmac road after leaving **Bossington.** A signpost announces the *'Diverted Coastpath Porlock'.* Go round the back of a farm, and turn right along a good path flanked by hedges.

Walkers above Hurlstone Point with Porlock Bay stretching beyond

Continue along a field path, then along another hedged path, through gates and gaps. Do not take a path on the right to the beach, but walk to a road, then turn right. At the end of the road, go down a few steps and turn left up a road leading into **Porlock.** This is Sparkhayes Lane, passing a campsite before reaching the **High Street** in Porlock, where you turn right, with most of the village's facilities to hand.

Follow High Street to a junction with a road leading to Porlock Weir, close to the **Old School Visitor Centre.** Keep left up past the Ship Inn, then bear right along the **Worthy Combe Toll Road.** When the houses run out, turn right down a track signposted as the Coast Path, overlooking pastures, marsh and the Porlock Ridge. A good track leads into woodland, then a narrow path climbs steeply for a short while. The route diverges, with a bridleway to the left and footpath to the right. Both are signposted for Porlock Weir and both meet later. Cross a stream and walk down to cross a road. Turn left along a lower road, then left again up the **Worthy Combe Toll Road.** Pass the white, corrugated St Nicholas Chapel and follow the road down to **Porlock Weir.**

PORLOCK & PORLOCK WEIR

Porlock is a small, compact village clustered around the 12th-century church of St Dubricius. Note that the tiny Chapel of the High Cross is located directly above the porch, reached by a squeeze stairway. Down the road is Porlock Weir, where a tiny harbour features lock gates that can be closed to form a marina. It is only a small settlement and features a number of craft workshops.

Facilities in Porlock include: a small range of accommodation, including a campsite; post office; shops; toilets; pubs and restaurants. Transport links include buses to Taunton, Minehead, Lynmouth, Lynton, Combe Martin, Ilfracombe, Braunton and Barnstaple via the Exmoor Coastlink service. The Old School Visitor Centre is worth a visit for background information. Facilities at Porlock Weir include: hotel accommodation; toilets; pubs and restaurants; and the same bus links as Porlock.

DAY 2
Porlock Weir to Lynmouth

The Coast Path leaves **Porlock Weir** through a gap between the Ship Inn and Anchor Hotel, signposted for Culbone and County Gate. The narrow path climbs uphill and becomes a field path, then links with a track leading up to the left of a farm. Turn right along a narrow road, which is the **Worthy Combe Toll Road,** leading to a handsome double-arched tollgate. The left arch is the Toll Road, while the right arch is the way to Culbone Church.

A broad path climbs from the tollgate and passes under a couple of arches. There has been a series of landslips on the wooded slopes, and the path detours above them. The woods are rich and varied, the higher parts predominantly oak and holly. A descent on a good track leads to **Culbone** and its lovely little secluded church. A refreshment cabin is available here, where you make your own tea and coffee and leave the appropriate money.

The track crosses a stream and if you want to visit **Culbone Church,** then head down to the right. Keep climbing to the left to continue along the Coast Path. A path on the right is signposted as an *'Alternative Permitted Coastpath to Lynmouth via Culbone Wood',* while the

If you want to cover the distance from Minehead to Lynmouth as your first day's walk on the South West Coast Path, you need to be very fit, or risk wearing yourself out and compromising yourself for the rest of the journey. The landscape between Porlock Weir and Lynmouth features wooded slopes obscuring views of the sea, with farm pastures at a higher level. Facilities are limited on this →

Start:	Porlock Weir (863479)
Finish:	Lynmouth Harbour (723496)
Distance:	20km (12.5 miles)
Cumulative Distance:	35km (22 miles)
Maps:	OS Landrangers 180 & 181, OS Outdoor Leisure 9
Terrain:	An ascent through woodlands gives way to farm tracks and field paths above Culbone. More woodland walking gives way to cliff paths and a gradual descent to Lynmouth.
Refreshments:	There is a refreshment cabin (DIY) at Culbone. The Exmoor Sandpiper Inn is just off-route at Countisbury.

← stretch, but in the event of difficulty you can detour to the main road at County Gate and bail out by linking with the Exmoor Coastlink bus service.

main route keeps climbing to the left, and soon leaves the woods. Walk up through fields to reach a road, then walk down the road and climb past **Silcombe Farm B&B.** The lane is flanked by hedges as it climbs, becoming grassy as it drops into a little valley where there is a stand of conifers. The lane makes its way round another little valley before reaching a road at 308m (1013ft).

Follow the road downhill, as signposted for County Gate, passing below the stout stone buildings at **Broomstreet Farm.** A lane leaving the farm dwindles to a field path. Watch out for a signpost beyond a gate where the Coast Path drops steeply down through a field and back into the woods. Cross a stream and look for the marker posts to spot the narrow path and gates around the slopes of **Sugarloaf Hill.**

After passing **Guildhall Corner** the path goes down steps into delightfully mixed woodlands. A junction is reached where the *'Alternative Permitted Coastpath'* comes in from the right, and a left turn is signposted for County Gate and Lynmouth. Head down to the right from a little gateway, cross a stream, then walk up the track signposted for the Coast Path. This is part of the County Gate Nature Trail, while below is the 'pinetum', featuring a

continued on page 36

variety of pines, including tall Wellingtonias. The woodland track leads up to a junction at **Steeple Sturt**; there is access uphill to County Gate if there is any need to intercept buses at the Exmoor National Park Visitor Centre.

The Coast Path runs downhill from the junction to cross a stream at **Coscombe** that forms the county boundary between Somerset and Devon. Walk up the track and turn down to the right to find the **Sisters Fountain** marked by a stout stone cross in the woods. Local lore maintains that Joseph of Arimathea drank from this spring on his way to Glastonbury. Follow a path uphill marked for Wingate Combe and turn right along a track to pass between **stone pillars** bearing the heads of wild boars.

Walk gently downhill from a house, but watch for a path rising to the left from a bend. This is again marked for Wingate Combe, and crosses a slope covered in rhododendrons. The path crosses two streams in **Wingate Combe,** then continues across a wooded, scrubby slope to a gate giving access to **Glenthorne Cliffs.** A wooded gully on the steep slope rejoices in the name of **Pudleep Gurt!**

Cross a little stream at Swannel Combe, followed by another gully at Chubhill Combe, then land on a track at a gate, stile and stream. Walk up to a bend on a narrow road, then walk down the road signposted 'Lighthouse'. The light is at the end of **Foreland Point,** Devon's most northerly point, though the road is only followed to a bridge spanning a stream down in the valley. Gorse, heather, bracken, bilberry and scree characterise this valley.

A path up to the left is signposted as the Coast Path to Countisbury.

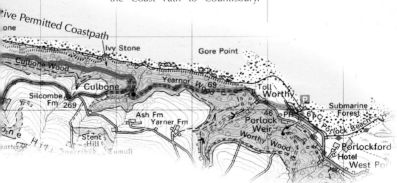

Steps are followed by a grassy path rising across a slope to a grassy gap. Turn left at the top to approach **Countisbury.** The Coast Path veers right before reaching the church of St John the Evangelist. You can walk through the churchyard to reach the **Exmoor Sandpiper Inn** on the main road. The cliff path runs parallel to the main road and eventually joins it for a stretch. When the road reaches a sign for the **Countisbury Lodge Hotel,** a path drops down to the right using steps on a wooded slope. Zigzags lead down through a beech wood with rampant ground cover, landing on a road just above the beach at Lynmouth. Walk though a pleasant park to reach a white-framed footbridge spanning the river at **Lynmouth.** The Bath Hotel is on the other side, while a right turn leads to the little harbour.

LYNMOUTH & LYNTON

Lynmouth nestles at the mouth of the River Lyn, while Lynton occupies the slopes high above, but buildings are stacked all the way up the wooded slopes. A cliff railway connects the twin villages, so there is no need to negotiate the steep streets and

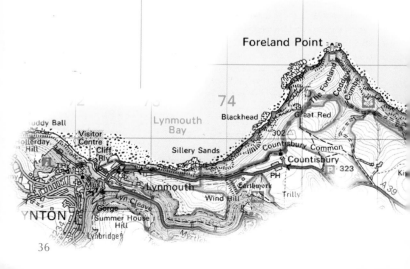

Boats moored at Lynmouth close to the Lynmouth Flood Memorial Centre

paths. Lynmouth was wrecked by a devastating flood in August 1952, killing 34 people; there is an exhibition in the Lynmouth Flood Memorial Centre. A sign at the Glen Lyn Gorge says it all: 'Opened 1854 Devastated 1952 Reopened 1962'. The Exmoor National Park Visitor Centre, between the harbour and cliff railway, is worth a visit. Note (after walking on foot between Porlock and Lynmouth) that in January 1899 the Lynmouth lifeboat couldn't be launched due to heavy seas, and was towed by men and horses over Porlock Hill to be launched at Porlock, to assist the vessel *Forrest Hall* off Hurlstone Point.

Facilities at Lynmouth and Lynton includes plenty of accommodation, including a youth hostel and campsite; banks with ATMs; post office; shops; toilets; pubs and restaurants. Transport links include buses back to Porlock, Minehead and Taunton, as well as ahead to Combe Martin, Ilfracombe, Braunton and Barnstaple via the Exmoor Coastlink service. Tourist Information Centre, Town Hall, Lee Road, Lynton, Devon EX35 6BT, tel: 01598-752225, email: tic@lynton-lynmouth.fsnet.co.uk

DAY 3
Lynmouth to Combe Martin

The Coast Path climbs from Lynmouth and heads for the popular Valley of Rocks. A road is followed down past Lee Abbey, but a new stretch of path has been opened round Crock Point. After working round the wooded slopes of Woody Bay, the path traverses steep slopes before crossing a deep, steep-sided valley at Heddon's Mouth. Although it returns to the cliffs, the path drifts →

Leave the harbour at **Lynmouth** and look for a gap between the Exmoor National Park Visitor Centre and the **Lynton & Lynmouth Cliff Railway.** Turn left up a flight of steps signposted for the Coast Path, Lynton, Valley of Rocks and Combe Martin. A zigzag tarmac path crosses the Cliff Railway twice, then a narrow road running between the Fairholme Hotel and North Cliff Hotel crosses it again. If you are tempted to use the Cliff Railway to avoid the ascent, it is necessary to walk back down to this road to continue. The road is the **North Walk,** a Victorian perambulation that narrows on a wooded slope before running out onto steep and rocky slopes as an easy tarmac path. When the path forks, keep low to the right and there are suddenly fine views of **Castle Rock** towering above the sea. Look out for feral goats as the path heads for a road and turning circle at the popular **Valley of Rocks.**

There is a signpost for the beach, but the Coast Path runs along the road. Up to the left is **Mother Meldrum's**

Start:	Lynmouth Harbour (723496)
Finish:	Combe Martin (576473)
Distance:	21km (13 miles)
Cumulative Distance:	56km (35 miles)
Maps:	OS Landranger 180, OS Outdoor Leisure 9
Terrain:	An initial steep climb from Lynmouth leads to an easy walk to the Valley of Rocks, Lee Bay and Woody Bay. Good cliff paths give way to a couple of deep valleys and a stretch of moorland walking. There is an ascent of Great Hangman before a final descent to Combe Martin.
Refreshments:	There is a café at Lee Bay and a hotel offering food and drink at Woody Bay. The Hunter's Inn is available off-route at Heddon's Mouth.

Cave, while later off to the right is a view of the 'White Lady', a shape formed by an irregular hole near the top of Castle Rock. The road is a toll road and leads through the Lee Abbey Estate. **Lee Abbey** is to the right and is a Christian conference centre. There are toilets at the bottom of the road and the Lee Abbey Tea Cottage is on the next uphill stretch.

Watch out for a Coast Path sign on the right, where a new stretch of path leads out of the woods, around **Crock Point,** then back into the woods. When the path climbs back up to the road, turn right to continue to Woody Bay, keeping right at a fork. A sharp left turn

← inland across the slopes of Holdstone Down and climbs to the summit of Great Hangman, the highest point on the South West Coast Path. Most walkers will be happy to finish at Combe Martin, though some may prefer to walk on to the bigger, bustling town of Ilfracombe.

Castle Rock towers above the sea as the route enters the Valley of Rocks

leads downhill, then *either* walk up to the **Woody Bay Hotel**, *or* turn right into the woods before reaching it.

The area round **Woody Bay** is protected as an SSSI and is noted for its 'hanging' oakwoods, threatened by invasive rhododendron and home to red deer. A clear woodland track runs down to a narrow road at **West Cottage.** Turn left as signposted for the Coast Path (or for 'America' on another signpost!). Follow the road up to a bend and through a gate, then climb a stony woodland path. The trees later bend over the path as it runs downhill. Cross over **Hollow Brook** at a little waterfall and leave the valley to cross a more open slope above the cliffs. Look out for razorbills and guillemots on the rocks. Follow a stony path across a steep slope of heather, rising past a couple of fine rocky viewpoints.

One rocky outcrop overlooks **Heddon's Mouth.** The path slices down across a steep, scrubby, stony slope into woods below. Turn left inland and upstream alongside a river, signposted as the Coast Path for Combe Martin. (This track eventually leads to the **Hunter's Inn.**) Turn right across a stone **footbridge,** walk downstream a little, then turn sharp left along a clear track, upstream and inland.

66

continued on
page 42

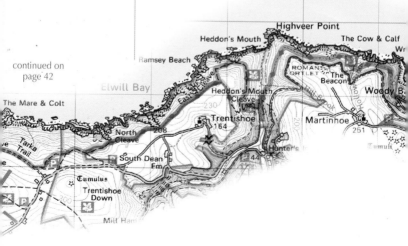

Watch for a sharp right turn uphill, signposted as the Coast Path for Combe Martin, leading up a wooded slope and through a gate. Zigzag up a steep slope of bracken, then head to the right along a path that contours back towards the coast high above **Heddon's Mouth.** The path swings left and later climbs up a steep slope of heather and rock. When a fence is reached on a stone-and-earth bank, turn right as signposted for the Coast Path. Cliffs fall steeply to the sea and there are fine views ahead, but the path is generally easy, using a grassy strip at the top of **East Cleave.** There are fields of sheep inland, then the path steps back from the cliff to avoid a landslip.

The path continues along the top of **North Cleave** and later runs down towards a patch of woodland, but avoids it by crossing a stile and heading inland across a field. The path climbs onto a more rugged moorland slope, running up through gorse and heather to reach a broad track. In the 19th century there was a plan to build a settlement in this exposed place. Turn right to follow the track across the slopes of **Holdstone Down,** later descending towards a valley with the broad dome of Great Hangman beyond. The track

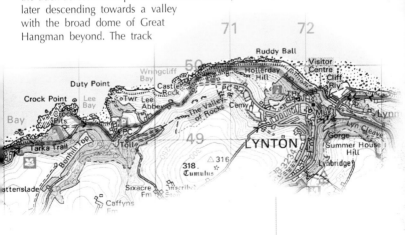

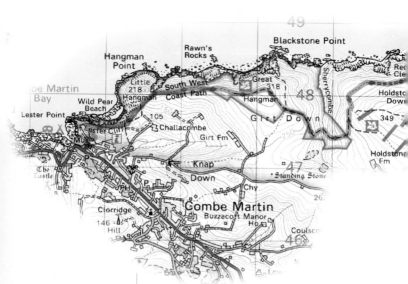

climbs uphill and heads inland, then is signposted down to a stream and footbridge in the valley of **Sherrycombe.**

Follow a path steeply up the other side of the valley, clipping a patch of woodland, then continuing up a slope of gorse and round a corner of a field. When a path junction is reached, walk straight onwards and uphill at a gentler gradient, following a good track to a sprawling cairn on the top of **Great Hangman.** This stands at 318m (1043ft), the highest point on the South West Coast Path. Enjoy the views back across Exmoor, as the route will leave the National Park by the end of the day. The coast of South Wales and Lundy Island are also in view.

Keep to the left of the cairn to follow a good path downhill. The path runs towards the smaller bump of **Little Hangman.** A climb to a bench on the summit is an optional extra, but the path roller-coasts along a cliff often covered in bushes, featuring only occasional views. Finally, the path is swallowed into the trees, passes a shelter and swings left downhill. Turn right at the bottom to enter **Combe Martin**.

COMBE MARTIN

Combe Martin stretches far inland from its little bay at the extreme western end of the Exmoor National Park. There were once schemes to develop a harbour, and even link the village with the former railway at Ilfracombe, but those plans were abandoned, along with its lead-mining industry. It might seem sensible to skip Combe Martin and head onwards to Ilfracombe, with its greater range of services, but the way is fiddly and could take you longer than expected.

Facilities include: B&B accommodation and a nearby campsite; post office; shops; toilets; pubs and restaurants. Transport links include buses to Lynmouth, Porlock, Minehead and Taunton, as well as to Ilfracombe, Braunton and Barnstaple via the Exmoor Coastlink service.

Tourist Information Centre, Sea Cottage, Cross Street, Combe Martin, Devon EX34 0DH, tel: 01271-883319, email: combemartintic@visit.org.uk

DAY 4
Combe Martin to Woolacombe

After the hilly days spent walking through the Exmoor National Park, the walk becomes a little gentler. There are plenty of ascents and descents, but they tend to be on a smaller scale. The route from Combe Martin to Ilfracombe is rather fiddly in places as the path works its way round a succession →

Follow the main road up Seaside Hill to leave **Combe Martin,** noting the Combe Martin Museum down to the right off a road bend. The Coast Path to Ilfracombe is signposted along quiet **Newberry Road,** running parallel to the main road. Although a path is followed parallel to the main road, it is later necessary to walk alongside the busy road to reach **Berrynarbor.**

Turn right downhill and continue down the **Old Coast Road,** where the tarmac gives way to a broad dirt road and track. Big beech trees and pungent ramsons grow alongside. Watch out for a stile on the right, where the Coast Path runs down to a **campsite.** Keep to the right-hand side of the campsite (unless visiting the little shop), to return to the main road and turn right. Pass a bus stop and follow a path parallel to the main road until opposite the **Watermouth Castle** theme park.

Start:	Combe Martin (576473)
Finish:	Woolacombe (457437)
Distance:	20km (12.5 miles)
Cumulative Distance:	76km (47.5 miles)
Maps:	OS Landranger 180, OS Outdoor Leisure 9, OS Explorer 139
Terrain:	Fiddly and convoluted paths require careful route-finding between Combe Martin and Ilfracombe. An easy cliff path leaves Ilfracombe, followed by a roller-coaster cliff path from Lee Bay to Morte Point. The final walk from Morte Point to Woolacombe is gentle and easy.
Refreshments:	Ilfracombe has plenty of shops, pubs and restaurants offering food and drink. A hotel and shop provide food and drink at Lee Bay. Detours inland can be made to the village of Mortehoe, which has a shop and inn.

At low water you can use a route along the shore at **Water Mouth,** but at high water continue with care up the main road before a path on the right gives access to a wooded slope. Both routes join again here and continue parallel to the road. A right turn at the edge of the wood reveals the Coast Path leading to the mouth of this scenic inlet. A steep flight of steps lead up to a fine viewpoint on **Widmouth Head,** but Ilfracombe remains hidden.

Walk down steps and follow the path around **Rillage Point** until it rises to a car park. Turn right and walk parallel to the main road, then follow the road down to **Hele Bay**, offering food and drink. Walk down the road towards the beach, then follow a path that works it way up a wooded slope to reach the top of **Hillsborough.** This is crowned with the rumpled earthen remains of a hillfort and offers a fine view over **Ilfracombe.** Follow a path downhill aiming for the harbour; keep to the left-hand side of the **harbour** to approach the centre of town.

← of little headlands and coves. Ilfracombe is full of distractions, then the Torrs Walk leads walkers away from town. An interesting rocky cliff-line stretches between Lee Bay and Woolacombe.

ILFRACOMBE

The bustling town of Ilfracombe developed around a wonderful natural harbour and has been a fishing port for centuries. The restored chapel dedicated to St Nicholas, on Lantern Hill overlooking the harbour, dates from the 14th century. In the

continued on
page 47

19th century the town developed as a splendid holiday resort, served by steamships and a railway (now gone), with rows of fine hotels. There are boat trips available, as well as summer steamer services to Lundy Island. You can forecast the weather as follows: 'Lundy high, sign of dry; Lundy plain, sign of rain; Lundy low, sign of snow'.

Facilities include: abundant accommodation of all types, including a nearby campsite; banks with ATMs; post office; shops; toilets; several pubs and restaurants. Transport links include buses back to Combe Martin, Lynmouth, Porlock, Minehead and Taunton, as well as ahead to Braunton and Barnstaple via the Exmoor Coastlink service. Buses also run to Lee Bay, Woolacombe, Croyde Bay and Saunton. National Express buses run from Ilfracombe to London. Tourist Information Centre, The Landmark, The Seafront, Ilfracombe, Devon EX34 9BX, tel: 0845-4583630, email: ilfracombetic@aol.com

Leave the centre of **Ilfracombe** by following Capstone Road a short way, then a path over the rugged little hill (usually with a flag flying on the top) at **Capstone Point.** Walk down towards the curious upturned bucket shapes

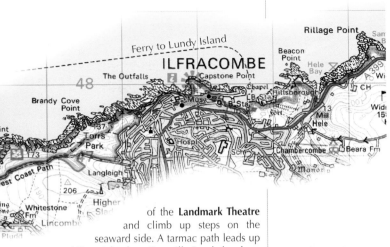

of the **Landmark Theatre** and climb up steps on the seaward side. A tarmac path leads up to a road. Turn right along Granville Road, then bear right as marked for the Coast Path up **Torrs Park Avenue.** Turn right at Avoncourt and follow the Coast Path as signposted for Lee to leave Ilfracombe. →

As the Coast Path continues, look out for signs and stiles as it wanders across grassy slopes away from town. Turn right along a clear track that is marked with an iron sign as '*Public Path – Please keep to it*'. The track is covered in short grass in places and eventually descends to a gate and a narrow road. Walk straight down the road, unless you are tempted by a path on the left leading to the village of **Lee.** The road steepens at the bottom, where a right turn leads to **Lee Bay.** The Lee Bay Hotel has a small shop alongside and offers accommodation, food and drink. There are toilets and a bus service back to Ilfracombe.

Follow the road uphill to leave Lee Bay, watching for a gate on the right near the top of the road. There is a National Trust sign for **Damage Cliffs** and a Coast Path sign for Woolacombe. The route becomes like a rollercoaster, with flights of steps leading into and out of a couple of little valleys. There is a lighthouse on **Bull**

The path known as the **Torrs Walk** has been hacked from the bedrock in places and as it wanders along the cliffs it begins to zigzag uphill. Watch out for a right turn leading to a **viewpoint** where you can look back towards Ilfracombe.

47

*An easy stretch of Coast
Path is followed from
Morte Point to
Woolacombe*

Point and the path crosses its access road. The path crosses a dip above **Rockham Bay**, where rickety steps allow access to the beach. Paths inland are signposted for the village of **Mortehoe**, which offers a little accommodation, including a campsite, a post office, shop and inn.

Keep to the Coast Path to reach rocky **Morte Point**, where a sharp left turn is made. The path becomes easier as it heads for the seaward side of Mortehoe village. Head towards the buildings, but turn right to keep below them. The path eventually joins a road between Mortehoe and Woolacombe, where there are a couple of hotels, toilets and a bus stop. The Coast Path wanders along a strip of grass between the road and the beach. **Woolacombe** is soon reached; you can either break at this point or head onwards for Croyde Bay, Saunton and Braunton.

WOOLACOMBE

Woolacombe is essentially a 20th-century holiday resort that has developed from a farming settlement, and has an astounding sandy beach.

Facilities include: accommodation of all types, including nearby campsites; bank with ATM; post office; shops; toilets; pubs and restaurants. Transport links include buses to Ilfracombe, Saunton, Braunton and Barnstaple. Tourist Information Centre, The Esplanade, Woolacombe, Devon EX34 7DL, tel: 01271-870553, email: woolacombetic@visit.org.uk

DAY 5
Woolacombe to Braunton

It's tempting on leaving **Woolacombe** to walk along the broad, sandy beach towards Baggy Point. This is fine if the tide doesn't push you close to the land, where slopes of soft sand prove heavy going. The Coast Path leaves by way of **Marine Drive**; when this climbs up towards **The Warren,** head off to the right along a path. Aim to follow the path between the sea and Marine Drive (the road is little more than a linear car park). Avoid spurs to right and left that lead either down to the beach or up to the road. At the same time, while walking through the scrubby dunes, look out for a path heading uphill to join a bridleway. This is signposted as the Coast Path and you turn right to follow it. The track narrows to a path then broadens again, climbing up to a road above a hotel and caravan site at **Putsborough Sands.** Refreshments and toilets are available.

Follow the road onwards and uphill a little, then turn right as signposted for the Coast Path. Although a track runs gently uphill, the path you take is signposted off to the right and runs towards the cliffs overlooking the sandy beach. Continue onwards across stiles and the path turns out to be pleasant and grassy, running well above a low cliff-line. The altitude is only 94m (308ft) as the path turns around dramatically rocky **Baggy Point.**

This is probably the easiest day so far, though much depends on how you feel after tackling the path to this point. Gradients are easy and there are a couple of fine, sandy beaches that beckon enticingly at low water. Breaks can be taken at Croyde Bay and Saunton, before a circuitous exploration of the dunes of Braunton Burrows. This extensive area often seems remote from the sea, and although it is a National Nature Reserve, a large part is used for military training. Sadly, →

Start:	Woolacombe (457437)
Finish:	Velator, Braunton (486357)
Distance:	25 kilometres (15.5 miles)
Cumulative Distance:	101km (63 miles)
Maps:	OS Landranger 180, OS Explorer 139
Terrain:	Easy paths and tracks, sometimes with the option of walking along sandy beaches.
Refreshments:	Food and drink are available at Putsborough Sands, Croyde Bay and Saunton.

← some walkers skip it entirely, even catching a bus all the way from Saunton to Westward Ho! – but if you start doing things like this, the chances are that you will keep doing it, leaving your long walk in tatters!

Note that there is a right turn at a junction, where you might have expected a left turn.

A good gritty path runs along the low cliff-line, passing a preserved whalebone and linking with a quiet road leading round **Croyde Bay.** One house offers teas and snacks immediately. Walk along the road and turn right along **Beach Road,** where more food and drink can be obtained, and there are toilets. **Croyde** lies inland from Croyde Bay and together they offer a range of accommodation, including campsites; post office; shops; toilets; pubs and restaurants.

Turn left along the sandy beach; in case of high water, hug the sandy shore and divert slightly inland to cross a footbridge over a stream flowing into the bay. At the far side of the bay, come ashore using a flight of steps (not the ones marked as 'Private'). Turn right as sign-posted for the Coast Path and Tarka Trail to Braunton. The path goes along the coast a little, then climbs to a road. Turn left along the road, then sharp right to follow a grassy path above and parallel to the road. This path runs across the slopes of **Saunton Down** and reaches the road near the **Saunton Sands Hotel.**

Just as the path reaches the busy road, there is a choice of routes. *Either* turn left to avoid the road, climbing back onto Saunton Down. This route links with a farm track that is followed to the right, then drops down towards **St Anne's Church** to rejoin the road. *Alternatively,* if you cross the busy road to reach the **Saunton Sands Hotel,** follow a circuitous route round

Looking back from Woolacombe to the adjacent village of Mortehoe

the hotel and down to a beach café and car park. Follow the car park access road inland, but step to the right along a path as marked. This rejoins the busy road, which is then followed past **St Anne's Church.**

At a crossroads near St Anne's Church, follow a narrow lane slightly downhill. A short path links the lane with a track, and a left turn along the track leads towards a **golf course**: beware of flying golf balls. Follow the track until signposts indicate a left turn, and take particular care crossing a fairway at that point. Waymarked paths lead away from the golf course, through patchy woodlands and open areas. There is a **military training area** to the right; stay on the clear

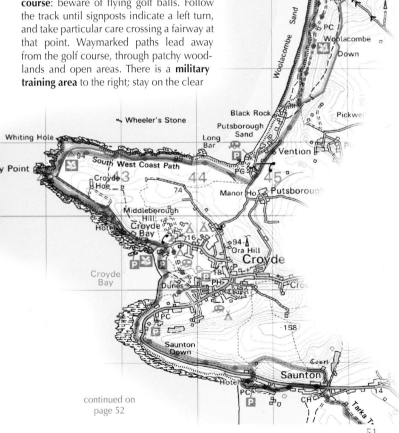

continued on
page 52

51

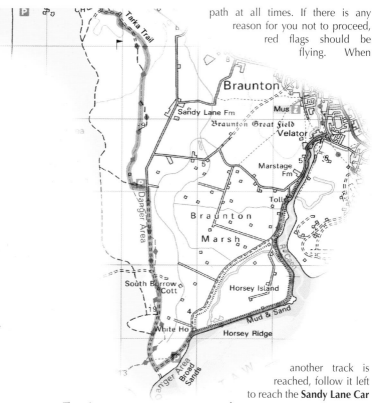

path at all times. If there is any reason for you not to proceed, red flags should be flying. When another track is reached, follow it left to reach the **Sandy Lane Car Park.** ←

There is an information board offering notes about the **Braunton Burrows National Nature Reserve.** It is one of the largest sand dune systems in Britain, made mostly of crushed, windblown shells. →

Leave the car park and turn right along a clear dirt road, barred to vehicles. It is known as the **American Road** and is often full of deep puddles. The military training area is still to the right. At length the track reaches the sea near **Crow Point**, a hooked spit that affords shelter to a few small boats. The villages of Instow and Appledore are seen across the mouth of the **River Taw,** but cannot be approached without a boat. Walkers may find it galling to be so close, yet spend more than a day trying to reach them!

Another dirt road, this time open to vehicles, begins the long journey inland. Follow it to the **White House,** where ferries once ran across the river mouth. Turn right as signposted for the Coast Path and follow an embankment around **Horsey Island.** The embankment was built in 1857 to reclaim the marshland, and the stone barns are locally known as 'linhays'. The grassy embankment leads inland alongside the tidal **River Caen.** Continue following it even though a road runs just below, to reach **Velator Quay**, built in 1853 as part of the marsh reclamation scheme. It was a thriving little port until the railway arrived in 1874. Use the riverside embankment until you have to follow the road again. When a roundabout is reached at **Velator** the route is practically in **Braunton.**

← These have been stabilised by marram grass and in some places colonised by woodlands. There are around 400 species of flowering plants, including orchids. Foxes, hedgehogs, rabbits, moles and small mammals thrive. Buzzards, kestrels and magpies are often seen, as well as a range of butterflies.

BRAUNTON

Facilities include: a range of accommodation, including a nearby campsite; bank with ATM; post office; shops; toilets; pubs and restaurants. Transport links include buses to Saunton, Croyde and Woolacombe, as well as Barnstaple. There are also buses to Ilfracombe, Combe Martin, Lynmouth, Porlock, Minehead and Taunton via the Exmoor Coastlink service. Tourist Information Centre The Bakehouse Centre, Caen Street, Braunton, Devon, EX33 1AA, tel: 01271-816400, email: brauntontic@visit.org.uk

The broad and sandy expanse of Croyde Bay at low tide

DAY 6
Braunton to Westward Ho!

This might seem like a long day's walk, but it is largely routed along old railway trackbeds and can be covered quickly. The trackbeds stretch from Braunton to Barnstaple, then from Barnstaple to Instow and Bideford. There's also a chance to catch a ferry between Instow and Appledore, saving a long walk via Bideford, but the ferry is subject to →

Return to the roundabout at **Velator** on the outskirts of **Braunton.** A tarmac cycleway is signposted for Barnstaple and soon crosses a road near the old **Wrafton station,** now a house. The railway line and its stations operated only from 1874 to 1970. Stout fencing on the right surrounds the RAF Search and Rescue base for 22 Squadron, where Sea King helicopters can be seen. The broad area of land that was formerly **Wrafton Marsh** was reclaimed in 1857. A roundabout and bus stop are passed at **RMB Chivenor.**

A well-wooded stretch of the old trackbed gives way to fine views across the estuary of the **River Taw.** There is access to a castellated restaurant at **Heanton Court.** Another wooded stretch is hemmed in between the estuary and main road, but the trackbed later drifts away from the road and runs close to the estuary. After passing an industrial site, the trackbed crosses **Yeo Bridge** to

Start:	Velator, Braunton (486357)
Finish:	Westward Ho! (433295)
Distance:	38km (23.5 miles)
Cumulative Distance:	139km (86.5 miles)
Maps:	OS Landranger 180, OS Outdoor Leisure 9, OS Explorer 139
Terrain:	Easy walking along broad, clear, level trackbeds for most of the way. Fiddly paths through woods and fields are used between Bideford and Appledore, giving way to grass and shingle banks near Westward Ho!
Refreshments:	Heanton Court offers food and drink near Braunton. Barnstaple has plenty of shops, pubs and restaurants. The old railway station at Fremington has a restaurant. Instow, Bideford and Appledore all have shops, pubs and restaurants.

enter **Barnstaple.** Keep close to the riverside to reach the **Long Bridge,** which dates from the 13th century, widened in 1798 and 1963. The South West Coast Path crosses it.

BARNSTAPLE

Barnstaple has a long been the administrative town of North Devon. A Saxon stronghold in the 10th century, it was surrounded by a wall to keep Danish invaders at bay. King Alfred made the town a Borough, creating one of the oldest Boroughs in England. The town was equipped with a mint and market Charter as it became an important commercial centre. In 1068 Barnstaple fell to the Normans and William the Conqueror held the town, while successive kings granted it further Royal Charters. Despite being far inland, Barnstaple had good access to the sea via the River Taw and developed a thriving shipping and naval tradition. The town changed hands frequently during the Civil War, yet continued to develop as a commercial centre. Museums illustrate its long history and heritage.

Facilities include: a range of accommodation, though campsites are rather distant; banks with ATMs; post office; shops; toilets; pubs and restaurants. Transport links include a railway with Wessex Trains services to Exeter. Buses run back to Braunton, Saunton and Croyde

← both seasonal and tidal restrictions. Some walkers skip this section altogether, getting a bus all or at least part of the way, but it is worth walking and should present no difficulties apart from the distance. Note that the trackbeds are also popular cycleways and can be busy on summer weekends. The remaining distance from Bideford to Appledore and Westward Ho! is along paths that can be fiddly in places, ending with a trudge along a shingle bank.

Walkers in a cutting on the old railway trackbed beyond Barnstaple

Bay, and ahead to Instow, Bideford, Appledore and Westward Ho! The Exmoor Coastlink service runs back to Braunton, Ilfracombe, Combe Martin, Lynton, Porlock, Minehead and Taunton. National Express buses run from Barnstaple to London and Birmingham. Tourist Information Centre, 36 Boutport Street, Barnstaple, Devon EX31 1RX, tel: 01271-375000, email: barnstapletic@visit.org.uk

Follow the road onwards after crossing the **Long Bridge** then turn right as signposted for Bideford and the Coast Path. A tarmac path runs from the end of the road through wooded surroundings. A right turn leads away

continued on
page 59

from town along another railway trackbed, which closed in 1982. There is a stretch alongside the estuary of the **River Taw**, then a grassy marsh to the right. The trackbed goes round an odd sort of shelter, while further along an old concrete navvy hut is also available for shelter. The trackbed pulls away from the marsh and goes through a cutting to reach the old **Fremington station**. This now houses the Fremington Quay Heritage Centre, a small restaurant, and a lookout tower equipped with binoculars and notes about the local birdlife. Fremington Quay was once described as 'the busiest port between Bristol and Land's End'.

Cross over a bridge spanning a tidal inlet and follow a long stretch of the trackbed away from the estuary. A curious upturned boat shelter is passed at a corner of the **Isley Marsh Nature Reserve** near Lower Yelland. At the far corner of the marsh there is a coastal path you can use instead of the trackbed. Pass the thatched **North Devon Cricket Club** and an MOD site, then a few cabins line the trackbed and there is access to the Wayfarer Inn. An old level crossing has been preserved at **Instow,** complete with gates, signal, signal box and rails.

INSTOW

Instow has a little accommodation, as well as a post office, shops, toilets, pubs and restaurants. There is a daily ferry between Instow and Appledore, from Easter to October, restricted to two hours of operation either side of high water, tel: 01237-476191. This ferry across the estuary of the River Torridge cuts 10km (6 miles) from

this day's walk and avoids Bideford. There are also bus services linking with Barnstaple and Braunton or to Bideford and Westward Ho!

The South West Coast Path continues along the old railway trackbed, hemmed between the road and the estuary. Pass a jetty where military boats are moored, then walk under a high main road bridge. The use of this bridge by walkers is not recommended; stay on the trackbed to reach **East-the-Water.** The old station site has been preserved and includes a restaurant in an old railway carriage and the Railway Carriage Visitor Centre in another. The old signal box is now a museum. Cross the **Long Bridge,** overhauled in 1925 after more than 600 years of service, to reach the little town of **Bideford.**

BIDEFORD

Facilities include: a range of accommodation; banks with ATMs; post office; shops; toilets; pubs and restaurants. Transport links include buses back to Instow, Barnstaple and Braunton, and ahead to Appledore and Westward Ho! National Express buses run from Bideford to London. There are day trips aboard the MS Oldenburg to Lundy Island. A visit to the island is highly recommended for anyone who can spare a day, with a chance to enjoy another 13km (8 miles) of spectacular coastal walking. Tourist Information Centre, Victoria Park, The Quay, Bideford, Devon EX39 2QQ, tel: 01237-477676, email: bidefordtic@visit.org.uk

Walk alongside the quays through **Bideford,** which have been raised and strengthened to resist flooding. A statue of Charles Kingsley is passed and the Tourist Information Centre is in the small park beyond. The quayside path is known as the **Landivisau Walk,** but the route is soon diverted away from the estuary and through the suburbs.

Follow the Coast Path signs up the gravel **Chircombe Lane** to pass under the high main road bridge again. Turn right along a narrow squeeze of a path down to the shore. Turn left, then drift inland a little as signposted along a road and paths. The route is fiddly, but well marked throughout. A path on a wooded slope passes through the grounds of the National Trust's **Burrough Farm.**

Once the shore is reached again, there is a choice of paths because of a breached embankment. *If the tide is out* you can follow the embankment and cross the breach easily, but *if the tide is in* you should detour inland a little as marked. Both paths approach the **Appledore Shipbuilders** and there is a detour inland to avoid the huge building. The route crosses a road, then a path leads to another road to pass well inland of the building. Follow **Hubbastone Road** and eventually reach the village of **Appledore,** passing a crane and walking along the quayside.

APPLEDORE

The village of Appledore overlooks the mouths of the Rivers Torridge and Taw. The older part of the village, dating back to the 16th century, is found around Irsha Street. Most of the houses along Appledore's quayside were built in the 19th century. Shipbuilding has always been an important industry; the sight of a huge ship-building shed appended to this charming little village comes as something of a surprise. Local yards built 200 ships in fifteen years during the Napoleonic Wars.

Facilities include: a little accommodation; post office; shops; toilets; pubs and restaurants. There are buses back to Bideford, Instow and Barnstaple, and ahead to Westward Ho! A ferry offers a direct link with Instow.

Walk beyond the car park and follow narrow **Irsha Street** through the older part of **Appledore.** Marvel at the rich and varied assortment of names on the houses. The Coast Path passes the **lifeboat station** and is rather narrow and overgrown as it clings to the top of a low cliff, quickly leading back onto a road. At low water it is possible to walk across the mudflats at **Skern,** otherwise follow the road and turn right at a crossroads to reach **Northam Burrows Country Park.**

Walk along a grassy expanse beside the road to reach the road-end amenity site at **Greysand Hill.** Stay on the grassy banks to reach the open sea again, then *either* walk along the sandy beach at low water, *or* crunch along the **Pebble Ridge** to reach **Westward Ho!** If the sandy beach is being followed, come ashore on a concrete ramp to reach an amusement arcade.

WESTWARD HO!

This nineteenth-century seaside resort was named after a novel by Charles Kingsley, and always includes the exclamation mark! It is said that the development did not meet with Kingsley's approval, who had a soft spot for Clovelly further along the coast.

Facilities include: a range of accommodation, including campsites; post office; shops; toilets; pubs and restaurants. Transport links include buses back to Appledore, Bideford, Instow, Barnstaple, Braunton, Saunton and Croyde Bay. National Express buses include a coast-to-coast service from Westward Ho! to Birmingham and Grimsby, and to London.

DAY 7
Westward Ho! to Clovelly

After the relatively easy interlude the Coast Path begins to resemble a roller-coaster again. The gradients are fairly gentle at first, but later there are some short, steep ascents and descents. Facilities are limited, unless you are prepared to move inland. With a bit of luck there will be some refreshment in the little village of Buck's Mills. The highlight of the day is undoubtedly the delightful village of Clovelly, →

Leave the amusement arcade on the seafront at **Westward Ho!** and follow the promenade past a long row of colourful beach huts. A coastal path beyond the huts links with the course of an old railway trackbed, which in turn leads along **Abbotsham Cliff**. The Coast Path later rises and falls, passing a ruined limekiln in one of the dips, then climbing over **Green Cliff**. Continue walking through gorse bushes, then cross a big stile and walk down a steep slope, ending with a flight of steps onto a cobbly beach at **Babbacombe Mouth**.

Climb steeply uphill on steps and continue along the top of **Babbacombe Cliff**. The path later heads downhill and passes a small dammed pool. (Note that this path has suffered a series of landslips and may be diverted across the cobbly beach.) Cross another rise and walk downhill, veering inland a little to **Peppercombe**. A track leads to a building, where there is an option to continue inland to Horn's Cross, which has a pub and post office store. Otherwise simply turn right, then left as indicated, climbing steps up a wooded slope. The path undulates, but generally climbs uphill, then

Start:	Westward Ho! (433295)
Finish:	Clovelly (316249)
Distance:	18km (11.25 miles)
Cumulative Distance:	157km (97.75 miles)
Maps:	OS Landrangers 180 & 190, OS Explorer 126
Terrain:	Easy walking at first, followed by a series of short, steep ups and downs. Some woodland paths can be muddy, but a fine woodland track is used at the end of the day.
Refreshments:	Possibility of refreshments at Buck's Mills, or inland at Buck's Cross. There are pubs and cafés around Clovelly.

runs along the edge of the wood and enters the fields alongside. A descent through the woods leads to steps, leading down to the little village of **Buck's Mills.**

There is a single B&B at Buck's Mills and sometimes there is a chance to obtain food and drink without having to detour inland to **Buck's Cross.** A steep tarmac path can be used to reach the

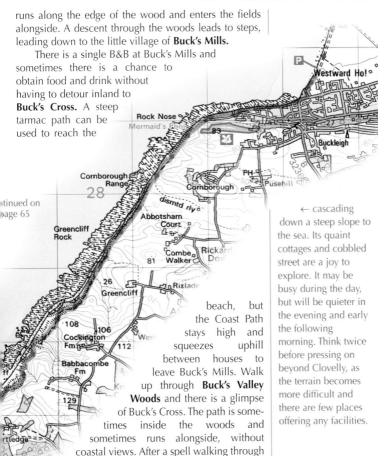

tinued on age 65

← cascading down a steep slope to the sea. Its quaint cottages and cobbled street are a joy to explore. It may be busy during the day, but will be quieter in the evening and early the following morning. Think twice before pressing on beyond Clovelly, as the terrain becomes more difficult and there are few places offering any facilities.

beach, but the Coast Path stays high and squeezes uphill between houses to leave Buck's Mills. Walk up through **Buck's Valley Woods** and there is a glimpse of Buck's Cross. The path is sometimes inside the woods and sometimes runs alongside, without coastal views. After a spell walking through fields beside the woods, the path drops down into the woods and crosses a footbridge.

Climb up to a broad track in the beech woods and turn right to walk gently downhill. The track, known as the **Hobby Drive,** loops round across a bridge, then climbs gently to reach a stone memorial bench. An inscription records that 'The new portion of road

63

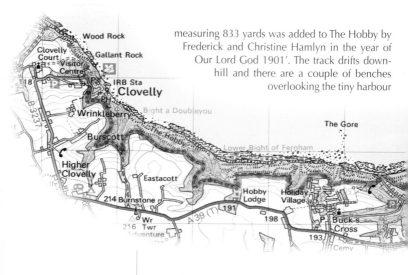

measuring 833 yards was added to The Hobby by Frederick and Christine Hamlyn in the year of Our Lord God 1901'. The track drifts downhill and there are a couple of benches overlooking the tiny harbour at Clovelly. Follow the track down across a couple of streams, then contour round to the top end of **Clovelly.** Although a path for the village centre is signposted down to the right, the Coast Path stays high and almost misses the village.

Steps lead up into the dense Buck's Valley Woods above Buck's Mills

CLOVELLY

Walkers should enter Clovelly, bracing themselves for an extraordinarily steep descent along the cobbly High Street, taking time to explore the cottages and little alleyways on the way to the harbour. The quay dates back to 14th century. The Cary family were Lords of the Manor until they transferred the estate to the Hamlyn family in 1730. There are 17th- and 18th-century inns. Throughout the 19th century, Clovelly's fishing industry declined as tourism increased. Vehicles are barred, and local folk use sledges to haul goods and provisions around the village. Small loads are pulled by hand, while larger ones require a donkey. A Land Rover runs up and down a steep back road between the harbour and the top of the village, useful for those who can't face the return climb.

Facilities include: a small range of accommodation, with some addresses further inland; post office; shops; toilets; pubs and cafés. There is a Visitor Centre at the top end of the village and several quaint cottages can be visited. Transport links include buses to Bideford and Barnstaple, with infrequent services ahead to Bude.

DAY 8
Clovelly to Hartland Quay

This may seem like a short day's walk, but it becomes increasingly difficult and some paths are steep and narrow. There is little point in pressing on beyond Hartland Quay as facilities are very limited until you reach Bude. Enjoy the rough and rocky coast, which is particularly dramatic in heavy seas. Hartland Point is one of the most significant points along the Coast Path, marking a sudden change of direction and a remarkable →

Leave the top end of **Clovelly** at the Lower Yard, where there are a couple of craft shops. Follow the tarmac road downhill to a junction, where a Coast Path signpost for Brownsham points through a stout black gate. (The narrow road running steeply downhill is the back road serving the little harbour.) Keep right along a grassy track and path along a woodland edge, then enter the woodland and pass a shelter. The woodland path is a bit of a squeeze, then there is a short stretch outside the woods, before a better path leads back into the woods. Pass the splendid **Angel Wings** shelter, built as a memorial in 1826 and restored twice. Continue along the path and generally keep right at junctions, or at least avoid those paths and tracks marked as private. A zigzag stretch leads onto a lower track that runs to **Mill Mouth.**

A Coast Path sign points straight across a little river; there is no footbridge, so be careful when the water is high. Follow a track inland from a ruin, then turn right up a zigzag woodland path to emerge in a field at a National Trust sign for **Brownsham.** Walk around the field edges then zigzag down into another wooded

Start:	Clovelly (316249)
Finish:	Hartland Quay (222248)
Distance:	17km (10.5 miles)
Cumulative Distance:	174km (108.25 miles)
Maps:	OS Landranger 190, OS Explorer 126
Terrain:	Wooded cliffs and valleys give way to easier walking through gentle fields. After turning round Hartland Point there is a series of valleys to cross and some steep slopes to climb.
Refreshments:	Possibly a refreshment hut near Hartland Point, otherwise nothing until the Hartland Quay Hotel is reached.

valley and cross a footbridge. Zigzag up the other side, first through woods, then later along the edges of fields. A memorial plaque reminds walkers of a Wellington bomber that crashed into the nearby cliffs. Follow the marked path along field edges, crossing another little wooded valley and a footbridge. Field paths equipped with stiles show the way onwards to a **trig point** at 152m (498ft).

Looking ahead, a 'radome' can be seen; this is quite close to Hartland Point, and makes a good reference point. Walk through the fields until the route turns around the cliffs of **Shipload Bay.** At this point, a grassy track could be followed inland to **East Titchberry,** where the National Trust maintain a 17th-century farmhouse with a three-storeyed malthouse. At nearby **West Titchberry** there is a farmhouse B&B. The Coast Path, however, leaves a corner on the grassy track and climbs above Shipload Bay to pass on the seaward side of the **Hartland Point Radar.** This was formerly a military site but is now used mainly for Air Traffic Control. Walk down to a small car park where there might be a refreshment hut. The whole nature of the walk seems to change at **Hartland Point,** suddenly becoming remarkably rough and rocky.

← change of scenery. The wooded slopes and valleys passed during the morning give way to bare and barren headlands later. Hartland Quay offers food, drink and limited accommodation; be sure to book in advance to avoid making detours inland.

Heavy seas batter exposed Hartland Point and its lonely lighthouse

67

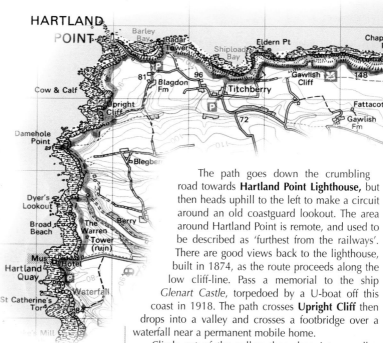

The path goes down the crumbling road towards **Hartland Point Lighthouse,** but then heads uphill to the left to make a circuit around an old coastguard lookout. The area around Hartland Point is remote, and used to be described as 'furthest from the railways'. There are good views back to the lighthouse, built in 1874, as the route proceeds along the low cliff-line. Pass a memorial to the ship *Glenart Castle*, torpedoed by a U-boat off this coast in 1918. The path crosses **Upright Cliff** then drops into a valley and crosses a footbridge over a waterfall near a permanent mobile home.

Climb out of the valley, then drop into a valley behind the rocky **Damehole Point.** Enjoy the rock scenery, from the slabby cliffs of the point to the ribs and pinnacles out to sea. Steps lead up a steep slope for a short way, then the path runs down into another valley, passing well below a house and crossing an arched **stone bridge.** Climb uphill again, looking back to the valley mouth to see a waterfall spilling onto the beach. The ascent is followed closely by another descent into the next valley. There is another house and you walk a little inland past it, then follow a path across a **stone bridge** hidden in a patch of woodland, spanning the **Abbey River,** named after 12th-century Hartland Abbey, situated upstream. Swing back towards the coast and climb onto the next headland, crossing a large sloping field. The ruins of a square **tower** with a large arch frames a view of Stoke Church for a moment. Keep just to the right of a cottage called the **Rocket House** to reach a minor road.

A track and path run downhill towards Hartland Quay. There are fine views back along the rugged coast, showing contorted strata and jagged headlands, before the **Hartland Quay Hotel** is reached. The former quay was battered by gales, neglected and finally crumbled away; the few buildings that remain are weatherbeaten. Food and drink can be obtained from a shop or bar. There are toilets and a small museum. Accommodation is offered at the hotel and there are a couple of B&Bs further inland, with a campsite at Stoke. Wise walkers will book a bed in advance.

The route from Hartland Quay to Bude is one of the most scenic and dramatic stretches of the South West Coast Path, but also one of the toughest. The path may be easy at times, but in other places it climbs steeply only to descend steeply, over and over again. Waterfalls often tumble from the valley mouths to the sea. This day can be very tiring in wet and windy weather. The best advice is to start early and take →

Leave the **Hartland Quay Hotel** and follow steps uphill. An easy stretch of path leads to a **waterfall,** then it moves inland behind a headland. Walk across a field bounded by a wall, then climb over a little headland and walk down to a twin-spout waterfall at **Speke's Mill Mouth.** Head inland to cross a footbridge. There is a choice of paths; *either* take the cliff path over the headland, *or* follow a gentler path up through a valley behind the headland. Either way, the route continues along the cliffs and the path rises gently with fields alongside. Pass some mangled, rusting winch gear, then note that a path can be followed inland from **Mansley Cliff** by those staying at Elmscott youth hostel. A swathe of gorse is passed before the path cuts slightly inland to a signposted road junction at **Sand Hole.**

Turn right along the road, then watch out on the right for the path leading back along the cliffs. Radio antennae stand in a field and the path runs fairly easily around **Nabor Point,** passing a National Trust sign for South Hole. Note the remaining earthen ramparts of **Embury Beacon** at 157m (515ft). This is an Iron Age fort

Start:	Hartland Quay (222248)
Finish:	Bude (208064)
Distance:	25km (15.5 miles)
Cumulative Distance:	199km (123.75 miles)
Maps:	OS Landranger 190, OS Explorers 111 & 126
Terrain:	One of the most difficult days along the whole of the South West Coast Path. The path is easy in parts, but sometimes climbs steeply and descends steeply over and over again. It can be very tiring, even though the final stretch to Bude is reasonably gentle.
Refreshments:	Possibility of refreshments at Morwenstow and Sandymouth, otherwise nothing until close to Bude.

that had to be hurriedly excavated in 1973 as the cliff edge was crumbling. Gorse grows along the cliffs and a gentle descent to **Knap Head** is followed by a sudden, steep, zigzag path down a scrubby slope. Stepping stones cross the stream above a waterfall at **Welcombe Mouth** and a small car park is passed.

Climb steeply up a scrubby slope and cross a field on top of the headland. The path drops down past **Ronald Duncan's hut.** This is often unlocked and visitors are welcome inside the one-roomed cabin, restored in memory of the poet and playwright who lived from 1914–82. There is information about him on the walls, as well as a fine view of **Marsland Mouth**. Continue down lots of steps on the steep slope, with a view of an old mill in the valley. Aim for a footbridge spanning **Marsland Water**. A sign welcomes you to Cornwall, or *Kernow*, to use its Cornish name, and you are immediately faced with the next ascent.

Walk up a broad path, then

continued on page 72

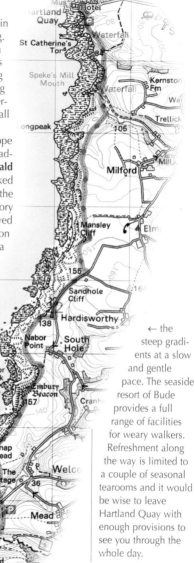

← the steep gradients at a slow and gentle pace. The seaside resort of Bude provides a full range of facilities for weary walkers. Refreshment along the way is limited to a couple of seasonal tearooms and it would be wise to leave Hartland Quay with enough provisions to see you through the whole day.

71

turn right to climb further uphill and round the top of **Marsland Cliff.** Keep an eye on the sea stack of **Gull Rock,** which displays striking zigzag strata. Head downhill along lots of steps and cross a **footbridge,** then climb steeply uphill. The path undulates across **Cornakey Cliff** and becomes vague. Swing right for a grassy descent to cross a small foot-bridge overlooking **Yeol Mouth.** Another steep climb gives way to gentler gradients over the grassy top of **Henna Cliff** at 130m (425ft). Go down a stony path on a steep slope of gorse and heather, crossing a **footbridge** at the bottom. Steps lead up onto **Vicarage Cliff** and alongside fields at the top.

MORWENSTOW

Morwenstow with its fine church is a hamlet a short step inland; food, drink and accommodation here are limited. The Bush Inn is at neigh-bouring Crosstown. There is an irregular bus service to Bude. When Parson Hawker occupied the vicarage at Morwenstow, from 1834–74, he had it rebuilt with chimneys shaped like the towers of his previous churches. Something of an eccentric, he also built a driftwood hut into the cliff face, easily visited by following a path signposted for 'Hawker's Hut'.

The path beyond **Morwenstow** zigzags down another steep slope of

continued opposite

72

gorse, passing a National Trust sign for **Tidna Shute** before crossing a footbridge. Climb up a slope of gorse; there is the option to detour to the right along the ridge of **Higher Sharpnose Point**, from an old lookout cabin. Keep left to continue along the Coast Path, past a crumbling cliff-line, then generally undulating for a while along a pleasant grassy path. A steep descent on a sweeping zigzag leads down to a foot-bridge in a valley overlooking a beach at **Stanbury Mouth**. Climb steeply uphill, keeping well to the right of a prominent **radar station**. Turn right as marked to follow the cliff path, crossing a dip at a National Trust sign for **Steeple Point**. The path appears to head out towards the sea before swinging down to the left to reach a car park and toilets at **Duckpool** in the Combe Valley.

Cross a footbridge and walk up a grassy slope to reach the clifftop again. The path leads downhill to cross a tiny footbridge at **Warren Gutter,** then climbs again. Pleasant grassy paths lead down to another footbridge at **Sandy Mouth.** A tearoom and toilets are available at a car park. The cliffs are low and the next ascent is easy, followed by a gentle walk down to cross a small foot-bridge near the cliff edge. The terrain is rolling and grassy, with no severe gradients, then steps lead down onto a cobbly beach in front of a huddle of cottages at **Northcott Mouth** where there may be refreshments.

Keep left, inland of a white building perched on **Maer Cliff,** then an easy walk along grassy paths leads to Crooklets Beach. Peer over the cliff edge to see how dramatically the rocks have been folded. There are already offers of accommodation, food and drink, as well as toilets. Cross a footbridge to leave **Crooklets Beach** by way of a curved row of beach huts. A path leads onwards for Middle and Summerleaze Beach and

Looking back along the rugged cliffs from the sandy beach at Bude

the little town of **Bude.** The Coast Path crosses the first small, **stone footbridge** you find on the **River Neet.**

BUDE

Bude, along with Flexbury and Stratton, is slightly set back from the coast. The little port enjoyed its best trading years in the late 19th century and was served by a short length of canal and a long railway line, though both were soon closed. There is a fine little museum near the canal. As a seaside resort its greatest asset is a splendid sandy beach.

Facilities include: a range of accommodation, including nearby campsites; banks with ATMs; post office; shops; toilets; pubs and restaurants. Transport links include summer Sunday buses back to Clovelly, Bideford and Barnstaple, and ahead to Widemouth Bay, Boscastle, Tintagel and Newquay. Longer bus journeys include destinations such as Plymouth and Exeter. Tourist Information Centre, Bude Visitor Centre, The Crescent, Bude, Cornwall EX23 8LE, tel: 01288-354240, email: budetic@visit. org.uk

DAY 10
Bude to Boscastle

The Coast Path crosses a stone footbridge on the River Neet in **Bude,** then heads straight away from the river. Turn right to pass the Bude Stratton Museum and walk alongside the **Bude Canal** to reach a restored lock gate at the seaward end. Cross the canal at the lock, turn right and go up steps beside the little lifeboat station. Turn right again and go up more steps beside **Efford Cottage,** built in 1820. Turn right along a tarmac path towards the coast, then swing left up a grassy slope to reach the Storm Tower on **Compass Point.** The octagonal tower dates from the 1830s but was rebuilt in 1880, matching the Temple of the Winds at Athens.

Follow the easy, gently rolling, grassy cliff path to **Upton,** where there are a couple of B&Bs. The Coast Path follows a narrow strip between the cliffs and a minor road. The Chough Hotel offers food, drink and accommodation, while the stretch of cliffs opposite form the **Phillip's Point Nature Reserve.** The ground cover changes from grass to flowery gorse scrub. After passing **Higher Longbeak** and **Lower Longbeak** the path descends gently to **Widemouth Bay.** Food and drink are available, with accommodation at the Bay View Inn.

The Coast Path from Bude to a little beyond Widemouth Bay is easy and never far from a road. The road has to be used on Penhalt Cliff, owing to landslips, then beyond Millook the route crosses Dizzard and a tough series of valleys and headlands on the way to Crackington Haven. This rocky cove is popular with geology students and the contorted strata in the cliff shows clear folding and faulting. High Cliff is one of the higher points →

Start:	Bude (208064)
Finish:	Boscastle Harbour (097914)
Distance:	27km (16.75 miles)
Cumulative Distance:	226km (140.5 miles)
Maps:	OS Landranger 190, OS Explorer 111
Terrain:	The early stretches of the Coast Path are easy, but become progressively more difficult through the day, with some short, steep ascents and descents, and narrow, rugged paths in places.
Refreshments:	There are pubs and shops at Widemouth Bay and Crackington Haven.

← on the Coast Path. The route onwards is quite rugged in places, with some short, steep ascents and descents. The crooked inlet to Boscastle Harbour isn't seen until the last moment and this is a natural place to break.

There are also toilets at the car park beside the sandy beach, but the sprawling settlement lacks character. There are plenty of buses running between Widemouth Bay and Bude.

Walk up the next grassy rise, then head gently downhill to a small development offering food and drink. The Coast Path climbs, then descends using a flight of steps. A diversion a short way inland leads across a wooded stream to a minor road at **Wanson.** Turn right and follow the road up past an **Outdoor Adventure Centre.** There is a short stretch of path to the right of the road, but landslips have even affected the course of the road on **Penhalt Cliff.** There is access to a campsite from this road. When a car park and viewpoint are reached at the top of the road, the Coast Path continues along the cliff. It is easy for a short way, then steps lead down a steep slope to the little settlement of **Millook.** Walk down the road through Millook, then up the road, looking back to see crumpled zigzag layers of rock on the cliff face.

The Coast Path is signposted on the right from a road bend. The path has been cut through the top of a slope covered in bushes and is mostly grassy and easy underfoot. There is a slight descent and the path shifts onto a

The Storm Tower on Compass Point is seen after leaving Bude

wooded slope at a National Trust sign for **Dizzard.** Climb from the oakwood and continue through fields over the highest part of the cliff at 164m (538ft). Continue along the top of a bush-covered slope, then go down steps into a steep-sided valley. There is a footbridge at the bottom then more steps lead uphill. When the path descends later, it follows a bushy ridge towards the sea at **Cleave.** The path turns sharp left and goes down to a footbridge, then steps lead up the next steep slope. The path now appears to head out onto **Pencannow Point,** but makes another sharp left turn and heads down to **Crackington Haven,** short-cutting a prominent bend on the road.

CRACKINGTON HAVEN

This little place is popular with geology students. It was once a busy little port where boats would simply run aground on the beach with cargoes of coal

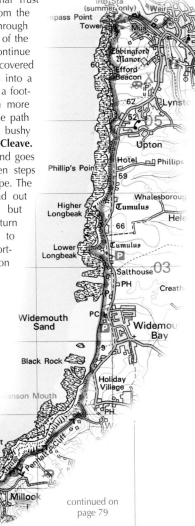

continued on page 79

and limestone, leaving laden with slate. A 19th-century plan to develop the adjacent Tremoutha Haven as a port came to nothing. A small range of facilities include: the Combe Barton Inn, offering food, drink and accommodation; a couple of shops; toilets and cafés. Transport links include buses back to Bude and onwards to Boscastle.

The path leaving **Crackington Haven** is reasonably easy, but has some steep and rugged slopes. Three footbridges are tucked into little valleys on the way round **Tremoutha Haven** to **Cambeak.** There is no need to climb out onto the headland at Cambeak as the Coast Path runs inland behind it and reaches the cliff edge a little later. A few steps run down to a footbridge, then uphill again. There is a grassy ascent before crossing a dip on a scrubby, bushy slope. The higher parts of **High Cliff** reach 223m (732ft), and you need to be careful as the grassy ground is pitted with rabbit holes on the descent.

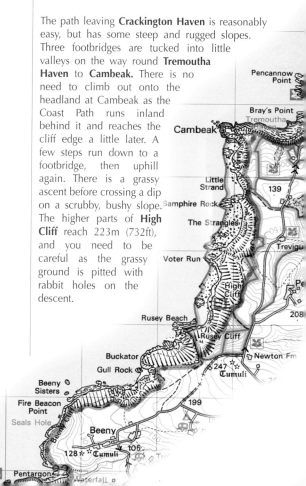

continued on
page 80

Cancleave
Strand

Millook

Dizzard
Point

Cumulus

Millook
Common

Byworth
Cliff

Chipman
Strand

Nature
Reserve

·164

Dizzard

·148

Cleave
Strand

·136

horn's Beach

Tresmorn

Whitemoor
147

Cleave

Tresmorn
Village

Higher
Crann

·31

St Gennys

Crackington
Haven

Drop down into
a valley and cross a small
footbridge, then climb in stages
across the steep and rugged slopes of
Rusey Cliff. Watch out for feral goats that
control the scrubby vegetation, and keep an eye
open for waymarks whenever a junction of paths
appears. Climb uphill, then head down into another
little valley with views back along the cliffs. The walk is
easy for a while, looking down on the prominent **Gull
Rock.** The path swings round towards **Beeny Cliff,** where
a narrow path leads downhill, steep and stony in places.
It basically contours around the cliff, but there are steps
climbing uphill too. The path swings round into a valley
at **Pentargon** and crosses a footbridge above a waterfall.
Steps lead uphill, then easier paths lead towards **Penally
Point,** with a sudden view over the crooked rocky inlet
of **Boscastle Harbour.** The path suddenly swings left and
runs down to a narrow road heading inland past a
variety of buildings to reach a bridge over a river.

BOSCASTLE HARBOUR

While there is no doubt that Boscastle Harbour is a
splendidly sheltered haven for boats, approaches made
in wild weather were fraught with danger. Sea stacks and
rock walls crowd around the inlet; large boats had to be
towed in carefully by rowboats, with additional steerage

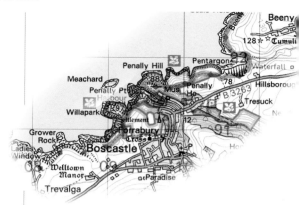

from men on the shore using ropes. The harbour was developed in the 16th century and enjoyed a good trade almost to the 20th century. The buildings alongside Boscastle Harbour rise inland to Boscastle itself.

Facilities include: a small range of accommodation including a youth hostel; shops; toilets; pubs and restaurants. Transport links include buses back to Crackington Haven and Bude, and ahead to Tintagel, Polzeath and Newquay. There is a Witchcraft Museum and a National Trust shop.

View out of the long, narrow, crooked inlet of Boscastle Harbour

DAY 11
Boscastle to Port Isaac

Leave **Boscastle Harbour** by crossing the bridge over the river to continue on the opposite side to the youth hostel. Follow a track towards the mouth of the narrow inlet, passing the little harbour wall. The scenery is splendid and there is the option to detour up to a white-washed building on the headland at **Willapark.** This was used by Customs officers and makes an excellent view-point. The Coast Path actually cuts across the back of the headland.

Walk down steps, then uphill and through some bushes, then down again and cross a **footbridge.** Walk uphill and along a track for a short while, then turn right along a path and enjoy fine views back along the coast. Keep an eye open to spot a fine rock arch to the right, known as the **Ladies Window.** The path undulates and there are views of rugged sea stacks. Steps lead down into **Rocky Valley**; after crossing a footbridge, turn right to find steps climbing up the other side. There are fine views through the mouth of the valley. The path

The Coast Path beyond Boscastle Harbour features several rugged little headlands and coves. Rocky Valley is particularly attractive, but most walkers are looking ahead for their first glimpse of the legendary Tintagel Castle. Make up your own mind about its Arthurian associations, but be careful how long you spend exploring the crumbling ruins. The coastline to →

Start:	Boscastle Harbour (097914)
Finish:	Port Isaac (995807)
Distance:	22km (13.75 miles)
Cumulative Distance:	248km (154.25 miles)
Maps:	OS Landrangers 190 & 200, OS Explorer 111
Terrain:	The first half of the walk has several short ascents and descents, but none are particularly difficult. On the second half of the walk, however, a particularly arduous series of steep ascents and descents are negotiated.
Refreshments:	There is a café near Tintagel Head, and more places offering food and drink in Tintagel itself. Refreshments can also be obtained at Trebarwith Strand.

← Port Isaac is rugged in places and includes a series of steep-sided valleys rather reminiscent of the walk from Hartland Quay to Bude. There are no facilities of any kind between Trebarwith Strand and Port Isaac, so ensure you have enough provisions for the distance.

undulates again across the slope, then runs downhill and crosses a deeply entrenched path above **Bossiney Cliffs.** Walk down to cross a footbridge, then climb up around the next slope and more steeply towards the next headland. You can *either* walk round the headland *or* simply skip it and continue more directly along the coast. Ignore the Camelot Castle Hotel, and look ahead to spot the bits of ancient masonry that constitute **Tintagel Castle** on Tintagel Head. The path drops down to **Castle Cove.**

TINTAGEL

Tintagel Castle is the legendary birthplace of King Arthur, and while there is little to back up the Arthurian claim, the site has at least 2000 years of history behind it. The site of a 5th/6th century stronghold and 13th-century castle, it has been in ruins since the 16th century. You can buy a ticket to explore the ruins, crossing a footbridge over the crumbling neck of land that links the Island to the mainland. There is an English Heritage shop and exhibition, the Castle Beach Café and toilets.

Facilities in the village of Tintagel include: a range of accommodation, including campsites; post office; shops; toilets; pubs and restaurants. The Old Post Office is a delightfully rustic stone building in the care of the National Trust. A Landrover service sometimes runs between Castle Cove and the village. Transport links include buses back to Boscastle and Crackington Haven, and ahead to Port Isaac, Polzeath and Newquay.

Walk a short way up the road from the **Castle Beach** Café and head up to the right

82

continued on page 84

Mo
Is
Tintagel
Dunderh
Po
Penhallic Poin
Treb
S
Gull Rock
Port Wi
Dennis Point
Backways Cove
Start Point
Tregonnick Tail
The
Mou
Tregardock Beach

along a zigzag path. This reaches the upper entrance to **Tintagel Castle**, while the Coast Path continues

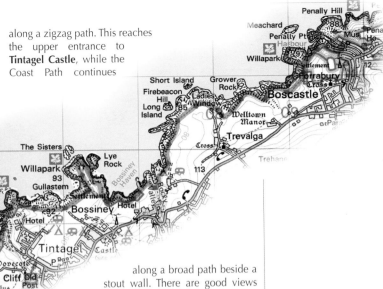

along a broad path beside a stout wall. There are good views back to Tintagel Head as the path makes its way to the prominent St Materiana's Church. Turn right at this point and continue along a clear track to reach the clifftop Tintagel youth hostel. Continue along the cliff path.

Gull Rock is a prominent feature out to sea, and National Trust signs announce **Glebe Cliff** and **Bagalow** as the route unfolds. While passing the quarried slopes at **Lanterdan,** look out for a prominent pinnacle of rock. Slate quarrying has been carried out for 500 years at 10 different locations. Even the rough spoil has found a use in the zigzag 'curzyway' Cornish hedgebanks. The Coast Path drops down to **Trebarwith Strand,** where heavy seas pile up dramatically in a narrow rock inlet. Note that food and drink cannot be obtained between here and Port Isaac.

Climb up a path flanked by an assortment of nets and buoys, turning left up a short stretch of road, then right to pick up the Coast Path. A steep flight of steps leads high above Trebarwith Strand. Cross a field at the top of the cliff, then drop down into a valley, crossing both wooden and stone footbridges. Climb in a sweeping zigzag with a good view out of the valley mouth into **Backways Cove.** The path continues easily on grass, passing some gorse scrub and a National

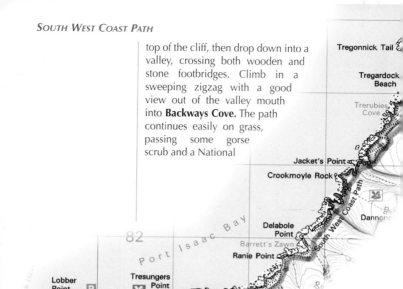

Trust sign for **Treligga Cliffs.** Walk down into a valley and inland a little to cross a stone slab footbridge. There is access to **Tregardock Beach** to the right.

Follow the path up onto **Tregardock Cliff,** which is easy enough, and pass a National Trust sign for **Dannonchapel,** beyond which comes the toughest part of the day's walk. A steep and stony path leads down the ridge of **Jacket's Point** towards the sea. Swing left down to a footbridge above a waterfall. Climb lots of steps on a steep slope beside a huge wedge-shaped cut in the cliff. Keep high around the cliff, basically picking a way round the edge of a field, then head down into another valley. The valley is not so deep or steep-sided, and there is no footbridge over a small stream. Climb out of it and walk through fields before dropping into the next valley to cross another small stream. The path climbs a slope of grass and gorse beside a crumbling cliff above **Barrett's Zawn.** After

crossing the top of the cliff there is a steep descent down a slope of gorse into another valley. Cross a small stream and climb uphill, then continue through fields over the top of **Bounds Cliff.** Stout granite stiles are crossed as each field is passed, then another slope of gorse leads into a little valley. Cross a footbridge, then head up and around the slope and back alongside fields again. The path runs close to the sheer cliffs a couple of times and reaches a road near the Headlands Hotel at **Port Gaverne.**

The Coast Path is signposted on the left side of the hotel, omitting a small headland. A path and a steep, narrow road lead quickly down to the **Port Gaverne Inn.** Follow a road uphill from the beach to reach the top end of **Port Isaac.** The Coast Path is signposted off to the right, along a track and tarmac path, then follows a narrow road down into the village.

PORT ISAAC

Neighbouring Port Gaverne was once a thriving port for shipping slate. Port Isaac is essentially a fishing village given over to tourism. Take time to explore the nooks and crannies, poky alleyways and characterful buildings that are piled up around the cove. Fishy smells emanate from an odd-shaped building by the little beach, where you can inspect the day's catch.

Facilities include: a small range of accommodation; post office; shops; toilets; pubs and restaurants. Transport links include buses back to Tintagel and ahead to Polzeath and Wadebridge.

DAY 12
Port Isaac to Padstow

There are a number of small valleys to cross beyond Port Isaac and Port Quin, but they are not too difficult and the walk becomes easier later. A fine path leads to Port Quin along the splendidly rugged coast. The little settlement was formerly a fishing harbour and is now simply an attractive huddle of buildings. Fine rock scenery can be enjoyed all the way around Pentire Point before the path works its way around the calmer recesses of →

A narrow road leads uphill out of **Port Isaac,** overlooking the beach and leading towards the **Hathaway B&B.** Turn right in front of the building and climb up a flight of granite steps. Walk round the edge of a field and drop gently and easily into a valley to cross a footbridge at **Pine Haven.** Climb a long flight of steps up a steep slope of gorse. The path rises and falls as it makes its way round the coast, with good views.

Turn round **Varley Head** and follow steps downhill, looking ahead to see the path snaking away to Kellan Head. There are a few steps down past some big boulders on the way, then lots of steps lead up and down before another climb onto **Kellan Head.** Turn round the headland and look inland along a narrow inlet to the little settlement of **Port Quin.** A path flanked by bushes leads there, but the only facility is a water tap as you reach the road. A sign indicates that the Long Cross Hotel lies inland if food and drink are needed.

Follow the minor road uphill from the slipway and watch for a stone stile on the right. A path leads back towards the mouth of the inlet, but cuts inland behind a

Start:	Port Isaac (995807)
Finish:	Padstow (920755)
Distance:	19km (11.75 miles)
Cumulative Distance:	267km (166 miles)
Maps:	OS Landranger 200, OS Explorer 106
Terrain:	While there are a few steep-sided valleys on this stretch, the route becomes easier as it progresses and paths are good around the headlands. Sand dunes are crossed before a ferry is used between Rock and Padstow.
Refreshments:	There is only a water tap at Port Quin. Food and drink can be obtained at Polzeath and Rock.

headland where there is a 19th-century folly. Pass between two fenced-off **mine shafts** and follow the path gently uphill onto **Trevan Head.** Walk downhill and cross a stream, then follow the path over the roof of a cave. There is also a little cave to the left of the path at the top. Walk down a bushy slope and cross a little stream, then climb again and look out for a big hole to the right where the sea pounds through an arch. Keep right at a path junction and walk up onto **Carnweather Point.**

The path is grassy at first, then moves through gorse, shifting towards sheer cliffs. The path drops, then climbs over **Com Head,** then undulates towards **Rumps Point.** There are two headlands at the end of the point, as well as the islet of The Mouls. The Coast Path swings left before the end of the point, so explorations are optional. Climb gradually and enjoy the fine rocky coast to reach **Pentire Point,** with views over Padstow Bay and the estuary of the River Camel, with Padstow in the distance. The path descends gently across a grassy slope. There is a detour across a slope of gorse around a small rocky inlet, then another detour round the little sandy bay at **Pentireglaze Haven.** The path leads up to a road, but a patchy Coast Path can be followed in front of the houses at **New Polzeath.** The road ends and a tarmac path continues. *Either* walk down steps onto a sandy beach, *or* follow the path in among the houses if the tide is in. A left turn followed by a right turn leads to the road at the head of the beach in **Polzeath.**

← Padstow Bay to cross the River Camel. Make sure that the ferry is running from Rock to Padstow, to avoid a lengthy detour inland to Wadebridge.

A Coast Path walker crosses Brea Hill to reach the ferry at Rock

POLZEATH

Facilities at Polzeath include: a small range of accommodation, including nearby campsites; post office; shops; toilets; pubs and restaurants. Transport links include buses back to Port Isaac,

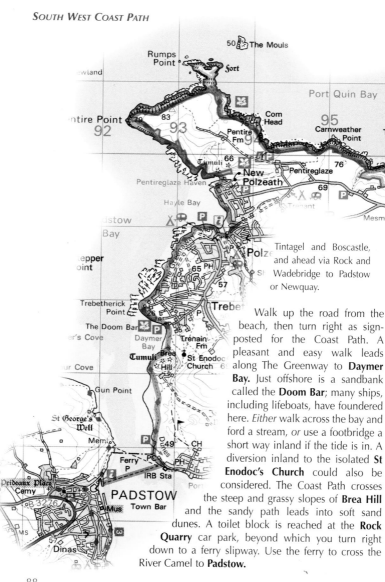

Tintagel and Boscastle, and ahead via Rock and Wadebridge to Padstow or Newquay.

Walk up the road from the beach, then turn right as signposted for the Coast Path. A pleasant and easy walk leads along The Greenway to **Daymer Bay.** Just offshore is a sandbank called the **Doom Bar**; many ships, including lifeboats, have foundered here. *Either* walk across the bay and ford a stream, *or* use a footbridge a short way inland if the tide is in. A diversion inland to the isolated **St Enodoc's Church** could also be considered. The Coast Path crosses the steep and grassy slopes of **Brea Hill** and the sandy path leads into soft sand dunes. A toilet block is reached at the **Rock Quarry** car park, beyond which you turn right down to a ferry slipway. Use the ferry to cross the River Camel to **Padstow.**

The ferry from Rock to Padstow operates all year round at frequent intervals, but not on Sundays between the end of October and beginning of April. When the tide is high the ferry heads for the harbour at Padstow, but at low water lands a little further north. Tel: 01841-532239 for timetable details. Fares are quoted as returns, though walkers can request a single. The ferry avoids a lengthy detour inland to Wadebridge.

PADSTOW

Padstow still has a few fishing boats in its harbour, but today is mainly a tourist resort, with the chance to indulge in a boat trip. It can be very busy, but is well worth exploring and its narrow streets are full of charm and interest. Sir Walter Raleigh was Warden of Cornwall while at the Court House, while Prideaux Place is a fine Elizabethan manor house. St Petroc's Church dates from the 6th century.

Facilities include: plenty of accommodation, including a campsite; banks with ATMs; post office; shops; toilets; pubs and restaurants. Transport links include the Western Greyhound bus along the coast to Harlyn Bay, Porthcothan, Bedruthan Steps, Mawgan Porth and Newquay. Buses also run inland to Wadebridge, Bodmin and Bodmin Parkway for connections to the railway. Tourist Information Centre, Red Brick Building, North Quay, Padstow, Cornwall PL28 8AF, tel: 08841-533449, email: padstowtic@visit.org.uk

DAY 13
Padstow to Porthcothan

A fairly short and easy day's walk, which should allow time for a thorough exploration of Padstow in the morning. The route takes in two significant headlands, Stepper Point and Trevose Head. There are also several sandy beaches, a couple of which are well placed for a lunch break at Trevone or Harlyn Bay. Although there are several places to stay along the coast and inland, they are limited to a few clusters of addresses rather than centres of accommodation.

Take careful note as you step ashore from the Rock to Padstow ferry. You walk only a short way, then the Coast Path is sharp right uphill as signposted. A gate gives way to a tarmac path leading up to a granite cross **war memorial.** Walk down a clear track, but avoid paths and a track leading down to the right to the shore. **St George's Well** is passed on a bend, then the path reaches a sandy beach at **Harbour Cove.**

It is possible to walk across the beach, but the Coast Path moves inland and hugs field boundaries, crossing a track and using a boardwalk in a wetland area. The route crosses, and even follows part of another track, before shifting away from the beach. When a group of buildings are reached at **Hawker's Cove,** head up to a road, but leave it almost immediately and pass between two rows of cottages. The Coast Path continues to **Stepper Point.**

Pass below the **coastguard** lookout, then climb towards a daymark tower. Walk along the cliff coast to pass the deep crater called **Pepper Hole,** then turn round the clifftop overlooking **Butter Hole.** The path is grassy but later there is gorse scrub. Enjoy splendid cliff scenery from **Gunver Head** to another deep crater called **Round Hole,** then walk towards the beach car park at **Trevone Bay.**

Start:	Padstow (920755)
Finish:	Porthcothan (858721)
Distance:	22km (13.75 miles)
Cumulative Distance:	289km (179.75 miles)
Maps:	OS Landranger 200, OS Explorer 106
Terrain:	Easy walking on good paths set at gentle gradients. Rugged headlands separate a succession of sandy beaches.
Refreshments:	Food and drink can be obtained at Trevone, Harlyn Bay and Treyarnon Bay.

TREVONE BAY

Facilities include: a small range of accommodation, including a campsite; post office; shops; toilets and a café. Transport links include the Western Greyhound bus back to Padstow and ahead to Harlyn Bay, Constantine Bay and all points to Newquay.

The path away from **Trevone Bay** is a bit fiddly at first, but leaves the sandy beach and uses a clear track above a rocky beach. An easy, rolling, grit-surfaced path continues, either along the cliff edge or tucked into the fields alongside. Steps lead down onto a sandy beach at **Harlyn Bay** and a bridge is used to cross over a river. The Harlyn Inn offers food, drink and accommodation. A sign on the way to the beach points out that the Coast Path heads along the **beach**. At high water this will not be passable, in which case you might retire to the inn and wait until the tide receeds.

Walk along the sandy beach and *either* come up onto the low cliff before the stone house at the far end, *or* come ashore at it using a slipway. Follow the path gently up onto **Cataclews Point,** then continue and cross

Looking around rugged Mother Ivey's Bay to the lifeboat station

a beach access road. The path moves inland a step to pass behind Mother Ivey's Cottage, then returns to the cliffs around **Mother Ivey's Bay.** The path climbs gently uphill and there is a view of a prominent lifeboat station.

However, the path heads straight inland before that point, climbing

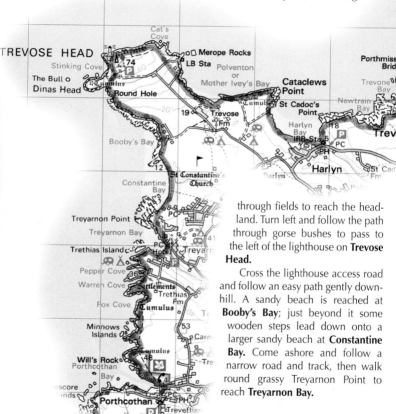

through fields to reach the headland. Turn left and follow the path through gorse bushes to pass to the left of the lighthouse on **Trevose Head.**

Cross the lighthouse access road and follow an easy path gently downhill. A sandy beach is reached at **Booby's Bay**; just beyond it some wooden steps lead down onto a larger sandy beach at **Constantine Bay.** Come ashore and follow a narrow road and track, then walk round grassy Treyarnon Point to reach **Treyarnon Bay.**

TREYARNON BAY

Facilities include: a little accommodation, including a youth hostel and campsite; toilets and a café.

92

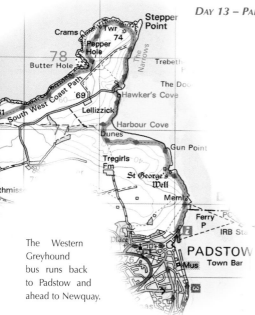

The Western Greyhound bus runs back to Padstow and ahead to Newquay.

Walk beyond **Treyarnon Bay youth hostel** and the café, then drop down to the head of the sandy beach. Ford a stream and climb inland behind a clifftop cottage. An easy grassy path leads onwards round several little headlands and coves. There are also rugged little stacks, including the **Minnows Islands,** often beaten by heavy seas. The Coast Path suddenly swings round to reveal the inlet of **Porthcothan Bay,** then the path heads for the road in the scattered little village of **Porthcothan.**

PORTHCOTHAN

Facilities include: a little accommodation, including a nearby campsite; post office; shop; toilets and pub. Transport links include the Western Greyhound bus running back to Padstow, and ahead to Mawgan Porth and Newquay.

93

DAY 14
Porthcothan to Newquay

A fairly easy day's walk, though some parts feature paths that can be rather steep and narrow. The coast is often very scenic, with little headlands and coves; Bedruthan Steps is one of the more popular places and a steady procession of visitors wander down the stone-paved path to view the spectacular beach with its line of rugged stacks. Mawgan Porth makes an ideal lunch stop, then a fairly straightforward path leads to Newquay. The town can be →

Leave **Porthcothan** by walking down past the Porthcothan Bay Stores, but do not reach the beach. Keep left and walk between the houses and the low cliff edge. As the path turns round a headland, there are splendid views of the cliffs and battered stacks of the **Trescore Islands.** Walk down to the head of a narrow inlet at **Porth Mear** and cross a footbridge. There is a series of little headlands and coves; signs warn walkers to keep inland of a series of white posts as the cliff is crumbling in places. Pass the top of the **Pentire Steps** and follow the path to a stone-paved path at **Bedruthan Steps.**

The beach is studded with highly individual rocky stacks, called (north to south) Diggory's Island, Queen Bess Rock, Samaritan Rock, Redcove Island, Pendarves Island and Carnewas Island. The Coast Path climbs inland, rather than down the steps, then heads off right before reaching a National Trust information centre, café and toilets. There are occasional Western Greyhound bus services along the road, heading to Padstow and Newquay.

The path continues through gorse and eventually descends around **Trenance Point** to pass below

Start:	Porthcothan (858721)
Finish:	Newquay Harbour (806620)
Distance:	18km (11.25 miles)
Cumulative Distance:	307km (191 miles)
Maps:	OS Landranger 200, OS Explorer 106
Terrain:	Mostly fairly easy, though the path is a little steep and narrow in places. The surroundings become increasingly urban towards the end.
Refreshments:	Shops and pubs at Mawgan Porth, food and drink at Watergate Bay.

...goes down to drink from the stream at rocky...

← overpoweringly busy after the open cliffs and some walkers may be inclined to press onwards to a quieter place for the night.

Trenance. Walk along the beach, except at high water, when you should stay on dry land and cross a bridge over the River Menalhyl to reach **Mawgan Porth.**

TRENANCE & MAWGAN PORTH

Facilities include: a range of accommodation, including nearby campsites; post office; shops; toilets; pubs and restaurants. Transport links include the Western Greyhound bus service back to Padstow and ahead to Newquay.

Walk up the road from the beach to leave **Mawgan Porth.** The Coast Path is signposted on the right, leading up around the headland of **Berryl's Point** and down around rocky **Beacon Cove.** Cross a footbridge on the way out onto **Griffin's Point,** where the scant remains of an Iron Age fort can be studied. The fence has been moved back on **Strasse Cliff** as the path has occasionally been lost to landslips. A narrow path squeezes down to a road beside the Watergate Bay

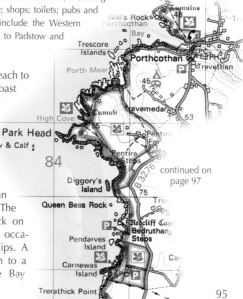

continued on page 97

95

Hotel. There are other hotels around **Watergate Bay,** and refreshments can be obtained. The road is also on the Western Greyhound bus route to Newquay. The bus stop is beside a toilet block.

The Coast Path leaves the road just beyond a little car park near the **Watergate Bay Hotel.** Follow a clear path uphill; note how the fence has been moved back to accommodate landslips. When buildings are reached at **Trevelgue,** keep to the path as it works its way around the headland to the seaward side of the Paradise Cove Hotel. **Trevelgue Head** is actually an island, and footbridge allows it to be visited even at high water. The path swings back towards the road at **Porth Beach,** in effect a suburb of Newquay, with hotels, take-aways, shops and bus services.

It is possible to walk around **Porth Beach** when the

Walkers descend stone steps on their way to see Bedruthan Steps

tide is out, but at high water follow the main road uphill from the **Mermaid Inn**. At the top of the road, just beside a bus shelter, the Coast Path is signposted apparently inland, but it actually goes down steps and doubles back underneath the main road. **Porth Bean Road** leads back down to the beach. Follow a tarmac path gently uphill from the beach and keep climbing to join a blocked-off road. Follow the road onwards past an access point for **Lusty Glaze Beach,** then turn right and walk along a pleasant grassy swathe away from the road. **Cliff Road** is joined at a toilet block and is followed all the way into **Newquay.** Walk down **North Quay Hill** to reach the **harbour.** It could be a good idea to walk on by referring to the next day's route description, maybe seeking accommodation for the night at **Pentire.**

NEWQUAY

Originally known as 'Towanblistra', a 'new quay' was constructed in the 16th century and the town prospered as a port. The thriving fishing industry was augmented by a brisk cargo trade, and the construction of a railway to the harbour. When the trade around the harbour

97

Looking across Newquay Harbour to some of the town's clifftop hotels

began to decline, Newquay's fortunes were buoyed up by tourism, and the town is blessed with the largest range of facilities yet seen on the South West Coast Path. There is a zoo at Trenance Gardens.

Facilities include: abundant accommodation of all types, including nearby campsites; banks with ATMs; post office; a large range of shops; toilets; pubs and restaurants galore. Transport links include a handy airport with flights to London Gatwick and Stanstead. Wessex Trains connect with Virgin Trains to Scotland and Great Western trains to London Paddington. Bus services include the Western Greyhound covering the coast back to Padstow, and other services inland. Buses run ahead to Crantock, Holywell and Perranporth. National Express buses run to London, and to Brighton via Plymouth, Bridport, Weymouth, Poole and Bournemouth. Tourist Information Centre, Municipal Offices, Marcus Hill, Newquay, Cornwall TR7 1BD, tel: 01637-854020, email: info@newquay.co.uk

DAY 15
Newquay to Perranporth

Leave **Newquay** by walking down **North Quay Hill** almost to the **harbour,** but turn left to follow a narrow road signposted as the Coast Path. A long flight of steps and a path lead up to the whitewashed **huer's hut.** This is thought to date from the 14th century, and was used by a man to raise a 'hue' when he observed shoals of fish in the sea. It may previously have been a hermitage where a monk tended a beacon fire.

The path continues along the cliffs, then an old tarmac road leads down to a car park on a narrow neck of land where you can cross and make a short circuit around **Towan Head.** Continue around the seaward side of the prominent Headlands Hotel to reach a car park and toilets at **Fistral Beach.** *Either* walk along the beach, *or if the tide is in,* use a path a short way inland behind the vegetated dunes. Join a road and turn right, climbing gradually uphill from a row of hotels. Walk to the end of **Pentire Point East,** then double back until a car park is reached. Food, drink and local bus services are found here.

Turn right down **Riverside Crescent;** a battered road signposted for the Fern Pit Café and ferry. If the tide is in

After exploring a couple of easy headlands beyond Newquay, the tidal inlet of The Gannel has to be crossed, by seasonal ferry if the tide is in, or by tidal footbridge when the water is low. The footbridge by the ferry is approached using a private path, and the Coast Path uses another tidal footbridge further inland. If the tide is in and there is no ferry, then either make a lengthy detour inland, or hire a taxi or catch a bus to Crantock. →

Start:	Newquay Harbour (806620)
Finish:	Perranporth (756542)
Distance:	17km (10.5 miles)
Cumulative Distance:	324km (201.5 miles)
Maps:	OS Landranger 200, OS Explorer 104
Terrain:	A fairly easy day, but complicated because a tidal inlet has to be negotiated after leaving Newquay. A series of headlands and sandy beaches is passed through the day.
Refreshments:	Food and drink can be obtained at Pentire, West Pentire and slightly off-route at Holywell.

← Other headlands and sandy beaches are negotiated in turn; note that there is an Army Training Area on Penhale Point. The day's distance is short; if walkers continue beyond Perranporth, a series of smaller villages offers a reasonable range of facilities.

The Gannel from the Crantock shore, seen at low tide

and the ferry running use the private zigzag path downhill from the café to get the **ferry** to the other side of **The Gannel.** There is also a low-tide footbridge if the café and path are open. The ferry usually runs daily, either side of high water, from the end of May mid-September, tel: 01637-873181 for current details of services.

Officially, the Coast Path doesn't use the ferry but continues down the road and along **Riverside Avenue.** Keep right and continue along **Pentire Crescent,** but avoid the first footpath you see signposted for Crantock. Continue along the road, turning right along **Penmere Drive,** right again along **Trevean Way,** then right along a footpath down to **The Gannel.** There is a **tidal footbridge** spanning the river channel; when you cross it you should aim for the left side of another tidal creek straight ahead. Turn right across a concrete slab at the head of this creek, then walk up a narrow road a short way. Turn right along a footpath near **Penpol,** passing through wooded and open areas to walk alongside **The Gannel** again. Continue along this path with a view across to the Fern Pit Café and ferry.

The path becomes a track at some houses, then turn right as signposted for the Coast Path near a **café.** Cross a car park and continue along a path over hummocky, vegetated dunes. There is a maze of paths, but by keeping well back from the shore it is possible to traverse directly from the dunes to a path running between the fields and cliff edge above **Crantock Beach.** Cross a beach access path seaward of the **Crantock Bay Hotel.** The cliff path leads around the end of the grassy **Pentire Point West.**

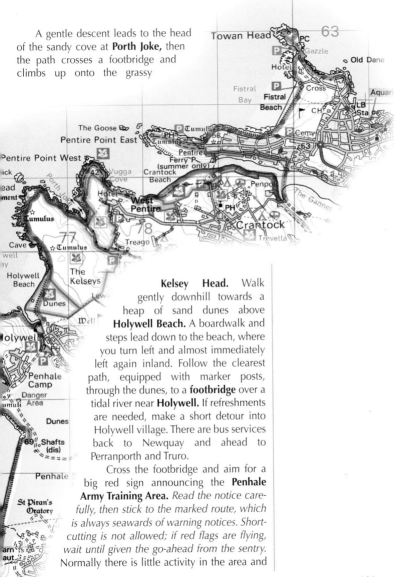

A gentle descent leads to the head of the sandy cove at **Porth Joke,** then the path crosses a footbridge and climbs up onto the grassy **Kelsey Head.** Walk gently downhill towards a heap of sand dunes above **Holywell Beach.** A boardwalk and steps lead down to the beach, where you turn left and almost immediately left again inland. Follow the clearest path, equipped with marker posts, through the dunes, to a **footbridge** over a tidal river near **Holywell.** If refreshments are needed, make a short detour into Holywell village. There are bus services back to Newquay and ahead to Perranporth and Truro.

Cross the footbridge and aim for a big red sign announcing the **Penhale Army Training Area.** *Read the notice carefully, then stick to the marked route, which is always seawards of warning notices. Short-cutting is not allowed; if red flags are flying, wait until given the go-ahead from the sentry. Normally there is little activity in the area and*

continued on page 102

101

the path simply works its way around **Penhale Point,** keeping away from mine shafts and the shabby cabins sprawling inland. The cliffs around **Hoblyn's Cove** are sheer and the path is flanked by fencing until it passes a stone house. After turning around **Ligger Point** the path cuts across a very steep grassy slope, with unseen cliffs below. Follow the marker posts down to the sandy **Perran Beach**, just before which there is an interesting pool under a rock arch to the right.

Broad and sandy Perran Beach can be followed onwards, but high water can obstruct the way. The Coast Path picks its way across the steep slope above the beach; whether you follow the beach or the slope, you have the option of switching to the other at a prominent access point. Either way, the route heads past **Crotty's Point** to reach the seaside resort of **Perranporth.** Depending on the state of the tide, *either* hug the shore and link roads and walkways to enter the town, *or* walk across the sandy beach. Note the curious rock arches on the other side of the little bay, then climb up steps onto the cliffs above the town.

PERRANPORTH

Facilities include: a range of accommodation, including a youth hostel and nearby campsites; post office; shops; toilets; pubs and restaurants. Transport links include buses back to Holywell and Newquay, and ahead to St Agnes, Porthtowan, Hayle and St Ives. National Express buses run from Perranporth to London, and to Brighton via Newquay, Plymouth, Exeter, Bridport, Weymouth, Poole and Bournemouth.

DAY 16
Perranporth to Portreath

Walk up **Cliff Road** to leave **Perranporth.** There is a grassy area between road and cliff, but be sure to walk up the road behind Droskyn Castle, towards the youth hostel perched on the cliff edge at **Droskyn Point.** The Coast Path is signposted up to the left before the hostel, and after a short ascent it runs gently downhill and roughly contours across a heathery slope. Capped mine shafts can be seen, as well as spoil heaps and levels. Go through a gap in a crumbling outcrop of granite at **Cligga Head.** Watch carefully for marker posts as there is a network of paths ahead on a rugged moorland slope covered in heather and gorse. The cliff edge is crumbling in places, then the clifftop path runs through gorse and there is an **airfield** inland. Pass concrete bunkers, then follow the path down into a valley called **Trevellas Coombe.** Head inland, walking between a narrow road and a river to reach the **Blue Hills Tin Streams.** This is an interesting site, open all year except Sundays, demonstrating how tin ore is crushed, washed and smelted. Although the actual mine closed in 1897, the tin streams developed as an attraction since 1975. Refreshments are available.

The hustle and bustle of Perranporth very quickly gives way to bleak, rugged cliffs and narrow paths. Old mine shafts, engine houses and chimneys dominate the scene; St Agnes was once a thriving mining area. Most of the mines have been capped, but stay away from old buildings and shafts. The cliff walk is quite arduous in places, but there are a handful of little villages and sandy beaches, so food, drink and relaxing interludes are →

Start:	Perranporth (756542)
Finish:	The Square at Portreath (657454)
Distance:	20km (12.5 miles)
Cumulative Distance:	344km (214 miles)
Maps:	OS Landranger 203, OS Explorer 104
Terrain:	Rugged cliffs often feature narrow, stony paths with some short, steep ascents and descents. Old mines are very much in evidence.
Refreshments:	Available at the Blue Hills Tin Streams, pubs at Trevaunance Bay, a café at Chapel Porth and pubs at Porthtowan.

← available. Bear in mind that accommodation is quite limited and it is wise to book your bed ahead. There is a long and empty stretch beyond Portreath.

Cross a road bridge below the Blue Hills Tin Streams and walk uphill, then follow a steep track up to the right signposted as the Coast Path. Walk along a path just to the right of the track, passing a gate and later drifting towards the cliffs before descending to **Trevaunance Cove.** Land on a road beside the Driftwood Spars Hotel and Restaurant, then cross over and walk up the road opposite. Turn right and bear right as signposted for the Coast Path. This leads to another road, which you follow to the left, then continue off the end of the road to reach **Trevaunance Point.**

TREVAUNANCE BAY & ST AGNES

The old harbour at Trevaunance Bay has been destroyed by storms. Ore shipments from the tin mines formed the mainstay of trade, but the mines have been closed for a century and the area is slowly turning to tourism.

Facilities between the bay and village include: a small range of accommodation, including nearby campsites; post office; shops; toilets;

continued on page 106

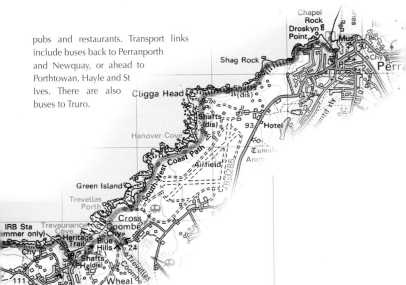

pubs and restaurants. Transport links include buses back to Perranporth and Newquay, or ahead to Porthtowan, Hayle and St Ives. There are also buses to Truro.

Climb up a flight of steps above **Trevaunance Point** and follow a marked path across a slope of heather and gorse. Pass a National Trust sign for Newdowns and swing round rugged **St Agnes Head.** Another National Trust sign announces **Tubby's Head** and the path straightens out alongside a drystone wall. Watch out for a descent to the right, and follow a path down towards an old engine house on the slope, passing just below it. Continue round the slope and keep an eye on the marker posts – there is a network of criss-crossing paths – but eventually the route heads down to **Chapel Porth.** The National Trust runs the Chapel Porth Beach Café and there are toilets.

The paths you see climbing straight uphill from Chapel Porth are marked as dangerous, so head inland parallel to the narrow road, then swing sharp right and follow a stony track uphill. Keep an eye on the marker posts in an area of spoil heaps and follow a path that later overlooks the sea again. This leads down to **Porthtowan,** landing on a road-end and following the road inland to **The Unicorn,** which offers food and drink.

PORTHTOWAN

Facilities include: a little accommodation, including a campsite; post office; shop; toilets; pub and restaurant. Transport links include buses back to Perranporth and Newquay and ahead to St Ives.

The Coast Path turns sharp right beyond **The Unicorn,** following a road up to the **Beach Hotel.** Continue beyond the hotel to the top of the road, then follow a clear track onwards, set back a little from the cliffs. Looking ahead, a **flue**

chimney can be seen and the track runs just to its left. Also to the left is a stout fence surrounding an extensive MOD property on **Nancekuke Common.** The path passes a sign pointing out that the route crosses MOD property, and warns of dangerous cliffs and mine shafts.

The path proceeds easily alongside the fence, then steps run down into a dip in the cliff-line and climbs the other side. Further along is another dip, also crossed

using steps. The path leaves the MOD property and the sea is full of rugged stacks. The path passes a car park and runs down towards a white **Day Mark.** Turn left to reach a road, then follow **Lighthouse Road,** overlooking the compact little harbour at **Portreath** and continue down into the village to reach **The Square.**

The rocky shore near Trevaunance Cove before St Agnes Head

PORTREATH

The little harbour with its solid stonework contrasts markedly with the modern sprawl of the village. Trade centred around exports of copper and imports of coal, though fishing was also important.

Facilities include: a small range of accommodation; post office; shops; toilets; pubs and restaurants. Transport links include buses inland to Redruth and Camborne for further connections or access to main line railway services.

DAY 17
Portreath to St Ives

Although the Coast Path has some steep ascents and descents after leaving Portreath, it levels out and runs easily along the cliffs and around the headlands to Gwithian. There is no habitation, but there are a couple of handy cafés. Choose between a walk over the dunes of The Towans, or a long beach walk if the tide allows. Agonise over whether to follow busy roads from Hayle to Lelant, or catch a bus or train to →

Leave The Square in **Portreath** and follow **Beach Road** to a sand and pebble beach, the last place to get food and drink for a while. Swing left away from the beach, then right as signposted for the Coast Path up a road called **Battery Hill.** Pass the Battery House and walk down to the end of the road. Turn left as signposted, then *either* climb up steps to the right onto a headland, *or* walk straight up a little valley to reach the cliffs. The scenery along the cliffs is remarkable, especially around **Ralph's Cupboard.**

Although the clifftop path is easy, there are two steep-sided valleys to cross using flights of steps. The path is easy and almost level again on **Reskajeage Downs,** running from one little car park to another. The latter car park is surrounded by gorse bushes, then there are a couple more small car parks tucked into the gorse. The path pulls away from the road and turns round another little headland, from **Deadman's Cove** to **Hell's Mouth.** Hell's Mouth Café is easily reached from the rock-bound cove.

Continue along the Coast Path, which links with a track, then cross a field and continue out onto a gorse-

Start:	The Square at Portreath (657454)
Finish:	St Ives Harbour (518408)
Distance:	29km (18 miles)
Cumulative Distance:	373km (232 miles)
Maps:	OS Landranger 203, OS Explorers 102 & 104
Terrain:	A couple of steep-sided little valleys lead to easy cliff and headland walking. Soft sand dunes give way to a detour inland by road from Hayle to Lelant, then a variety of paths lead onwards to St Ives.
Refreshments:	The Hell's Mouth Café and Godrevy Café fill an empty stretch of coast, followed by refreshments around Gwithian. There are a number of shops and pubs around Hayle, Lelant and Carbis Bay.

covered headland. This is **The Knavocks** and the path continues round a point and gently downhill with increasingly good views of **Godrevy Island** and its lighthouse. Follow the path round to a car park and toilets, then use a grassy path beside a minor road to reach **Godrevy Café** at another car park.

At the bottom end of the car park, use a boardwalk and steps down to the **Red River.** Turn left, cross a footbridge, then turn right towards the beach. Turn left along a path on a shingle bank overlooking a **gravel pit** and the sea. Climb up a few steps at the end of the bank and turn right to follow a broad path between a lifeguard cabin and toilets.

A café is available in an old coastguard lookout nearby, uphill among some chalets. Another café can be found further along, inland from a car park near **Gwithian.** There is also a little accommodation, a pub and bus services back to Newquay or ahead to St Ives.

The broad path gives way to a maze of waymarked paths through **The Towans.** Be sure to follow the Coast Path markers to negotiate this extensive belt of sand dunes; a long beach walk is also available at low water. **Gwithian Towans** gives way to **Upton Towans**, then a car park is passed below some mobile homes. **Phillack Towans** comes next, then an old car park is passed.

← continue. St Ives in summer is horribly busy, but is too interesting to leave without an exploration, and as the Coast Path beyond is so rough and remote, make arrangements before leaving town.

A razor-edged rocky cove at Ralph's Cupboard beyond Portreath

The route heads gradually down towards the beach, crossing a narrow beach access road at a lifeguard cabin. A soft, sandy path leads uphill, then more waymarks show the way back onto vegetated dunes at **Mexico Towans.** Head down towards the beach below more mobile homes and follow the path across **Riviere Towans.** Toilets are reached near the **Penellen Hotel,** then the path continues round the coast, nudging into a chalet development.

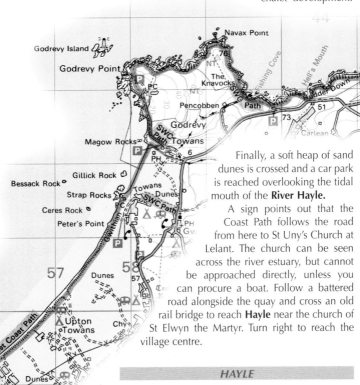

Finally, a soft heap of sand dunes is crossed and a car park is reached overlooking the tidal mouth of the **River Hayle.**

A sign points out that the Coast Path follows the road from here to St Uny's Church at Lelant. The church can be seen across the river estuary, but cannot be approached directly, unless you can procure a boat. Follow a battered road alongside the quay and cross an old rail bridge to reach **Hayle** near the church of St Elwyn the Martyr. Turn right to reach the village centre.

HAYLE

This sprawling village wins no points for prettiness, and its industrial past is all too evident. It does offer a number of facilities such as: a small range of accommo-

continued on page 112

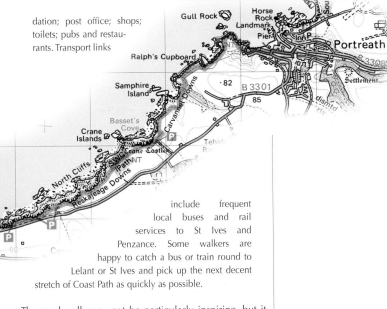

dation; post office; shops; toilets; pubs and restaurants. Transport links include frequent local buses and rail services to St Ives and Penzance. Some walkers are happy to catch a bus or train round to Lelant or St Ives and pick up the next decent stretch of Coast Path as quickly as possible.

The road-walk may not be particularly inspiring, but it takes little more than an hour to get from Hayle to Lelant. Follow the road under the **railway viaduct** and swing right to pass back under it. If time is not pressing you could turn right and follow an embankment around a **tidal lagoon,** otherwise stay on the busy road.

Use the pavement on the right until it peters out, then use the one on the left. Turn right as signposted for Lelant at the **Old Quay House,** which offers food and drink. Keep right at other road junctions to follow the main road through **Lelant,** passing a B&B, post office and the Badger Inn. The main road turns left, but keep straight on down a minor road to reach **St Uny's Church.**

There is a waymark and a path just to the left of the church. When the path reaches a **golf course,** swing right down a deep rut and beware flying golf balls until the safety of a railway bridge is reached. Pass under and turn left before the old **Ferry House** to follow a path beside the railway.

Bushes alongside the path gradually obscure views and completely enclose the path. A tarmac path climbs steeply to the **railway**; turn right and head downhill as signposted for the beach and **artist's studio.** The Coast Path avoids both and runs round the well-vegetated headland of **Carrack Gladden** to reach Carbis Bay.

Again, don't go down to the beach; when steps lead down to it, climb uphill instead, then walk down the road from the railway station to reach **Carbis Bay.** The beach is dominated by the Carbis Bay Hotel; there is a beach café and toilets. Follow a path uphill just beyond the hotel. Steps lead up to a footbridge over the railway, then a path alongside the railway later becomes a road. Pass the white-washed **Baulking House**, formerly a huer's lookout.

Walk down through a crossroads to follow a tarmac path across the railway and land beside the beach below the railway

station at **St Ives.** Refreshment is immediately available, and a path behind beach huts gives way to one alongside a linear garden. Continuing towards the town centre leads along **The Warren,** with access to a whole series of narrow streets and alleyways. Head for the little **harbour.** If there is any time to spare, visit the promontory known as **The Island,** crowned by the restored **St Nicholas Chapel.**

ST IVES

The town's name can be traced back to St Ia, a 5th-century Irish missionary and daughter of a chieftain. The natural harbour was protected by The Island, or St Ives Head, and was developed in the 18th century. After a long history as a fishing port, St Ives has become associated with arts, crafts and tourism. There are a couple of museums to visit. In the summer months the town is packed; most coastal walkers would happily leave it in search of quieter cliff paths, but take the time to explore it first.

Facilities include: abundant accommodation of all types, including nearby campsites; banks with ATMs; post office; shops; toilets; plenty of pubs and restaurants. Transport links include a railway linking with main line services, for direct Virgin Trains to Scotland and Great Western trains to London Paddington. There are frequent bus services to and from Penzance and Hayle, and along the coast to Zennor, Pendeen and St Just. National Express buses run from St Ives to London, Birmingham and Scotland. Tourist Information Centre, The Guildhall, Street-an-Pol, St. Ives, Cornwall TR26 2DS, tel: 01736-796297, email: ivtic@penwith.gov.uk

DAY 18
St Ives to Pendeen Watch

It is a good idea to leave St Ives early in the day and monitor progress from time to time without trying to hurry too much. A pack full of provisions will be useful, so that detours for refreshment don't add to the journey. If you have plenty of time, and the weather is good, this is one of the most spectacular parts of the South West Coast Path. If you try and rush it, and suffer poor weather, it becomes an arduous treadmill. Accommodation is limited and is →

Leave **St Ives** by way of **Porthmeor Beach,** signposted from various points around town. Keep to the landward side of the toilets, putting green and bowling green at the far end of the beach, following an easy tarmac path beyond some minor granite tors. The path becomes stony and heads for **Clodgy Point,** then the ground is bouldery and may be muddy as the path climbs uphill. An easier stretch leads to a track, but this quickly becomes a narrow path again. For a while there are no habitations in view.

Walk along a stretch of boardwalk near **Pen Enys Point,** then notice how the **Trevalgan Holiday Farm** has staked out a trail along part of the Coast Path. This includes a recently constructed 'ancient stone circle' called the **Merry Harvesters!** A trig point is passed at 97m (318ft) on a plateau of gorse scrub at **Carn Naun Point.** The view ahead stretches to the lighthouse at Pendeen Watch.

Drop down into a valley and rise a little to cross a stream, pouring from the valley mouth as a waterfall. Walk round and across a slope, noting rugged rocks below. The path runs up and around little headlands and

Start:	St Ives Harbour (518408)
Finish:	Pendeen Watch (380358)
Distance:	22km (13.5 miles)
Cumulative Distance:	395km (245.5 miles)
Maps:	OS Landranger 203, OS Explorer 102
Terrain:	A rough and remote stretch, often along narrow and sometimes vague paths, with numerous short steep ascents and descents. One of the more difficult stretches.
Refreshments:	None actually on the route; detours inland lead to pubs at Zennor and Boswednack.

coves, crossing bouldery slopes before heading down into another valley to cross a stream above **Wicca Pool.** Climb up granite steps, then turn right towards the coast again. The path runs down through awkward boulders, almost to the bouldery shore, then climbs again.

Cross a couple of streams then contour high above **Porthzennor Cove.** Take a right turn downhill a little, then climb up to an attractive tor. Walk round **Zennor Head** and enjoy splendid views down into Pendour Cove. It is possible to head inland to **Zennor** and the Tinner's Arms. There is also a small museum if time can be spared; hostel accommodation and a campsite are available.

Be sure to make a right turn as indicated for

← always inland, so book your bed in advance, or be prepared to use the bus service to reach a more far-flung address. Ancient promontory forts on the remoter parts of the coast give way to ruined tin mines towards the end of the day.

Looking from rocky Zennor Head to the promontory of Gurnard's Head

Pendeen Watch on a granite marker stone. Lots of overgrown stone steps lead down to a footbridge. Climb uphill and walk round the top of **Pendour Cove** and an adjacent cove, then head downhill for a while. The path climbs up past a blocky tor, then runs downhill and uphill again. Walk around a slope and cross a

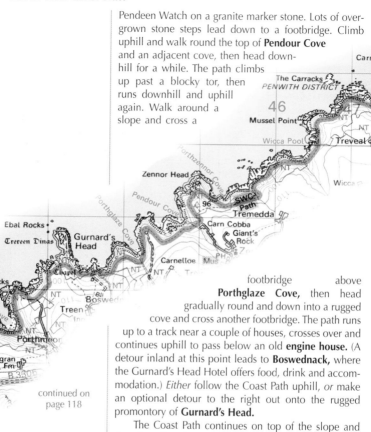

footbridge above **Porthglaze Cove,** then head gradually round and down into a rugged cove and cross another footbridge. The path runs up to a track near a couple of houses, crosses over and continues uphill to pass below an old **engine house.** (A detour inland at this point leads to **Boswednack,** where the Gurnard's Head Hotel offers food, drink and accommodation.) *Either* follow the Coast Path uphill, *or* make an optional detour to the right out onto the rugged promontory of **Gurnard's Head.**

continued on page 118

The Coast Path continues on top of the slope and there is a view down to a stack in a rocky little cove just beyond Gurnard's Head. After turning round a rocky little headland, cross a stream using a rock-slab footbridge at **Porthmeor Cove.** The slopes beyond can be wet and muddy and the Coast Path has been rerouted slightly. Climb uphill and have a look at a prominent headland. The ancient fortification of **Bosigran Castle** can be visited and the cliffs are popular with rock-climbers.

Descend in the rough direction of a **ruin,** but keep to the left of it to spot a tiny stone-arch footbridge. Climb uphill and follow the path in and out, up and down, along a tangled clifftop. A tower of rock crowned with a big boulder is passed at **Chair Carn.** Cliffs often look as if they have been constructed with cyclopean masonry and there are fine views. The path may be rough and muddy in places, but after passing a **crumbling ruin** becomes pleasant and grassy.

Bouldery stepping stones cross another wet area, then the path is grassy and level and runs alongside an embankment of earth and boulders. The path forges onwards through gorse, then descends steeply, zigzagging to some stepping stones across a waterfall-filled stream above **Portheras Cove.** Steps and a bouldery path lead up the other side of the valley, then turn right along a track that becomes pleasantly grassy. A couple of gates are passed and a sign indicates B&B and cream teas up at **Pendeen Manor Farm.**

The track zigzags down towards a huddle of huts beside **Portheras Cove.** Turn left up a gravel track, passing a gate at a large turning space, then follow the road uphill and keep left of the lighthouse at **Pendeen Watch.** The lighthouse is open for visits. Views inland reveal the villages of Lower Boscaswell, **Pendeen** and crumbling ruins associated with the tin mines. If you are not staying at Pendeen Manor Farm, you will either have to move inland to Pendeen for refreshment and accommodation, or continue further along the Coast Path.

117

PENDEEN

Evidence of the former tin-mining industry around Pendeen is prominent. Old chimneys, engine houses and winding gear can be seen. The past glories of the industry can be appreciated by visiting the Geevor Tin Mine, which was working as late as 1990. Tin was mined either by digging down into a vein until it became flooded, or digging up through a vein from the foot of a cliff. When

Map labels:

Robin's
Porthmeor P(
Porthmeo
Great
Zawn
Halldrine Cov
37 Porthmoina Cove
Boskran Castle
NT
The Wra or
Three Stone Oar
The Mozens
Brandys
Whirl Pool
NT
141
Rosem
Greeb Point
Pendeen Watch
69
Carn
Chair Carn
3
Long Carn
PC
The Enys
fogou
Pendeen House
Clough
South West Coast Path
Chypraze
Morvah
119
120
Settle
Portheras Fm
116

mighty engines were designed to pump out floodwater, mines were sunk even deeper and extended far out beneath the seabed.

Facilities include: a small range of accommodation, including a nearby campsite; post office; shops; pubs and restaurants. Transport links include buses back to Zennor and St Ives, and ahead to St Just and Penzance.

DAY 19
Pendeen Watch to Porthcurno

A granite marker stone up the road from the lighthouse at **Pendeen Watch** marks the course of the South West Coast Path as it runs down into a gentle valley set back from the cliffs. The path rises and falls, gradually making its way down to **Trewellard Zawn,** beyond which is a wasteland of ruined buildings, chimneys and engine houses. (You could detour inland to visit **Geevor Tin Mine.**) Cross a footbridge and turn right, then left, then take the second turn on the right, and keep straight on for **Levant.** There is a small car park above the restored **beam engine.**

Follow the track onwards across a moorland of gorse and heather to reach a **solitary house,** then turn right as marked along a path that links with another track. This appears to head for a pit wheel frame, but another waymarked right turn reveals a path leading through some old buildings instead. The path becomes a good track, passing more chimneys and engine houses. The buildings of the **Old Crowns Mine** are perched attractively on the cliff face.

When the track bends inland, take a grassy track to the right, which leads to old ruins at **Kenidjack.** The headland is also the site of an Iron Age fortification. A

Pendeen's ruined tin mines give way to classic Cornish cliff walking en route to Cape Cornwall, formerly given all the accolades now heaped on Land's End. After following rugged paths to Sennen, an easier path leads to Land's End. This can often be very busy, not just because of its attendant tourist trap, but simply because it is a place that inspires people. Despite the crowds, the cliff scenery is excellent. Some of the best cliff scenery along the South West Coast →

Start:	St Ives Harbour (518408)
Finish:	Minack Theatre at Porthcurno (386220)
Distance:	26km (16 miles)
Cumulative Distance:	421km (261.5 miles)
Maps:	OS Landranger 203, OS Explorer 102
Terrain:	The path is often rough and narrow, sometimes vague, with numerous short ascents and descents. Some parts are quite difficult, others quite easy.
Refreshments:	Food and drink are available at intervals at Cape Cornwall, Sennen, Land's End, and Porthgwarra.

← Path occurs soon after leaving Land's End, so allow plenty of time to appreciate each headland and cove. Bear in mind that accommodation can be sparse in places.

path drops down to a narrow track, where you turn left inland, but drop down another path on the right. This appears to lead towards ivy-clad ruins and a **chimney,** but another right turn reveals a path passing below them, crossing a **footbridge** over a stream.

Turn right and zigzag uphill, following the path high above **Porth Ledden,** then head downhill to join a road near a toilet block. Turn right and walk down towards the hump of **Cape Cornwall,** easily recognised on account of its landmark chimney. Refreshments are sometimes available here, and inland at **St Just** are shops, pubs, restaurants, a small range of accommodation, and bus services.

The Coast Path continues from the bottom of the Cape Cornwall road and is marked just above some huts. The path climbs steeply uphill but levels out on top. Be careful not to be drawn inland along a road, but follow a clear track down to a minor road in the **Cot Valley.** There is a youth hostel up the road to the left, but turn right to continue along the Coast Path by walking back towards the sea at **Porth Nanven.**

A narrow path leads to a tiny footbridge over a stream, then the Coast Path runs uphill. Keep right at a junction to reach a little tor above the sea. The path works its way across the slope, passing old mine shafts,

A Coast Path walker hurries past the Levant beam engine at Pendeen

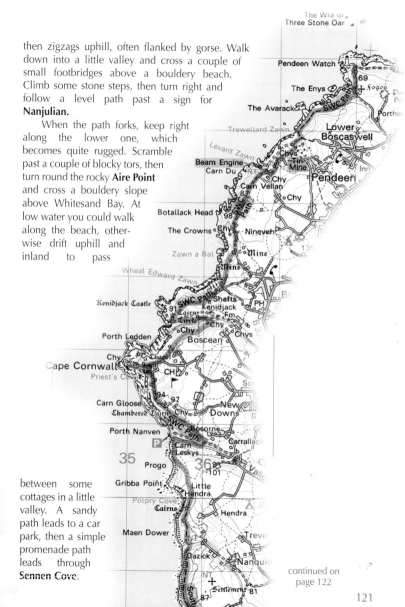

then zigzags uphill, often flanked by gorse. Walk down into a little valley and cross a couple of small footbridges above a bouldery beach. Climb some stone steps, then turn right and follow a level path past a sign for **Nanjulian.**

When the path forks, keep right along the lower one, which becomes quite rugged. Scramble past a couple of blocky tors, then turn round the rocky **Aire Point** and cross a bouldery slope above Whitesand Bay. At low water you could walk along the beach, otherwise drift uphill and inland to pass between some cottages in a little valley. A sandy path leads to a car park, then a simple promenade path leads through **Sennen Cove.**

continued on page 122

121

Aire Point

Carn Aire

Gurland Fm

Settlement 81

87

Treg

Whitesand Bay

Tre Fm

Cairn

Escalls

Carn Barges

Cowloe

Carn Towan

The Tribbens Jetty

LB/Sta

Sennen Cove

Pedn-mên-du

Inn

MS

Irish Lady

78

86

Gamper

Mayon Cliff

Mayon

Maen Castle

P

Dr Syntax's Head

101

Cemy

Kettle's Bottom

Standing Stone

PH

LAND'S END

The Peal

71

Inn

Dr Johnson's Head

Hotel

A 30

Carn Kez

85

Armed Knight

Theme Park Carn Greeb

cross

Enys Dodnan

Trevilley

Tumuli

Pordenack Point

67

80

60

Carn Boel

Zawn Reeth

Mill Bay or Nanjizal

79

Carn Lês Boel

fort

Pendower Coves

Zawn Kellys

Carn Barra

55

Rôskestal

Rosp Cro

Folly Cove

68

St Levan

Black Carn

P

48

Porth Loe

Porthgwarra

66

Landmarks

Carn Scathe

Gwennap Head

Hella Point

Polostoc Zaw

SENNEN COVE

The little fishing harbour is sometimes a tangle of nets; in the middle of it all you can look at local arts and crafts in the old round house from which fishing boats were once hauled onto dry land.

Facilities include: a small range of accommodation, including a nearby campsite at Sennen; shops; toilets; pubs and restaurants.

Leave **Sennen Cove** by walking into the car park at the harbour end of the village and turn left. Walk up a flight of steps and turn right, then follow a path up to an old clifftop lookout. A well-trodden path leads onwards, passing close to **Majon Cliff** and its Iron Age fort to reach **Land's End**.

LAND'S END

Land's End may be thronging with visitors, milling around the 'First and Last Refreshment House in England' or waiting to have their pictures taken beside the famous signpost. Every so often someone sets out from here to walk to John O'Groats, or travel-worn wayfarers arrive having walked from Scotland. The latest end-to-end record – 9 days 2 hours 26 minutes – was set on 13 May 2002 by a runner, Andrew Rivett. A little inland is the Land's End Hotel, offers of food and drink and souvenirs galore, and all the trappings of what is essentially a big outdoor theme park.

Take the well-blazed path downhill and cross a footbridge, passing close to the visitor farm at **Carn Greeb.** The crowds melt away suddenly, missing out on some particularly attractive cliffs and stacks, including the awesome arch of the **Armed Knight.** Be sure to walk around **Pordenack Point,** rather than short-cutting behind it, then continue round the next rugged headland to reach **Mill Bay.**

The Armed Knight is a pierced islet off the coast of Land's End

A rugged slope is crossed above the bouldery bay and a solitary house overlooks the scene. Drop down to cross a footbridge, then climb uphill and take the second path on the right. Steps lead onto the headland, which ends with the attractive point of **Carn Lês Boel.** Follow the easy cliff path onwards, which leads to the National Coastwatch Station on **Gwennap Head.** Pass a couple of curious daymarks and walk down to a road at **Porthgwarra**, where teas and toilets are available.

Follow a track off the end of the road to reach a path junction, then turn left up a slope covered in bushes. Pass a large boulder and continue along the top of the slope. A descent leads past **St Levan's Holy Well,** then over a footbridge. Climb up above a small sandy cove and pass the headland of **Pedn-mên-an-mere.** A car park is reached near the **Minack Theatre.** The little village of **Porthcurno** is directly inland.

PORTHCURNO

- There are two curious attractions here. The Minack Theatre and visitor centre sit on a cliff edge in a remarkably imaginative setting. Inland is the Museum of Submarine Telegraphy, illustrating how telegraph cables were laid beneath the sea to connect far-flung parts of the Empire. There is also a Secret World War II communications bunker.

Facilities include: a small amount of accommodation; post office; toilets; Cable Station Inn; beach café; bus services back to Land's End or ahead to Penzance.

DAY 20
Porthcurno to Penzance

A long flight of stone steps runs downhill from the **Minack Theatre.** When the path levels out, avoid the spur leading down onto the beach at **Porth Curno,** but keep left and pass beyond the head of the beach. Turn right and follow a path up a bushy slope, often set well back from the cliffs. Turn right at a junction and follow a clear path almost on the level for a while. Later another path on the right leads only to the **Logan Rock.**

If you do not wish to visit the headland, walk straight onwards, following a more rugged path across a small stream. Forge on through gorse bushes, turning round **Cribba Head** to descend to **Penberth.** A large area paved with stone slabs was used for landing fish, and a river is crossed by a stone-slab bridge. Note the restored capstan winch, lobster pots, nets and chains. There are toilets, then the path continues just seawards of the **cottage** nearest to the sea.

Climb up a rugged slope, again largely flanked by bushes, and watch out for a waymarked right turn. The path is set well back from the cliffs, and later drops down zigzag steps to cross a little footbridge above a

This is an attractive stretch, often rugged and sometimes difficult, but with some relatively easy stretches. There are open views from the headlands, scenic coves, and a couple of wooded areas, which are unusual on this coast. Mousehole is a quaint and attractive village, but the walk beyond it is a slog along roads through Newlyn to reach Penzance. However, Penzance is a big and bustling town and has a great range →

Start:	Minack Theatre at Porthcurno (386220)
Finish:	Penzance railway station (476306)
Distance:	18km (11.25 miles)
Cumulative Distance:	439km (272.75 miles)
Maps:	OS Landranger 203, OS Explorer 102
Terrain:	Rugged for most of the way, with several short, steep ascents and descents. Easier walking on the approach to Mousehole gives way to a long road-walk into Penzance.
Refreshments:	Tea garden at St Loy. Restaurant at Lamorna Cove. Plenty of pubs and restaurants in Mousehole and Newlyn.

← of facilities, as well as buses and trains to all parts of the country.

boulderly beach in the rocky cove of **Porthguarnon.** Steps lead up the other side and a sign points to a campsite inland.

Continue onwards with good views of blocky cliffs leaning back from the sea. The path becomes broad and grassy, but watch out for a descent to the right, marked for Lamorna. The path runs down to a house and garden at **St Loy**; after passing it watch for a stile on the right marked for the Coast Path. Go down steps on a wooded slope to reach a track. *Either* cross the track to go down to the shore, *or* turn left for teas at **Cove Cottage B&B.**

Turn left and walk carefully along the bouldery beach to leave St Loy, and watch for the path climbing back up onto the cliffs from a **large recumbent boulder.** The exotic woods and the slope beyond can be overgrown. Drop down over some granite boulders on **Boscawen Point,** then continue along the undulating path, flanked by bushes or flowery banks. It climbs up towards some houses, then a track is followed almost all the way down to a lighthouse at **Tater-du.**

The path runs between hedges and is fairly easy. A gate on the left leads to the 'Derek and Jeannie Tangye Minack Chronicles Nature Reserve – A Place for Solitude'. Pass a little headland with a prominent upright block of granite. The path is rough and rocky on the way round to **Lamorna Cove** where there is a restaurant and toilets.

Head for the toilet block across a concrete bridge to find a path that

continued on page 128

climbs between two houses on a rugged slope. Continue out beyond the cove to a tor on a headland at **Carn-du.** The path drops downhill, then runs along the coast, rising through mixed woodland dominated by Monterey pines. This is **Kemyel Crease Nature Reserve**. The path drops down from the wood and weaves about across an uneven slope. It then climbs to the top of the slope to an old lookout.

The path becomes much easier and is flanked by hedges and trees, leading to houses and a minor road. Turn right down the road to pass the **Carn Dhu Hotel** and Wild Bird Hospital. Watch out for the **Lowenna B&B** on the left, and turn immediately right down a narrow road. Walk straight down from

Merlin Place and turn left to pass cottage gardens along a narrow road above the sea. Pick a way round the harbour at **Mousehole** using narrow streets.

127

MOUSEHOLE

The fishing fleet that once filled the harbour is now sadly depleted. The village has turned to arts, crafts and tourism. The last native Cornish speaker, Dolly Pentreath of Mousehole, died 200 years ago. However, the language is now being studied by 3000 or more people and around 500, including a handful here, are thought to speak it fluently.

Facilities include: a range of accommodation; post office; shops; toilets; pubs and restaurants. There are regular buses to and from Newlyn and Penzance.

Follow the road signposted for Newlyn and Penzance, leaving **Mousehole** by way of the Old Coastguard Hotel. Use a broad footpath and cycleway alongside the road, passing the **Penlee lifeboat station.** There is a memorial to the eight crew members of the *Solomon Browne* lifeboat, lost on 19 December 1981. The path runs below the road, then joins it to continue through **Newlyn.** Again, aim to stay close to the harbour.

NEWLYN

The harbour is packed with fishing vessels and there are fishy smells from a number of buildings. Take a look at a variety of memorials along the way, including one maintaining that the *Mayflower* put to port on 16 August 1620 before finally sailing to America.

Facilities include: a small range of accommodation; post office; shops; toilets; pubs and restaurants. The Pilchard Works, signposted upriver from the harbour, is worth a visit.

Small fishing boats pulled up from the rocky beach at Penberth

There are regular bus services to and from Mousehole and Penzance.

Cross the lowest bridge over the river near the **Seamen's Mission,** then follow the road past the Tolcarne Inn. A tarmac path runs through the **Bolitho Gardens,** above a shingle beach. Aloes and bamboo grow here. A broad promenade path continues towards Penzance and passes several offers of food, drink and accommodation. After passing the **Jubilee Pool,** follow Battery Road around the harbour, passing the Isles of Scilly Travel Centre at the Weighbridge, tel: 0345-105555. The Trinity House **National Lighthouse Centre** is available for a visit, otherwise cross a swing-bridge and continue to **Penzance railway station.**

PENZANCE

Mousehole, Newlyn and Penzance have long histories as fishing ports. All were attacked in 1595 by Spanish vessels based in France. Being on the end of a peninsula, the few visitors generally arrived by sea, but by the 1850s Penzance was the terminus of a railway and began to develop a thriving tourist industry. Sometimes it gets just a bit too crowded.

Facilities include: abundant accommodation, including a youth hostel and nearby campsites; banks with ATMs; post office; plenty of shops; toilets; several pubs and restaurants. The town has one of the best ranges of services along the South West Coast Path. Transport links include: Virgin Trains Cornish Scot running through the Midlands and Northern England to Scotland, as well as Great Western trains to London Paddington and local Wessex Trains services. Local bus services cover Penwith and far beyond. National Express buses leave Penzance for destinations including Plymouth, London, Birmingham and Scotland. Ferry and helicopter services reach the Isles of Scilly for more coastal walking. Tourist Information Centre, Station Road, Penzance, Cornwall TR18 2NF, tel: 01736-362207, email: pztic@penwith.gov.uk

DAY 21
Penzance to Porthleven

Start at the railway station in **Penzance** and walk past the Tourist Information Centre, aiming for Penzance Yacht Club. Look out for a **cycleway** on the left and follow it between the railway line and a stout sea wall. The cycleway has a view inland to the Heliport and seawards towards Marazion and St Michael's Mount.

Pass a level crossing and toilets, then the **Station Restaurant,** car park and more toilets. The Coast Path joins a road, but you can leave it a little further along and follow a path through an arc of greenery between the road and beach. This leads to the **Folly Field**, a recreational area next to the ancient market town of **Marazion**.

MARAZION & ST MICHAEL'S MOUNT

Originally called 'Margtiasiewe', there has been a settlement at Marazion since 308BC, and Henry III granted it a Charter in 1257. Ferries depart for St Michael's Mount, and there is a tidal causeway. The island can be visited free, but there is a charge for climbing the Mount and exploring the buildings, including the remains of a

The walk from Penzance to Marazion is level and easy. If there is time, take a ferry or tidal causeway to the historic and atmospheric St Michael's Mount. From Marazion to Praa Sands the route uses narrow, undulating paths and tracks, gradually becoming more difficult. Beyond Praa Sands the cliffs are higher and the route becomes a roller-coaster. Most villages along the way offer accommodation, food and drink, →

Start:	Penzance railway station (476306)
Finish:	Porthleven Harbour (628258)
Distance:	23km (14.25 miles)
Cumulative Distance:	462km (287 miles)
Maps:	OS Landranger 203, OS Explorers 102 & 103
Terrain:	Easy tracks and paths, gradually becoming more rugged and difficult, ending with a series of ascents and descents on narrow cliff paths.
Refreshments:	Plenty of food and drink at Marazion. Inn and refreshment hut at Perranuthnoe. Inn and cafés at Praa Sands.

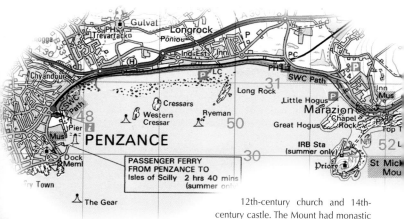

← but Porthleven is an ideal distance for a day's walk from Penzance.

12th-century church and 14th-century castle. The Mount had monastic links with Mont St Michel off the coast of Brittany. St Michael's Way signposted from Lelant to St Michael's Mount, commemorating a pilgrim route to the distant shrine of Santiago de Compostela in Galicia.

Facilities include: a range of accommodation; post office; shops; toilets; pubs and restaurants. The old town hall is now the Marazion Museum. Transport links include frequent buses to and from Penzance, and ahead to Praa Sands, Porthleven and Falmouth.

Leave **Marazion** by following Fore Street and Turnpike Hill, passing **The Old Toll House.** The road leaves the village and passes **Mount Haven Hotel** before a right turn is marked as the Coast Path down the access road for **Chymoryah East.** Turn left before reaching the house, following a path and steps down into a field. Continue down to the rocky shore and turn left, then climb up a **metal stairway.** There are tamarisk hedges along the low cliff, then a National Trust sign announces **Trenow Cove.** The path reaches a track and is diverted inland, but watch for a path on the right, marked by yellow arrows, leading back to the coast.

Follow the path around **Boat Cove.** Turn round a little point and follow the path to a car park and toilets at **Perranuthnoe.** Just down the beach road is a refreshment hut, while inland the Victoria Inn offers food, drink and accommodation. There are also buses back to Penzance and ahead to Praa Sands and Porthleven. Cross the road to continue along a narrow path, keeping right along a waymarked track. Turn right down a path before the last building, but turn left along a low cliff path and avoid dropping onto the beach. Field paths with stiles lead gradually round a rocky bay overlooked by **Acton Castle.** Gorse slopes give way to the fine rocky **Cudden Point.**

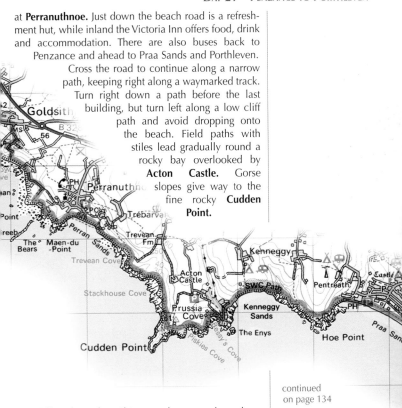

continued on page 134

Follow the path until it passes huts on a slope above **Prussia Cove.** Keep left to avoid paths leading down into the cove, then keep right of a thatched house and turn right to walk up a track. Turn right again at a junction to pass between **granite pillars** and follow another track downhill. This bends left and passes between curious, curved buildings, heading down to a small ford. Follow the track uphill below a neat row of cottages, to reach an **old quarry.**

Go past a gate to follow a path across a lushly vegetated slope, with views down onto **Kenneggy Sands.**

133

Cross a small stream and follow a path cut through bushes to reach **Hoe Point.** Turn round the point then tunnel through taller bushes and head for **Praa Sands.**

PRAA SANDS

Facilities include: a little accommodation, including nearby campsites; post office; shop; toilets; pub and restaurants. Transport links include buses back to Penzance and ahead to Porthleven and Falmouth.

The Coast Path goes down onto the beach in front of the **Welloe Rock Inn** and Beachcomber Café. You may notice layers of clay and peat along the beach; there was once fenland here, but the sea cut into it and windblown sand smothered it. Climb up steps and turn right across **Praa Green.** Turn left along a clear path at the far end, then turn right along a sandy path through an area of scrub. The path leads up to a road and a right turn leads through the **Sea Meads private estate,** full of holiday homes. Leave the estate and turn right down to a road-end, continuing along a path that passes an access point for the beach.

Climb gradually up across a slope, passing from **Lescleave Cliff** to **Rinsey Head.** Follow the path as marked, well back from the headland, then go through a car park and pass a National Trust sign for **Rinsey Cliff.** There is an old engine house, then the path forks. Keep right and walk downhill, closer to the rocky coast. The path climbs and there is a fork at a field. Keep left and pass above old mine buildings and a **chimney.** The path zigzags downhill, climbs steps, and drops into a dip where there is a stream and beach access.

Climb again and follow the path as it wanders along the cliffs, climbing a couple of times to pass deep bites in the cliff face. Pass below a prominent **white house,** then pass a **cross** commemorating seamen who were buried along the cliffs, before the passing of Gryll's Act (1808) allowed

The Welloe Rock Inn rises above the broad beach at Praa Sands

them to be interred in the nearest conse-crated ground. Follow a broad path, then bear right at a road junction to walk down into **Porthleven.** The road passes the **Ship Inn** and continues alongside the **harbour.** Turn right round the head of the harbour.

PORTHLEVEN

The harbour's early 19th-century granite quays handled a considerable amount of shipping, though lost trade as the railways arrived. Fishing remains important, though tourism is big business.

Facilities include: a range of accommodation; post office; shops; toilets; pubs and restaurants. Transport links include buses back to Penzance and ahead to Falmouth.

DAY 22
Porthleven to The Lizard

This day is full of interest. Early on the Loe Bar is crossed, which blocks a freshwater lake. A fine old church is embedded into a hillside at Gunwalloe Church Cove. The site of an early Marconi station is remembered on Poldhu Point, where the first trans-Atlantic signals were transmitted (the Morse letter 'S', repeated over and over from here and received at St John's in Newfoundland on 12 December 1901). Between Mullion Cove and The Lizard the cliffs are spectacular, with attractive groups of rugged stacks, such as at Kynance Cove. The Lizard Point is the southernmost point on the British mainland, and much less crowded than Land's End.

Walk round the harbour at **Porthleven,** passing the **clock tower** building at the far pier. Walk up Cliff Road and continue along **Mount's Road,** walking straight onwards at a road junction down to a road-end car park. Turn left up a path and link with a broad coastal path that eventually leads down to a house. Cross the gritty sandspit of **Loe Bar** and look inland to Loe Pool, once a tidal inlet; there are footpaths around the shore. Walk up past a **white cross** erected in memory of the 100 crew of HMS *Acton*.

Continue along the path and watch for a junction, dropping down to the right for the Coast Path. This runs close to a crumbling edge and passes rusty old winches at **Gunwalloe Fishing Cove.** There is a café, or you could follow the road a short way inland to **Halzephron Inn** for food, drink and accommodation.

Walk along a track and step to the left of a house on the cliff edge. Walk up a path to continue along the cliffs,

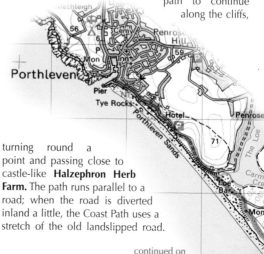

turning round a point and passing close to castle-like **Halzephron Herb Farm.** The path runs parallel to a road; when the road is diverted inland a little, the Coast Path uses a stretch of the old landslipped road.

136

continued on page 138

Start:	Porthleven Harbour (628258)
Finish:	Most Southerly Café, The Lizard (701115)
Distance:	22km (13.5 miles)
Cumulative Distance:	484km (300.5 miles)
Maps:	OS Landranger 203, OS Explorer 103
Terrain:	Easy paths and tracks progressively give way to narrower and more difficult paths, though in many places the ground is level. There is a series of little valleys with steep descents and ascents.
Refreshments:	Café and nearby pub at Gunwalloe Fishing Cove. Beach Café at Poldhu Cove. Restaurant at Mullion Cove. Café at Kynance Cove.

Turn right to continue along the cliff path, enjoying splendid scenery around **Halzephron Cliff.** Walk down towards **Winnianton Farm** and a toilet block at a sandy bay.

This is **Gunwalloe Church Cove.** The church of St Winwalow is pressed into a hillside and has a separate belfry. Look inside and note how its granite pillars lean. The building is mainly 15th century, though has 13th/14th-century features. The original manor house of Winnianton was founded in the 11th century.

Leave the church to either cross a stream on the beach or use a **footbridge** hidden in reedbeds a little further inland. The path follows a crumbling edge at **Carrag-a-Pilez** and passes a little car park. Walk down a road to **Poldhu Cove.** There are toilets and the Poldhu Beach Café, and bus services back to Helston and ahead to The Lizard, or to Truro and Perranporth.

Rather than pass the beach café, take the next turning up to a big retirement home on the headland, formerly the **Poldhu Hotel.** Step down to the right of the road as marked, then follow the path as it climbs steps and runs along a fine cliff to a **Marconi monument.** Marconi's Poldhu station served from 1900 to 1933; the land was given to the National Trust in 1937. Go past an old kissing gate, marked by a granite pillar, then fork down to the right and pass seawards of a **white**

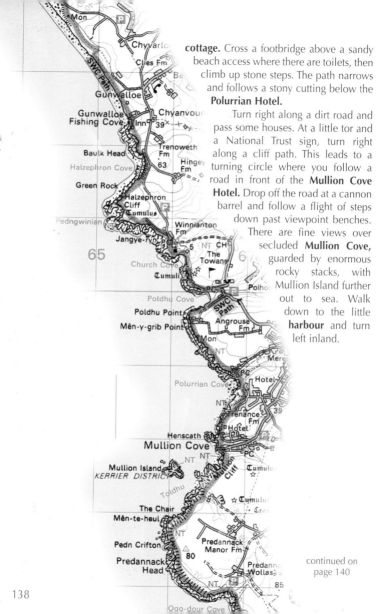

cottage. Cross a footbridge above a sandy beach access where there are toilets, then climb up stone steps. The path narrows and follows a stony cutting below the **Polurrian Hotel.**

Turn right along a dirt road and pass some houses. At a little tor and a National Trust sign, turn right along a cliff path. This leads to a turning circle where you follow a road in front of the **Mullion Cove Hotel.** Drop off the road at a cannon barrel and follow a flight of steps down past viewpoint benches. There are fine views over secluded **Mullion Cove,** guarded by enormous rocky stacks, with Mullion Island further out to sea. Walk down to the little **harbour** and turn left inland.

continued on page 140

138

MULLION & MULLION COVE

Facilities include: a range of accommodation; post office; shops; toilets; pubs and restaurants. Transport links include buses from Mullion back to Poldhu Cove and Helston, or ahead to The Lizard.

Leave **Mullion Cove** by walking up the road from a café, turning right round the back of a house to follow the route marked Coast Path uphill. There are brief but splendid views of the cove, then the path runs up a slope of thorny scrub. At the top are the **Mullion and Predannack Cliffs,** part of The Lizard National Nature Reserve, noted for a variety of plants including rare Cornish heath. The cliffs support kittiwakes and gulls, while stonechats and skylarks are common over the heaths. The variety of plant species is maintained by grazing the area with Soay sheep and Shetland ponies.

Boats moored in the picturesque fishing harbour at Porthleven

The path runs along, then down across a little valley to cross a **stream** below a house. Walk uphill and along again across a slope of open flowery scrub. Pass through a gate onto the National Trust's **Predannack** holding, and turn round into a rocky cove.

There is a short descent to cross a little stream, then continue uphill and onwards, with gorse scrub alongside. Continue round a field edge and reach a Lizard National Nature Reserve sign that explains the long tradition of cattle grazing at **Kynance Farm.** The path to follow is the muddy one slicing behind **Vellan Head,** though you could walk round the headland if you wish. Veer inland and down into a valley at **Soap Rock,** then climb up and continue along the clifftop.

There are little headlands to visit, or they can be short-cut using paths behind them. There is a splendid view over rocky **Kynance Cove.** Walk down towards the stacks, then swing left to walk down steps to a huddle of cottages and cross a concrete slab over a stream. A café is available, otherwise go down steps to the **beach** and climb steps on the other side. The path is clear, but watch for a turn

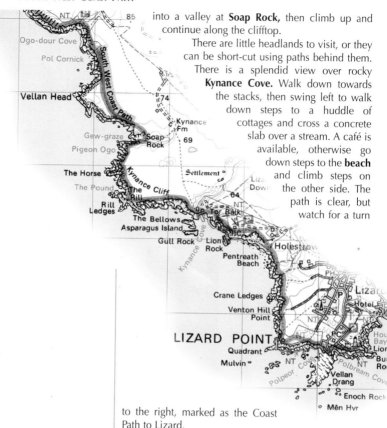

to the right, marked as the Coast Path to Lizard.

Keep seaward of a car park and toilets to continue along the path. The clifftops are rugged, then the path briefly cuts into a field. An English Nature sign is passed as the **Caerthillian National Nature Reserve** is entered. Enjoy the flowery grasslands and walk down into a valley to pass a rocky inlet, crossing two tiny streams divided by a rise. Walk uphill and along the cliffs again, passing an access point for Lizard village. Pass a National Trust sign for **Old Lizard Head,** with a view

Attractive rocky stacks and headlands at Kynance Cove near The Lizard

ahead to the lighthouse on the point. Walk downhill, passing another access point for the village, but turn right through tamarisks and climb up stone steps. The path leads to cafés; one of which is **The Most Southerly Café,** a fine place to take a break and enjoy the views.

THE LIZARD

Facilities include: a range of accommodation, including a youth hostel; post office; shops; toilets; pubs and restaurants. The multi-banded rock known as serpentine outcrops in the area and a range of ornaments are carved and polished and offered for sale at workshops. Transport links include buses to Mullion, Helston and even distant Perranporth.

DAY 23
The Lizard to Porthallow

After enjoying wonderful scenery around Lizard Point, the South West Coast Path embarks on a roller-coaster route through picturesque Cadgwith, then along the cliffs to Black Head, and later reaches the charming village of Coverack. An easy stretch around appropriately named Lowland Point is followed by the unsightly Dean Quarry, and then a couple of diversions inland to reach the tiny villages of Porthoustock and Porthallow. In due course there might be a better Coast Path in these parts, but take heart from the fact that the scenery improves the next day.

Leave The Most Southerly Café on the **Lizard Point** and pass in front of the serpentine shop to pick up the Coast Path. Pass the **youth hostel,** formerly the Polbrean Hotel, built in the 1860s as Polbrean Villa for the artist Thomas Hart. The path passes in front of a foghorn and **lighthouse,** open for visits. There is also a detour to the right to a deep crater, the **Lion's Den,** which collapsed in 1842. The Coast Path runs along easily, then goes down steps to cross a little concrete footbridge over a small stream where there is access down to a beach or up to Lizard village. However, continue in front of the **Housel Bay Hotel,** passing another access point for Lizard village.

The path passes The Lizard Wireless Station, which in 1901 received a signal from the Marconi station on the Isle of Wight. Pass the prominent Lloyds Signal Station, and National Coastwatch Station at **Bass Point.** Follow a track away from a house, but turn right for the Coast Path, which later passes a **lifeboat station** with an inclined cliff lift for access. Steps lead down to a huddle of curious houses at **Church Cove,** where you simply turn left uphill a few paces, then right as signposted for Cadgwith.

The path veers inland to avoid an old quarry. Pass alongside a couple of fields, then walk down across a gorse-filled valley to cross a footbridge over a little stream. Walk up and along the path, through deep scrub, then turn into a little valley and pass in front of a couple of cliff **chalets.** Follow the path above the crater called the **Devil's Frying Pan,** then turn left through a gate, and right down a narrow road. Continue down what appears to be a garden path at **Hillside,** keeping right as a road bend is reached to walk down a path into **Cadgwith.** Walk straight down the road and pass the harbour.

CADGWITH

Facilities include a small range of accommodation,

Start:	Most Southerly Café, The Lizard (701115)
Finish:	Porthallow (797231)
Distance:	25km (15 miles)
Cumulative Distance:	508km (315.5 miles)
Maps:	OS Landrangers 203 & 204, OS Explorer 103
Terrain:	Plenty of short but steep ascents and descents at first, followed by easier walking around Black Head and Coverack. The route shifts inland to Porthoustock and Portholland, using minor roads, tracks and field paths, where care is needed with route-finding.
Refreshments:	Cadgwith and Coverack have a small range of shops, pubs and restaurants.

shops, toilets, pubs and restaurants. Buses can be found up at Ruan Minor, heading back to The Lizard and Helston, or onwards to Coverack.

Follow the road up past **Cadgwith Cove Inn** then turn right as signposted for the Coast Path. Follow the path in front of a row of cottages overlooking the harbour, then turn left at a small **hut** with a chimney. The path rises and goes through a couple of fields before crossing a rugged slope set back from the coast. Walk through deep scrub and pass a gate, then turn right along a path flanked by hedgerows. Go through another gate and downhill, then turn right to a little cove at **Poltesco.** Stone steps lead down to a footbridge over a wooded river.

Walk straight on, keeping to the right of a ruin, heading uphill between unruly hedgerows to reach a fork in the path. Go either way as both paths join beyond a bouldery slope. Walk beside a putting green and continue along a path flanked by hedgerows. Head downhill and turn right, then continue down a road to reach a café and toilets at **Kennack Sands.** The beach can be very popular and the area is managed by English Nature as a National Nature Reserve. The low cliffs are of geological importance, displaying many layers of rock, while the landward slopes are rich in flowers.

Walk up towards the **toilets** and keep right, in front

of a house, avoiding the beach, to follow a path flanked by hedges. A concrete slab is used to cross a pool, then the path passes through a notch at the back of a headland. Walk down to a concrete block wall at the next cove, with a wooded valley rising inland. A patchy path climbs uphill, then runs across gentle slopes of gorse and heather

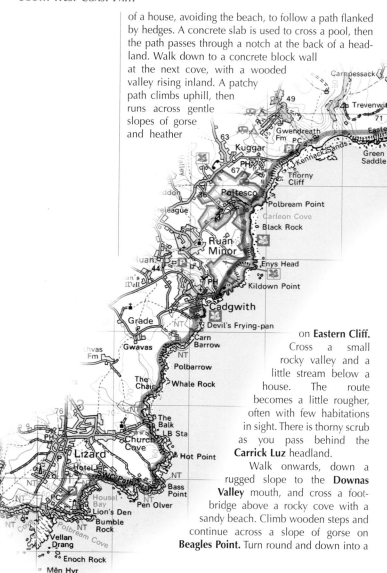

on **Eastern Cliff.** Cross a small rocky valley and a little stream below a house. The route becomes a little rougher, often with few habitations in sight. There is thorny scrub as you pass behind the **Carrick Luz** headland.

Walk onwards, down a rugged slope to the **Downas Valley** mouth, and cross a footbridge above a rocky cove with a sandy beach. Climb wooden steps and continue across a slope of gorse on **Beagles Point.** Turn round and down into a little valley to cross a footbridge over a stream, then walk up a rugged path and turn right to walk through gorse and

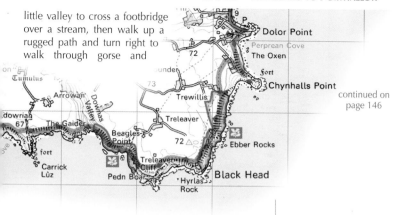

continued on page 146

heather scrub. The path leads to a white Coastguard lookout on **Black Head.**

Turn left just before the lookout to walk through the gorse bushes along **Chynhalls Cliff.** The path is gently graded, but rough in places, and a footbridge is crossed. Walk though patchy woodlands near a pig farm, where the path can be muddy. Take care not to be drawn along intersecting paths, but reach a road near **Chynhalls Farm** and turn right. This is a private road, where you head off to the left down steps towards **Chynhalls Point.** A gap is reached just before the point, where you turn left. Coastal views give way to a wooded path leading to a tarmac road at the top end of **Coverack.** Turn right down **School Hill,** then turn left to walk above the tiny **harbour.**

COVERACK

Facilities include: a small range of accommodation, including a youth hostel and nearby campsites; post office; shops; toilets; pubs and restaurants. Transport links include buses back to The Lizard and Helston and ahead to Porthallow and Helford.

The road out of **Coverack** runs around a bouldery, sandy cove. When the main road turns inland, a narrow road continues. Walk to the end of this road and down a track almost to a gate. Turn right down a path into a wood, then continue along the rugged path through wooded and scrubby areas. Cross a stream using **granite slabs,** and stepping stones through muddy areas.

Cross a bouldery wall and continue along a vague path round **Lowland Point. Dean Quarry** is ahead and you should read the notice that warns about blasting, any time between 1000 and 1830. Warnings are given either by red flags or sirens. Follow 'footpath' signs

faithfully through the quarry, passing under a conveyor belt above a pier, then down to a gritty grey beach at **Godrevy Cove.**

Set off around the beach, only to

The little harbour at Coverack, with Lowland Point seen in the distance

detour inland as marked, uphill beside a stream and through a kissing gate into the fields above. Watch for a gate revealing a woodland path, then follow this to a road and turn right up through **Rosenithon.** Turn right uphill again at a junction until the road levels out. Cross a slab-stile on the left, into a field, then drift to the right. The path leads down to a road, where you turn left and right down into the tiny village of **Porthoustock.** There are toilets here and beach access, but little else.

Follow the road uphill, then keep straight on along a track when the road bends right. Watch for footpath markers on the right and follow a vague path uphill, across a couple of fields. Continue straight along a road, which bends down left to a junction, where you turn right up to another junction. Just to the right is a narrow path flanked by hedges. Follow it downhill to the **Parc-an-tidno B&B** and Cider Press Barn. Walk along a concrete road and turn right down a tarmac road for the village of **Porthallow** and the Five Pilchards Inn.

PORTHALLOW

The village is more or less the halfway point of the South West Coast Path. Facilities include: a small range of accommodation; post office; shop; toilets; pub and cafés. Transport links include buses back to Coverack and The Lizard and ahead to Helford or Helston.

Check your tide tables for this day's walk. The tide needs to be out if you are going to cross Gillan Creek, but not so far out that it prevents the ferry from running between Helford and Helford Passage! Walking round Gillan Creek takes only an hour or so, but detouring round the Helford River would take all day. The ferry across the Helford River runs from April to October; failing that you could use Truronian bus services from Helford to Helford Passage, →

Start on the bridge near the **Five Pilchards Inn** and walk along Porthallow's grey, pebbly beach. Climb concrete steps and follow a path that tunnels through bushes. A field path leads towards more rugged slopes, where the narrow path runs through bracken and bushy areas. Pass a sign for Nare Point and go down around a field to get back onto the cliff path. Enter a field at **Nare Point** and almost reach a building on the end of the point. The view takes in a series of inlets ahead: Gillan Harbour, Helford River and Carrick Roads.

Follow a grassy track along the shore, obtaining intermittent views through gaps in the bushes alongside. Go through a gate and cross a footbridge over a miniature **wooded gorge.** There is plenty of thorny scrub and mud, but stick to the path to cross stiles and walk along **Trewarnevas Cliff.** The path runs uphill, completely enclosed by trees, then a right turn leads down steps to the shore, where there is a cove of moored boats at **Gillan Harbour.**

Walk up a concrete ramp and along a path behind **The Tower House.** Walk down a path through bushes to reach **Flushing Cove** and its pebble beach. The path

Start:	Porthallow (797231)
Finish:	Custom House Quay, Falmouth (812325)
Distance:	29km (18 miles)
Cumulative Distance:	537km (333.5 miles)
Maps:	OS Landranger 204, OS Explorer 103
Terrain:	Paths narrow and rugged in places, but ascents and descents are quite short. Wooded parts can be muddy. The tide needs to be out for Gillan Creek to be forded. Use a ferry to cross the Helford River.
Refreshments:	There are pubs at Helford and Helford Passage, and a beach café at Maenporth.

again runs through bushes, then reaches a signposted junction. The Coast Path is marked as straight ahead, down steps to the shore, where a **tidal ford** or slippery stepping stones lead to **St Anthony-in-Meneage.** If the tide is in, however, use the alternative marked route as described below.

The *alternative route* runs up a concrete lane and straight up a road passing a house called **Dolton.** A Coast Path signpost points to the right, up through fields. Go through a gate, then turn right after the next gate to reach a stile. Cross diagonally up a field to reach a ladder stile and minor road. Turn right down the road to reach a road junction and bus stop at the head of **Gillan Creek.** Turn right, following the road as it rises on a wooded slope, then descends to the tiny village of **St**

← though that would take several hours. Assuming all goes well, the walking is fairly easy and often very scenic, ending in bustling Falmouth – with more ferries to sort out for the following day.

Gillan Creek at high water: you will not be able to wade across

Anthony-in-Meneage. This alternative route adds an extra 3km (2 miles) to the day's walk.

· St Anthony-in-Meneage, or 'in the Land of the Monks', was served from the 13th century from Tywardreath Abbey. It probably stands on the site of an old Celtic church. Follow the road past the church and uphill. Watch out at the top of the road for an **iron gate** well away to the right. Go through the gate and walk up through a field to reach a bushy part of the headland. This can be explored, but return to this field to continue walking around the edge.

The route leads inland alongside the **Helford River** and the field path gives way to a muddy woodland path. Views of the long inlet are restricted, though three tiny coves are passed along the way. When a **house** is reached, follow a track uphill, then turn right downhill from a road bend. Look for a few steps up to the left, where the Coast Path follows another muddy path. Pass close to the **Helford River Sailing Club,** then at a junction beside a chapel/gallery, walk down a narrow road to a ford and footbridge at **Helford.**

Swing round the other side of the inlet by road, passing offers of cream teas, the post office shop and thatched **Shipwrights Arms.** A signpost indicates the public footpath to **Helford Point and Ferry.** Walk down to the point, check the ferry times, and open a brightly coloured sign to call the ferry.

HELFORD

Facilities include: a small amount of accommodation; post office shop; toilets; café; pub and restaurant. Transport links include buses back to Porthallow, Coverack and The Lizard, or to Helston for further connections. The Helford River ferry operates daily from April to October, subject to tidal and weather restrictions, tel: 01326-250770. If you call the ferry by opening the hinged sign, please remember to close it again before boarding.

The ferry reaches **Helford Passage,** and the Ferryboat Inn. Turn right to continue along the Coast Path, signposted for Durgan. Follow a field path with occasional views of the Helford River through the woods, then walk down to a road at **Durgan** and pass the Old School House.

The road runs uphill on a wooded slope, with granite pillars supporting a stout chain alongside. Avoid using the beach access on the right, but walk further

continued on page 152

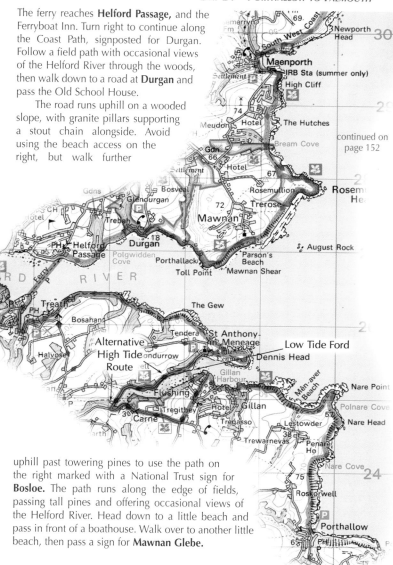

uphill past towering pines to use the path on the right marked with a National Trust sign for **Bosloe.** The path runs along the edge of fields, passing tall pines and offering occasional views of the Helford River. Head down to a little beach and pass in front of a boathouse. Walk over to another little beach, then pass a sign for **Mawnan Glebe.**

Walk through thick gorse and thorny scrub around **Toll Point,** then along a field path towards a wooded slope near **Mawnan.** Don't go up to the church; if you do find yourself heading that way, drop back down into the wood to continue. Turn round a point and walk through more thorny scrub, then pass fields and cross a foot-bridge to continue towards **Rosemullion Head.** Turn round the headland on a slope of short turf and enjoy the views around other headlands and inlets.

Keep low and walk through a wooded patch at **Nansidwell,** then follow a field path and cross a valley mouth. Climb up past tall pines and continue along, before squeezing between back gardens and scrubby cliffs, tunnelling through bushes. Turn around a point on a field path, walk down

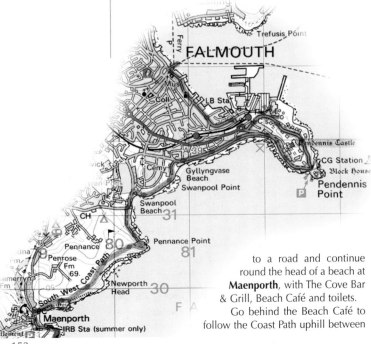

to a road and continue round the head of a beach at **Maenporth,** with The Cove Bar & Grill, Beach Café and toilets.

Go behind the Beach Café to follow the Coast Path uphill between

Looking across Carrick Roads from Pendennis Head to Zone Point

hedges, later completely enclosed by bushes, then alongside a **golf course** and into woodland. Turn left down through the woods and the path leads out onto a road. Turn right down the road to pass The Three Mackerel to reach **Swanpool.** The pool on the landward side of the road is often full of swans and ducks. The beach can be busy and toilets are available. Pass in front of the Swanpool Beach Café, then continue along a concrete block, and follow a ribbon of tarmac path up and down to the next beach.

White sand **Gyllyngvase Beach** abuts Falmouth. There are toilets, the Queen Mary Gardens and Gyllyngvase Beach Café Bar. Turn right along Cliff Road to follow tarmac garden paths parallel to the low cliffs. Set off along the road around **Pendennis Head** against the one-way flow of the traffic. Beware of paths that seem to offer coastal walks, as they end abruptly. Enjoy the view, then follow the road to **Falmouth.**

Head for the town centre as signposted and the harbour is on the right. Note beautifully restored Arwenack House, which is mostly 16th century, but has 14th-century fragments. There is a ferry for St Mawes from the **Custom House Quay,** on the right after Trago Mills. You can also follow the road through the centre of

Falmouth, passing the Church of King Charles the Martyr, to use ferry services from the **Prince of Wales Pier.**

FALMOUTH

Ships used to sail around Pendennis Head to reach Penryn, until Falmouth properly developed as a harbour and took over the export of tin. Pendennis Castle and its counterpart at St Mawes date from the mid-16th century, though Falmouth's harbour didn't really expand until the mid-19th century, aided by a rail link. Until then hundreds of ships anchored in Carrick Roads, rather exposed to the weather. A variety of cargo is shipped though the docks, which are currently rather quiet.

Facilities include: plenty of accommodation, including a youth hostel on Pendennis Head; banks with ATMs; post office; a variety of shops; toilets; an abundance of pubs and restaurants. There are boat trips and tours of the docks. Transport links include a railway, connecting with main line services at Truro. Bus services include routes back to Helford Passage and The Lizard peninsula, and inland to Truro to link with connecting buses to St Mawes, Portscatho or Portloe. National Express buses leave Falmouth for Plymouth, Exeter, Poole, Bournemouth and along the south coast to Eastbourne. Tourist Information Centre, 28 Killigrew Street, Falmouth, Cornwall TR11 3PN, tel: 01326-312300, email: falmouthtic@yahoo.co.uk

DAY 25
Falmouth to Portloe

Start by getting a ferry from Falmouth to St Mawes, either from the Custom House Quay or Prince of Wales Pier. The ferry runs all year round but check times in advance, tel: 01326-313201. Enjoy the splendid views as you cross Carrick Roads; Pendennis Castle and St Mawes Castle, both open to visitors, guard either side of the inlet.

ST MAWES

Facilities include: a small range of accommodation; banks; post office; shops; toilets; pubs and restaurants. Most walkers simply transfer from one ferry to another, but if time can be spared St Mawes is worth exploring.

The ferry from St Mawes to Place is seasonal, from May to September. Check sailing times in advance, tel: 01209-214901. At high water the ferry will drop passengers at a pier close to Place, but at low water the landing may be at a flight of steps a little further away. Watch for herons and egrets roosting in trees by the water.

Walk inland along a narrow road signposted for **St Anthony's Church.** Turn right along a path, passing a

The day starts with two ferry journeys; check the times carefully and ensure that the Falmouth–St Mawes one will link nicely with a smaller ferry to Place. Your walk doesn't actually start until you reach Place, so don't leave it too late. If the ferries aren't running, bus services offer some assistance, though travelling from Falmouth to St Mawes takes hours, and there is no bus to Place. The Coast Path is reasonably easy to Portscatho, →

Start:	Custom House Quay, Falmouth (812325)
Finish:	Portloe (937394)
Distance:	22 kilometres (13.75 miles)
Cumulative Distance:	559km (347.25 miles)
Maps:	OS Landranger 204, OS Explorer 105
Terrain:	Easy walking at first, getting progressively more difficult.
Refreshments:	Portscatho has shops, pubs and restaurants. The Pendower Beach House Hotel and Nare Hotel also offer food and drink.

← although the village isn't seen until the last moment, so the whole coast looks rather empty. Walking round Gerran's Bay is also fairly easy, though becomes more difficult en route to Nare Head, and there are several ascents and descents before the little village of Portloe.

stone coffin, gravestones and the church. Walk up to a track and turn right down it, followed by a left turn up another track. Follow a field path with fine views back across Carrick Roads and continue towards a lighthouse, but turn left up a tarmac path before reaching it. Take the second turn to the right, marked as the Coast Path, up a tarmac path and steps to reach a narrow road at the top.

Turn right to reach the late 19th-century battery on **St Anthony Head,** where there are toilets in a bunker. There are information boards about the gun emplacements, the flowers of the surrounding heath and the birds on the cliffs. From the bird observation point kittiwakes, cormorants and shags can often be spotted.

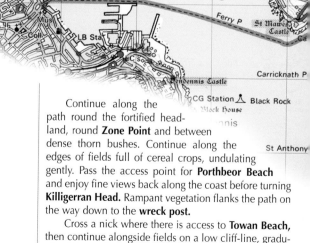

Continue along the path round the fortified headland, round **Zone Point** and between dense thorn bushes. Continue along the edges of fields full of cereal crops, undulating gently. Pass the access point for **Porthbeor Beach** and enjoy fine views back along the coast before turning **Killigerran Head.** Rampant vegetation flanks the path on the way down to the **wreck post.**

Cross a nick where there is access to **Towan Beach,** then continue alongside fields on a low cliff-line, gradually rising and enjoying flowery banks. There is another beach access, and a path leading inland to a campsite at Treloan Farm. A cottage is reached at **Pencabe,** where a left turn suddenly reveals the village of **Portscatho.**

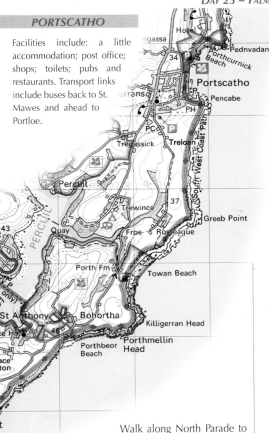

PORTSCATHO

Facilities include: a little accommodation; post office; shops; toilets; pubs and restaurants. Transport links include buses back to St. Mawes and ahead to Portloe.

continued on page 158

Walk along North Parade to leave **Portscatho,** which continues as a path past Tregerein Guest House and along the cliffs. The path drops down and up steps either side of a beach access at **Porthcurnick.** Use this access, or visit a nearby refreshment hut and then go down to the beach. Walk up a concrete ramp and road, then turn right at a gate where the Coast Path is signposted along the next stretch of cliff. Pass the National Coastwatch Station on **Pednvadan Point.** The path works its way along the coast, then drops down a wooded slope to **Porthbean Beach.**

Turn left, then left again to head inland, but fork right along a path flanked by bushes. The way ahead is sometimes among the bushes and sometimes alongside fields. Avoid a left turn inland, but also avoid steps to the right down to a beach. Cross a small footbridge and walk uphill, then down through a small wooded patch at **Treluggan Cliff.**

Slopes of bracken are followed by bushes. Turn left uphill and inland at a big white house called **Pendower Court.** Turn right along a narrow road down to Pendower Beach House Hotel, and cross a small concrete footbridge over a stream. Cross a sandy heath and climb up stone steps to leave **Pendower Beach,** finding a road and toilets at the top.

Turn right uphill, then right again as signposted for the Coast Path to Carne. The path is easy enough, then is diverted uphill, inland and around **The Nare Hotel.** Follow the road down to the right, along the

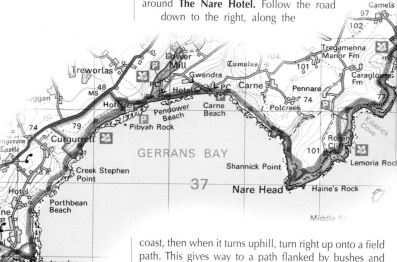

coast, then when it turns uphill, turn right up onto a field path. This gives way to a path flanked by bushes and bracken. Walk uphill, then down into a valley full of gorse and cross a footbridge over a stream. Climb uphill again, from a rough slope into a field, then up another slope of gorse to the top field on **Nare Head.**

Walk along a path through gorse, cross another field, touching 100m (330ft) before crossing a stile to get back onto another slope of gorse. Walk downhill and a sign states *'footpath runs round head of valley and along fence to stile'.* Continue above the bouldery **Kiberick Cove,** then climb up and round the headland at **The Blouth,** crossing a curious stile on top of a stile.

Look down a grassy slope to spot the next stile. Walk down into a patch of woodland, down a slope of bracken

The little village of Portscatho appears quite suddenly on the route

towards the rocky shore, then up and across a couple of little footbridges. Wind uphill, passing in front of **Broom Parc** in a stand of pines. Walk up some steps, continue between hedges, then walk downhill with a sudden view of **Portloe.** Turn left, then right at path junctions to pass a toilet block on the way down to the tiny harbour.

PORTLOE

Facilities include: a small range of accommodation; post office shop and tearoom; toilets; pub. There are buses back to Portscatho and St. Mawes, or inland to Truro for further connections by bus and rail.

DAY 26
Portloe to Mevagissey

The cliff path leaving Portloe is rather rugged in places. West and East Portholland are tiny settlements with few facilities. An easy path runs over towards Caerhays Castle, then becomes a little more difficult on the way to Hemmick Beach. The route climbs onto Dodman Point and visits a tall granite cross on the summit, inscribed, 'In the firm hope of the Second Coming of Our Lord Jesus Christ, and for the encouragement of those who strive →

Walk up the road to leave **Portloe** via Fuglers B&B. Turn right down an access road, then right again between an old boathouse and chapel, both converted to dwellings. Turn left uphill, then right in front of cottages, then left up steps signposted for the Coast Path to reach **Flagstaff.**

A rugged path turns round a rocky brow, then crosses a small stream. Walk up some steps, then follow the path as it undulates, before climbing more steps up from a National Trust sign at **Tregenna.** The rugged path runs across a bushy slope, down a wooded slope, and into a valley full of bracken. Cross two footbridges, climb uphill and drift inland before making a right turn to descend a grassy path between gorse bushes. The path steepens and narrows, then steps descend to a footbridge at **West Portholland.** The beach is grey grit and shingle, with an old limekiln.

The Coast Path is routed along a minor road to **East Portholland,** though you can walk along a sea wall between the two tiny villages. There is an old chapel, toilets, post office, tearoom and a small summerhouse for rent. Follow the road past the sandy beach and pass the far row of cottages, then zigzag up a track that

Start:	Portloe (937394)
Finish:	Mevagissey (015448)
Distance:	20km (12.5 miles)
Cumulative Distance:	579km (359.75 miles)
Maps:	OS Landranger 204, OS Explorer 105
Terrain:	Rugged paths at the beginning and in places around Dodman Point, but most other stretches are easier.
Refreshments:	Cafés at East Portholland and Porthluney Cove. There are pubs and restaurants at Gorran Haven, and a pub at Portmellon.

becomes flanked by bushes. Turn right at a gate and walk down around a couple of fields, then up to a road. Turn right down the road to find **Caerhays Castle** on the left and **Porthluney Cove** on the right. There is a beach café and toilets. Continue along the road a little to find the Coast Path signposted on the right.

Walk up towards a corner of a small wood, then turn right and cross a stile. Follow a fence up to another stile and enter a wood. Climb up some steps, then down, then walk through fields. Steps lead down to a little footbridge at **Lambsowden Cove.** Follow a rugged path on a scrubby slope, then stay on the cliff edge through fields, descending steps to a house beside **Hemmick Beach.** A stream crosses the road, and a left turn leads to **Boswinger** and its youth hostel. The Coast Path follows the road to the right.

Walk up the road to find steps on the right and a National Trust sign for **The Dodman.** The path climbs steeply, then drops to pass round a rocky cove, climbing again to reach the end of the point. The path is rugged and crosses a scrubby slope along the way. A stout **granite cross** stands on top, and there are fine views from a stance of 114m (375ft).

Continue along a narrow path, then alternate between field paths, bushy paths and scrubby slopes, passing a National Trust sign for **Lamledra.** The path works its way above **Vault Beach** and out towards a

← to serve Him, this cross is erected. AD1896'. The path has one or two difficult moments before it reaches Gorran Haven, but the continuation via Chapel Point to Mevagissey is easier.

Looking back to Portloe and its tiny harbour from the cliff path

headland. There is access to the beach on the right beyond a stile, but keep left to turn round the point of **Pen-a-maen** on a slope of gorse and bracken. Although there is a view of **Gorran Haven** ahead, there are cliffs in the way. Climb up to pass them, then walk down steps to land on Foxhole Lane at the **harbour.**

GORRAN HAVEN

Facilities include: a small range of accommodation; post office; shops; toilets; pub and restaurants. Transport links include a rather circuitous bus route to Mevagissey. There are summer ferries from Mevagissey to Fowey.

Walk up **Church Street**; the footpath signposted to the right offers a view of the beach, but leads back onto Church Street beside the little church of St Just. Continue up the road and pass Mount Zion Church, then turn right along **Cliff Road.** (To the left is the Llawnroc Inn.) At the top of the road

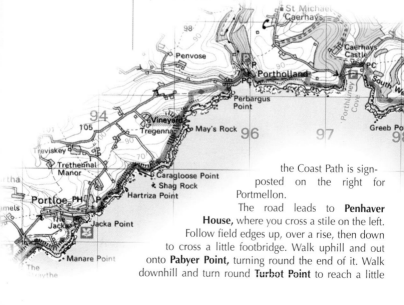

the Coast Path is sign-posted on the right for Portmellon.

The road leads to **Penhaver House,** where you cross a stile on the left. Follow field edges up, over a rise, then down to cross a little footbridge. Walk uphill and out onto **Pabyer Point,** turning round the end of it. Walk downhill and turn round **Turbot Point** to reach a little bay with a beach of white pebbles. Cross an access road at **Chapel Point**; there is no access to the attractive buildings on the point.

The path crosses grassy slopes and becomes a bit more rugged, then leads up to a road. Turn right along **Chapel Point Lane** and drop down to a junction. Turn right down into **Portmellon** and walk round the head of the beach to the 17th-century Rising Sun Inn, which offers food, drink and accommodation. Walk up **Portmellon Road,** passing hotels and B&Bs en route to **Mevagissey**. At a road junction, the Coast Path runs down through a park with splendid views over

Taking a break on Pen-a-maen before reaching Gorran Haven

the harbour and the coast ahead. Walk down the road; *either* go down steps or alleys on the right to reach the **harbour,** *or* follow the road into the centre of town.

MEVAGISSEY

The first recorded mention of this settlement was in 1313, and boats have been built here since 1745. The town's first electric street lights were powered by generators fed with pilchard oil! Fishing is still moderately important, though the town is essentially a tourist resort and can be very busy.

Facilities include: a large range of accommodation; bank; post office; shops; toilets; pubs and restaurants. There is the Mevagissey Museum, and a little aquarium. Transport links include buses back to Gorran Haven and onwards to Pentewan, St Austell and Par. There are also ferries from Mevagissey to Fowey. Tourist Information Centre, St George's Square, Mevagissey, St Austell, Cornwall PL26 6UB, tel: 01726-844857, email: jenny@mevagissey-cornwall.co.uk

DAY 27
Mevagissey to Polmear

Start at the head of **Mevagissey** harbour and walk towards the museum. Watch out for a narrow concrete path rising to the left, above the harbour. This is marked as the Coast Path, but if you find yourself at the Mevagissey Museum at the far end of the harbour, simply climb more steeply up flights of steps. Either way, continue up steps to the **coastguard lookout**, then cross an open green space at the top of the cliffs.

Pass seawards of the houses along a bushy path, then walk between gardens and rugged cliffs. Drop into a valley and cross a little footbridge, then walk up steps. Continue either alongside fields, or through rough patches around **Penare Point.** Walk downhill and cross a footbridge over a wide, muddy area. Follow the path uphill, to the right, swinging left, to emerge at the top near a busy road. Turn right and follow a path parallel to the road, but screened by bushes. Cross the **Pentewan Sands Holiday Park** access road and walk along the pavement beside the busy road. Turn right for **Pentewan** and walk to The Square in the middle of the village.

The Coast Path leaves Mevagissey and resembles a roller-coaster, with plenty of short ascents and descents, steep at times. Inland views reveal what appear to be snow-capped peaks, actually the towering spoil heaps from china clay works around St Austell. The harbour at Charlestown traded extensively in china clay and there is an interesting Shipwreck & Heritage Centre. The rest of the day is easy, ending with →

Start:	Mevagissey (015448)
Finish:	The Ship Inn at Polmear (088535)
Distance:	18km (11.25 miles)
Cumulative Distance:	597km (371 miles)
Maps:	OS Landranger 204, OS Explorers 105 & 107
Terrain:	Plenty of ascents and descents for the first half, sometimes steep or rugged underfoot. The rest of the walk is easy.
Refreshments:	Food and drink can be obtained at Pentewan, Charlestown and Par.

← a diversion around a china clay works at Par Docks, where everything looks rather grey and dusty. Walkers may keep moving beyond Par and Polmear, walking round Gribbin Head to reach Fowey.

PENTEWAN

Facilities include: a little accommodation; shop; toilets; pub. There are buses back to Mevagissey and Gorran Haven, and ahead to St Austell for further connections by bus or rail.

Looking along the cliffs of St Austell Bay after turning Black Head

Follow the Porthpean road, **Pentewan Hill,** climbing steeply from The Square to leave Pentewan. Turn sharp right along The Terrace and pass **All Saints Church.** At the end of the road is a

continued on page 168

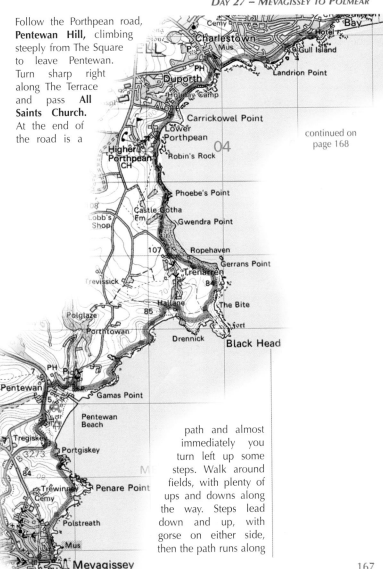

path and almost immediately you turn left up some steps. Walk around fields, with plenty of ups and downs along the way. Steps lead down and up, with gorse on either side, then the path runs along and around a little cove. Cross a little **footbridge** and walk up more steps. Continue along, before dropping down into a wooded valley, where steps lead down to a footbridge. Turn right downstream in the woods to reach tall pines near a house at **Hallane Mill.**

Turn left inland, past a gate, then right over a stile and back towards the coast. See how the river enters the sea as a waterfall. Steps lead uphill, then the path runs along and down towards the humped promontory of **Black Head.** A big block of granite stands in memory of Cornish poet A. L. Rowse.

The path leading out onto **Black Head** is optional, otherwise make a sharp left turn round the memorial stone and head for a patch of woodland. Climb up onto a cliff path and continue beside fields. Walk along **Ropehaven Cliffs,** managed as a nature reserve, then down into woods, but turn left and uphill again at a bench. The clear woodland path leads to a track, where

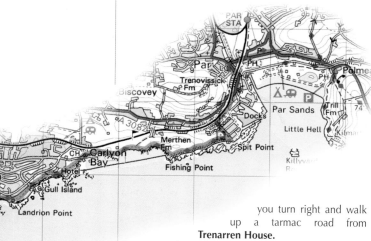

you turn right and walk up a tarmac road from **Trenarren House.**

The Coast Path is signposted up from the right of the road, and runs between fields and wooded cliffs. Walk down steps to a footbridge over a stream, and climb steps on the other side. Walk over the top and follow a fence down to a tiny footbridge over a stream. Climb up more steps and cross another rise, then walk down to a track leading down to a road at **Porthpean.**

The Coast Path is immediately above the beach, in front of the **Porthpean Sailing Club.** Walk down a ramp towards the beach, then along a concrete wall past toilets, to reach a 'falling rocks' sign. Climb up a long flight of granite steps, then cross a wooded rise and walk downhill. The route is along the backs of houses, then through another wooded area, before passing inland of the late 18th-century **Crinnis Cliff Battery.** Walk down a path to the Pier House Hotel & Restaurant beside the harbour at **Charlestown.** Access across the sea lock may be barred, so walk round the head of the harbour to reach the far side.

CHARLESTOWN

This late 18th-century port was built by Charles Rashleigh from Menabilly. Ore was shipped from nearby mines, but the china clay industry provided the main cargo. Facilities include: a little accommodation; post office shop; toilets; a couple of pubs and restaurants. The Shipwreck & Heritage Centre is located at the head of the harbour. There is a greater range of facilities at nearby St Austell, with bus services and main line railway connections. Tourist Information Centre, Southbourne Road, St Austell, Cornwall PL25 4RS, tel: 01726-879500, email: tic@cornish-riviera.co.uk

Walk round to the far end of the **harbour** and turn left. A tarmac path leads up past toilets, then the path begins to drift inland through fields. Turn right to regain the cliffs, then right again in front of the **Porth Avallen Hotel.** The path is flanked by bushes, then crosses a green space in front of the **Carlyon Bay Hotel.** Cross another green space, then walk through an old car park and cross the access road to the Cornwall Coliseum. Continue along a bushy path, then walk alongside the **Carlyon Bay Golf Course,** towards a china clay works on **Spit Point.**

The quaint old stone harbour at Charlestown is worth exploring

Turn left inland along a dusty tarmac path beside the perimeter fence of the works. Cross a footbridge over a series of pipes and continue alongside the railway to reach a busy road. Turn right past the **Port of Par** access point, and walk under a rail arch to reach a junction at The Par Inn.

Turn right over a level crossing and walk under another rail arch, then follow the road all the way through the village of **Par,** passing the Church of the

Good Shepherd. Bear right at a junction to continue into
Polmear, passing under the Par Docks Road to reach the
Ship Inn. There is an access road for the Par Sands
Holiday Park, though the Coast Path stays well clear of
the beach.

PAR & POLMEAR

Facilities include: a small range of accommodation; post
office; shops; pubs. There are bus services back to St
Austell for further connections, and ahead to Fowey.
There is an important junction at Par where the line for
Newquay branches from the main line railway.

DAY 28
Polmear to Polperro

Headlands and coves come one after another throughout this day's walk. Some are hidden, such as the little cove at Polkerris, shortly beyond Par Sands. Gribbin Head is prominent, having been in view for the past couple of days, and bears a candy-striped daymark. Explore the bustling little town of Fowey, or catch one of the regular ferries across the River Fowey to Polruan. This will commit you to a rugged cliff walk with no readily available accommodation or other facilities until you reach Polperro. Strong walkers might continue to Looe, the next town, but Polperro's little alleyways and quaint old buildings deserve a decent inspection.

The Coast Path is signposted just to the left of the Ship Inn at **Polmear.** The path climbs up a hollow way overhung by trees, then heads off to the right to run closer to the coast. The way ahead is easy; if anyone was tempted to include **Par Sands,** there is a path climbing up to join the Coast Path. Walk along the coast and uphill for a while, then head down a path through bushes with a

Looking from Poltridmouth to Polruan after rounding Gribbin Head

Start:	The Ship Inn at Polmear (088535)
Finish:	Polperro (208509)
Distance:	21km (13 miles)
Cumulative Distance:	618km (384 miles)
Maps:	OS Landrangers 200 & 201, OS Explorer 107
Terrain:	Fairly easy at first, but a little more difficult after turning Gribbin Head. The cliff coast from Polruan to Polperro is quite difficult, with lots of ascents and descents that prove tiring late in the day.
Refreshments:	Food and drink readily available at Polkerris, Fowey and Polruan.

view down onto the little harbour at **Polkerris.** Walk down between the Rashleigh Inn and the Lifeboat House Beach Shop and café. There are also toilets.

Turn left on the beach and head back inland a little, then turn right up a path and stone steps. A zigzag path leads up a slope of tall beech trees. Walk down through fields to run close to the coast again, then cross rather more rugged slopes that are sometimes flanked by gorse. The path runs close to fields from time to time and eventually leads round **Little Gribbin** towards **Gribbin Head.** *Either* aim for the prominent red-and-white **Gribbin daymark,** erected in 1832, *or* stay faithful to the cliff path to turn round the headland. Either way, descend to a small beach at **Poltridmouth** and cross a couple of little footbridges. Turn right as signposted for the Coast Path and head round to a smaller beach, where there is a house beside a concrete wall holding an attractive pond in place.

Cross the outflowing stream and turn right up a wooded path onto **Lankelly Cliff.** The path is worn down to bare rock in places and there are steps. Continue along a roller-coaster path around field edges, then down into a valley to cross a tiny footbridge. Walk up and down again to reach a tiny beach at **Coombe Hawne.** Another uphill stretch leads over to Allday's Fields and **Covington Wood.** Walk down through the wood on a clear path, again worn down to bare rock, to reach **Readymoney Beach.** The beach is tiny and over-looked by 16th-century St Catherine's Castle. Food, drink and toilets are available.

Walk up the Readymoney Road and along the Esplanade to reach **Fowey.** Keep following the road to the town centre if you want to explore, otherwise find the ferry signposted on the right for Polruan. In bad weather it sometimes runs from the Town Quay, in which case you continue into the town. The ferry runs daily and regularly throughout the year; check times on 01726-870232.

FOWEY

The sheltered tidal river mouth at Fowey is deep and has long been used for anchorage. At the end of the 14th century, following an attack by Spanish ships, a stout chain was attached to blockhouses on either side of the river mouth. Although china clay is still exported from Fowey, the river often looks more like a marina, full of pleasure boats. The town is well worth exploring. Its narrow streets are full of character; the waterfront colourful and scenic; there is a museum and aquarium.

Facilities include: a good range of accommodation; banks with ATMs; post office; several shops; toilets; plenty of pubs and restaurants. Transport links include a bus service back to Par and St Austell for further connections. Tourist Information Centre, 4 Custom House Hill, Fowey, Cornwall TR11 3PN, tel: 01726-833616, email: foweytic@visit.org.uk

POLRUAN

Facilities include: a small range of accommodation; post office; a few shops; toilets; pubs and restaurants. The local Polruan Bus provides services to and from Polperro and Looe.

Leave **Polruan** by climbing uphill from The Quay and Lugger Inn, either by road or using a flight of steps. Turn right along **West Street** to pass the Russell Inn, then turn left up **Battery Lane** to pass the Headland Gardens. The path skirts a car park and passes the **National Coastwatch Station.** Walk along a road, past a school, then turn right to get back onto the path.

The Coast Path follows an undulating course, crossing a small stream, then gradually gains height to overlook **Lantic Bay.** Follow the path as it dips down

continued on page 176

across a scrubby slope above the bay. Take care when climbing not to be drawn down the beach access path at a stile. Turn left uphill instead, then turn right downhill. Again the path swings right down towards the beach, so turn left to continue along the Coast Path around **Pencarrow Head.**

The path cuts across a scrubby slope, passing above a **small cottage** that was once used as a lookout. When the path enters a field, swing to the right to continue. The route becomes a roller-coaster, crossing a couple of little footbridges separated by a stone step stile. Climb up to a gateway where paths diverge, and keep to the right for the Coast Path.

Drop steeply into **West Combe** and cross another footbridge above a waterfall at **Lantivet Bay.** There is access to Lansallos Beach by turning right; turn left for the Coast Path. Turn sharp right just before a gate and follow the path as it rises across a scrubby, bushy slope. Contour across the slope, descend into a valley and cross a footbridge over a stream.

Climb steeply up a narrow path, passing an obelisk **daymark**; along with a bell out to sea, warns sailors of the Udder Rock offshore. Cross the top of a rise, then walk down steps on a slope of gorse. Cross a footbridge over a stream, then climb up steps on another slope of gorse. Walk over the top and more gently down the other side to turn

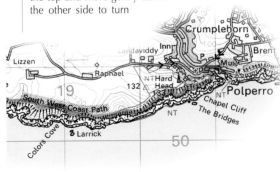

round **Raphael Cliff.** There are fine views, then steps drop steeply downhill.

Walk up and down across a slope, over a small stream and pass a National Trust sign for **Chapel Cliff.** There is another steep climb, which levels out a bit, and the slope becomes covered in bushes until trees completely enclose the path. As soon as a few houses appear ahead, walk down to the right along the path closest to the cliffs. Turn right at a rocky stance that offers a fine view over the harbour at **Polperro.** A tarmac path continues downhill, and steps to the right lead down to the **harbour.** Turn left and pass the Blue Peter Inn and toilets, then the Polperro fish landing area and walk to the head of the harbour, crossing a river at the 16th-century **House on Props.**

POLPERRO

Despite the crowds of tourists, Polperro still has a small fishing fleet and great character, with buildings crammed together along tiny alleyways and narrow streets. Visit the Polperro Heritage Museum of Smuggling & Fishing.

Facilities include: a range of accommodation; post office; shops; toilets; pubs and restaurants. Polruan Bus services provide links back to Polruan and ahead to Looe.

An easy path runs from Polperro to Talland Bay. The path becomes a little more difficult, but a lot more attractive, on its way round the next headland. St George's Island can occasionally be visited on boat trips. Looe comes in two parts, West and East; although a road bridge is easily reached, there are ferries across the narrow tidal river. After a gentle walk to Millendreath Beach and a detour away from the coast, the terrain becomes more difficult on a →

Cross a river at the head of **Polperro** harbour, beside the House on Props, and turn right along **The Warren,** signposted as *'Public Footpath Talland Bay'*. The road is narrow and passes toilets while offering good views back across the harbour. Keep climbing as a path continues, losing sight of Polperro. Make a right turn at a fork, marked for Talland.

Walk downhill and turn around **Downend Point,** passing close to a granite cross war memorial. The path runs across a bushy slope and leads onto a narrow tarmac road. Follow this until it turns inland, then use a path on the right to stay above the sea. Turn right downhill, then left and right, to reach **Talland Bay.**

Follow a narrow tarmac road up from Talland Bay Café and pass the toilets, then turn right along a road to reach the **Smuggler's Rest Café.** There is a small car park opposite and the Coast Path runs up a flight of steps. The field path gives way to a track, which narrows when it reaches a patch of woodland. The path runs through bushes and up steps to **Hendersick.** Walk across a slope of grass and gorse, then up to a rocky outcrop above the **Hore Stone** for a view of St George's Island.

Walk downhill, then up steps, then keep high

Start:	Polperro (208509)
Finish:	Portwrinkle (360539)
Distance:	20km (12.5 miles)
Cumulative Distance:	638km (396.5 miles)
Maps:	OS Landranger 201, OS Explorers 107 & 108
Terrain:	After an easy start, and despite several easy interludes during the day, the Coast Path gradually becomes more difficult.
Refreshments:	Plenty of places offer food and drink at Talland Bay, Looe, Millendreath Beach, Seaton and Downderry.

around **Portnadler Bay.** Walk down steps and cross a footbridge over a stream, then follow a level path through bracken and fields to reach a road. Follow the Marine Drive or the grassy coastal strip alongside, around **Hannafore Point,** until you can overlook the circular Banjo Pier in **Looe Bay.**

Walk down the road and watch for the Coast Path dropping down to the harbourside. There is a small seasonal ferry from **West Looe** to **East Looe,** but it takes only a few minutes to cross the stone arches of the road bridge. *Either* walk along the harbourside *or* along the main shopping street, Fore Street, to reach **The Guildhall.**

← rugged, wooded slope. Beyond Seaton and Downderry a splendid cliff walk, closed for many years, offers a scenic and interesting route to Portwrinkle.

WEST LOOE & EAST LOOE

There are more facilities in East Looe than West Looe, including: a range of accommodation; banks with ATMs; post offices; plenty of shops; toilets; several pubs and restaurants. Transport links include a branch railway with Wessex Trains linking with main line services at Liskeard. Bus services include the Polruan Bus back to Polperro and Polruan, and other bus services ahead to Seaton, Downderry, Portwrinkle and Torpoint for Plymouth. The Old Guildhall Gaol & Museum offers plenty of history about the town. There are occasional boat trips out to St George's Island. Tourist Information Centre, The Guildhall, Fore Street, East Looe,

continued on page 180

179

Cornwall PL13 1AA, tel: 01503-262072, email: looetic@looetourism.freeserve.co.uk

Walk from **Fore Street** onto **Buller Street,** then turn left along **Castle Street.** Climb steeply up through a crossroads onto **East Cliff.** This road becomes a tarmac path climbing further uphill. Keep right at a fork and follow a gravel path through the bushes, then walk down another tarmac path. Pass houses and follow a road to a junction with **Plaidy Lane.** Turn right downhill almost to a **small beach,** but follow the road uphill and inland. Watch for

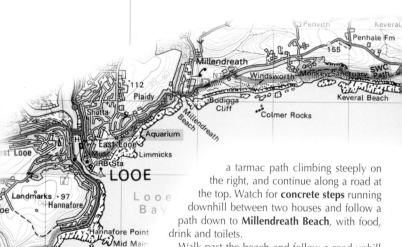

a tarmac path climbing steeply on the right, and continue along a road at the top. Watch for **concrete steps** running downhill between two houses and follow a path down to **Millendreath Beach**, with food, drink and toilets.

Walk past the beach and follow a road uphill inland. The tarmac peters out at **The Watch House** and a sunken path continues through a wood. Emerge on a road at **Bay View Farm** campsite, then walk along the road to find a Coast Path sign for Seaton, pointing to the right at a National Trust sign for **Bodigga Cliff.**

The path leads downhill from an open space and undulates across a wooded slope. Not far uphill is the Woolly Monkey Sanctuary at **Murrayton** (no direct access from the Coast Path). Pass a National Trust sign for **Struddicks.** Walk uphill, along a level path, then uphill again. Steps lead down on another wooded stretch. Turn right down a road called **Looe Hill,** then right again across a river and along Bridge Road at **Seaton.**

SEATON

The Seaton Valley Countryside Park lies across the road from a grey beach. Facilities include: a small amount of accommodation; post office shop; toilets; pub restaurant and beach café. There are buses back to Looe and ahead to Downderry, Portwrinkle and Torpoint for Plymouth.

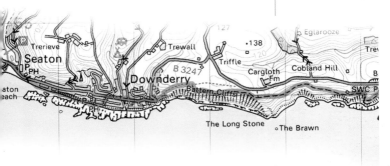

Leaving **Seaton,** the Coast Path signpost points ambiguously between the beach and the road climbing to Downderry. If the tide is fully in, then the path alongside the **sea wall,** which eventually drops onto the **beach,** may be impassable. When the tide is out, it makes sense to avoid the traffic on the road. Either way, there is access to **The Inn on the Shore,** supported by a stout retaining wall high above the shore. A path beside the inn links **Main Road** and the beach.

continued on page 182

DOWNDERRY

Facilities include: a small amount of accommodation; post office shop; toilets; pub; restaurant. Buses run back to Seaton and Looe and ahead to Portwrinkle.

Either follow the road through **Downderry,** *or* if using the pebbly beach, come ashore at a ramp and follow a road called Beach Hill inland, then turn right along **Main Road,** which is the B3247. The road crosses a dip and passes St Nicholas' Church, then rises to leave the village and bends sharply to the left. At the entrance to **Downderry Lodge** there is a Coast Path signpost and the path works its way up a wooded and bushy slope.

View from the cliffs beyond Downderry to the Long Stone

Near the top of the slope, turn right along a narrow path, which traces a crumbling, overgrown wall along **Battern Cliffs.** The path becomes easier and overlooks a wooded slope leading down to a fine beach, with the **The Long Stone** stack prominent. Views from the clifftop stretch far away to the urban sprawl of Plymouth.

Walk downhill to go through a small gate, then continue down some steps. The path climbs, then comes a series of ups and downs and more small gates. Pass below a wooden building and through another gate, where the path rises, then drops down steps. The path hugs the coast to reach the village of **Portwrinkle.** Follow the route as marked above the houses, before turning right down a road to a tiny harbour. Follow the coastal road overlooking the rocky shore to reach the **Whitsand Bay Hotel.**

Looking down from the cliffs to Portwrinkle and its miniscule harbour

PORTWRINKLE

Facilities include: a couple of B&Bs and a hotel with a restaurant; beach shop and toilets. The little village of Crafthole is only 800m (0.5 mile) inland and the Finnygook Inn offers food, drink and accommodation. There are buses back to Downderry and Seaton, and ahead to Torpoint for Plymouth.

DAY 30
Portwrinkle to Plymouth

The last day's walk in Cornwall, concluding some 450km (280 miles) since Marsland Mouth. If you follow the Coast Path exactly, it leads gradually inland beyond Portwrinkle to avoid a military firing range at Tregantle Fort. After running through the scattered holiday cabins on the rugged cliffs at Freathy, it describes a most circuitous course. A more straightforward route leads around Rame Head, conspicuous in distant views for a few days. After passing Cawsand and Kingsand an easy walk leads through the Mount Edgcumbe Country Park to Cremyll, where a ferry crosses the mouth of the River Tamar, saving a lengthy detour inland. Plymouth is the big city of the South West Coast Path, with the fullest range of facilities.

The Coast Path climbs uphill to leave **Portwrinkle** across the road from the Whitsand Bay Hotel. Climb up steps, then walk alongside the **golf course**. Go through a gate at a National Trust sign for **Trethill,** and follow the path until a line of marker posts and signs warn of a **military range** ahead. The path is diverted inland to a road, then runs parallel to the road up to 100m (330ft). **Tregantle Fort** sits low and solid on top of the hill; follow a road past it.

Turn right as signposted for Whitsand Bay. When the road bends down to the left, there is a path running parallel to it from a National Trust sign for **Tregantle.** Looking back to Portwrinkle, the sandy beach looks tempting, but is included in the military ranges. Follow the path to **Sharrow Point,** then follow the road up across a slope covered in holiday cabins at **Freathy.** The road rises, then drops a little to a junction where the **Whitsand Bay Holiday Park** is to the left. You may have already spotted a sign for the Cliff Top Café (off-route and its access track does not link with the Coast Path).

Turn right beyond a **post box and bus stop** to follow the Coast Path as signposted. Watch carefully for marker posts with arrows as you wind down among the cabins, eventually reaching a hollow with only a few cabins, before climbing back up towards the road. Veer right and walk downhill, passing more cabins while describing a broad loop across the rugged, bushy slope. When a grassy track is reached, follow it up towards the road again, then turn right down another path. This swings left and runs down past the whitewashed **Plymouth Wiggle Hut.** Continue across a bushy slope, then cross an access road near a row of cottages and climb steps inland to cross another access road to walk above **Polhawn Fort.**

A short field path leads to more rugged slopes and steps uphill. The path contours around **Rame Head,** with

Start:	Portwrinkle (360539)
Finish:	Admiral's Hard, Plymouth (462540)
Distance:	22km (13.5 miles)
Cumulative Distance:	660km (410 miles)
Maps:	OS Landranger 201, OS Explorer 108
Terrain:	Paths are mostly quite easy, though there are some rugged stretches and occasional short, steep ascents and descents. The latter half of the walk includes long stretches in woodlands.
Refreshments:	There is a café off-route at Freathy, and pubs and restaurants around Cawsand and Kingsand. Food and drink available at Cremyll while waiting for the ferry to Plymouth.

an optional detour across a gap to **St Michael's Chapel**, built in 1397, on top of the headland. Just inland is the National Coastwatch Rame Head Station. As you walk down towards the gap, note that the Coast Path runs off to the left, the clearest path across the rugged slopes.

An easy stretch of path leads from Rame Head towards the next point. When a bend on an old, narrow road is reached, keep right to walk gently downhill to **Penlee Point.** Look out for Queen Adelaide's Chapel on the right, actually a 19th-century folly. Follow the road into mature woodland, but watch for a track slicing down to the right. Follow a bit more road, then continue along the woodland track again. Pass a row of houses and follow a tarmac path through the woods, dropping

St Michael's Chapel on top of Rame Head was built in 1397

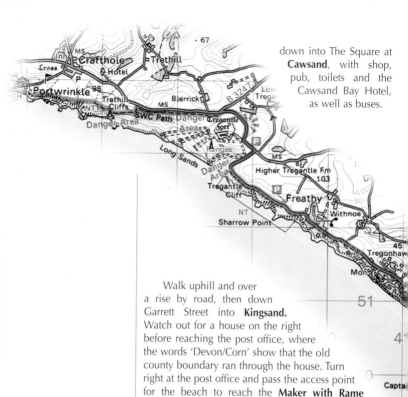

down into The Square at **Cawsand**, with shop, pub, toilets and the Cawsand Bay Hotel, as well as buses.

Walk uphill and over a rise by road, then down Garrett Street into **Kingsand.** Watch out for a house on the right before reaching the post office, where the words 'Devon/Corn' show that the old county boundary ran through the house. Turn right at the post office and pass the access point for the beach to reach the **Maker with Rame Institute.**

CAWSAND & KINGSAND

Facilities include: a small range of accommodation; post office; shops; toilets; pubs and restaurants. A bus service describes a loop between the Cremyll and Torpoint ferries, heading back to Freathy and on to Plymouth.

After passing the Institute, turn left when you see a street sign for **The Cleave,** then turn right up narrow **Heavitree Road.** Walk steeply uphill until you see a sign for **Lower Row,** then turn right to walk through a gate into the **Mount Edgcumbe Country Park.** A clear path runs up

186

across grassy slopes and leads into woodland, eventually reaching a road.

Turn right along the road, then turn left up a path. Keep left at a fork after an iron gate, then keep right along a level track in dense woodland. Pass an ornate **stone shelter**, then later climb up steps and zigzag above a landslip. Head down steps on the other side and drop down to the coast. Cross a footbridge over a wet area and continue through the woods. Walk through an open area below a **ruin** on a knoll, then through a tall gate and fence into the woods again.

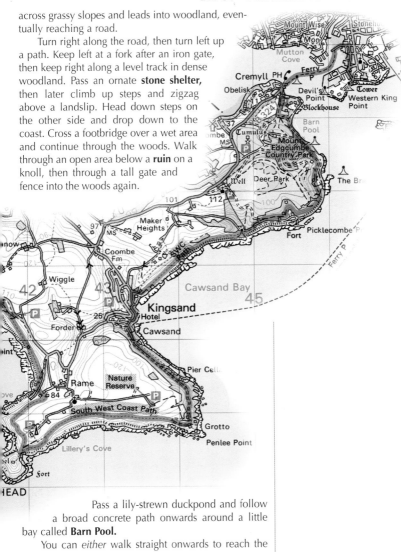

Pass a lily-strewn duckpond and follow a broad concrete path onwards around a little bay called **Barn Pool**.

You can *either* walk straight onwards to reach the

Smeaton's Tower dominates The Hoe and the Plymouth waterfront

Formal Gardens and Orangery Restaurant, *or* turn left up a broad concrete road with an avenue of trees alongside. When a junction is reached, there is a view to the left of **Mount Edgcumbe House,** but turn right to walk gently down another concrete road to reach the **Edgcumbe Arms** and ferry slip at **Cremyll.** The ferry (tel: 01752-822105) runs regularly throughout the year to Admiral's Hard at **Plymouth**. You can catch a bus into the centre of Plymouth, or keep walking along the newly developed 'Plymouth Waterfront Walkway'.

PLYMOUTH

This is the biggest city on the South West Coast Path, and there's lots to see. In the past, walkers were quite happy to take a bus to Turnchapel and get straight onto the next stretch of cliff path. Although Plymouth was devasted by bombing during World War II, many fine buildings survived, even around the dockyards. The Hoe is a fine grassy area dominated by Smeaton's red-and-white lighthouse; it was here that Sir Francis Drake concluded a game of bowls before going out to meet the Spanish Armada. Down below, the Barbican is well worth exploring, and many interesting places can be visited along the Waterfront Walkway.

Facilities include: a full range of accommodation, including a youth hostel; banks with ATMs; post offices; a mass of shops; toilets; pubs and restaurants galore. There is a railway with Virgin Trains to Scotland, Great Western trains to London Paddington and local Wessex Trains. An excellent local bus service helps with travel around the city, and into the surrounding area. National Express buses leave Plymouth for Penzance, Poole, Bournemouth, Brighton, London, Birmingham and Scotland. Tourist Information Centre, Island House, 9 The Barbican, Plymouth, Devon PL1 2LS, tel: 01752-304849, email: plymouthbarbicantic@visit.org.uk

DAY 31
Plymouth to Wembury Beach

Start at the ferry slip at **Admiral's Hard,** where a stone tablet in the ground reads 'Welcome to Plymouth. Please wipe your feet'. Head inland and *either* turn right along Strand Street, *or* along Cremyll Street, if you want the shop, toilets or pub. You get glimpses of the docks and pass the **Ede Vinegar Works.** Incidentally, the whole of this walk is dotted with code words from *The Nautical Telegraph Code Book*; you'll need a copy if you want to know what they mean!

Pass between the stout granite arch of the **Royal William Yard,** built in 1825, and the Butchers Arms, to reach a road junction at the **Artillery Tower** Restaurant. The building dates from the 15th-century. Enjoy the view of Drake's Island and The Sound; don't be tempted along the coastal promenade, which is a dead-end. Turn inland by road, passing toilets, and keep to the right-hand side all the way along **Durnford Street.**

This is a fine Georgian street; Arthur Conan Doyle worked as a doctor at No 1, and the street is studded with Sherlock Holmes quotations. Pass the **Royal Marines Barracks;** a limestone edifice; and turn right

The first half of this day's walk is an exceedingly convoluted trail through Plymouth. The route has recently been tidied up, and the 'Plymouth Waterfront Walkway' is a celebration of the city's heritage, a showcase for some unusual artistic features, and an integral part of the South West Coast Path. Keep an eye peeled for acorn waymarks on lampposts, or set into the pavement, and for the biggest Coast →

Start:	Admiral's Hard, Plymouth (462540)
Finish:	Wembury Beach (517484)
Distance:	22km (13.5 miles)
Cumulative Distance:	682km (423.5 miles)
Maps:	OS Landranger 201, OS Explorer 108, OS Outdoor Leisure 15
Terrain:	Urban for first half, with some busy roads and industrial areas. A wooded cliff gives way to a more open fairly easy low cliff-line.
Refreshments:	Plenty of places to eat and drink around Plymouth, and odd places at Pomphlett, Oreston, Turnchapel, Mount Batten and Heybrook Bay.

← Path marker on the entire trail! Get a booklet about the trail from the Tourist Information Centre. Walkers who are in a hurry could use the ferry from the Barbican to Mount Batten to avoid an 8km (5-mile) walk around Cattewater. The continuation to Wembury Beach is fairly easy and runs along a low cliff-line.

along **Millbay Road** to continue along Caroline Place towards **Millbay Docks.**

Walk straight past a roundabout and observe the 'Wall of Stars', commemorating celebrities who once sailed from Plymouth, then pass a stack of gold bullion lying unattended on the pavement! Walk up to the **Duke of Cornwall Hotel** and note the interlocking stones set into the pavement, illustrating how the Eddystone Lighthouse was constructed. Turn right along **West Hoe Road** and study its 'Wall of Industrial Memories', then continue along **Great Western Road** for another good view of The Sound from the 'Royal Navy Millennium Wall'. There is a concentration of hotel and B&B accommodation in this area.

Pass the West Hoe Pier and continue along **Hoe Road,** where you should divert up onto **The Hoe** and

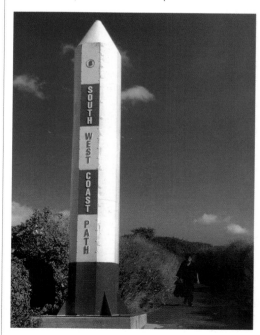

The biggest marker post on the entire South West Coast Path!

admire Smeaton's Tower, the original Eddystone Lighthouse. Walk down **Madeira Road,** with a stout sea wall below and the impregnable walls of the **Royal Citadel** above. One corner commemorates the 'Total Eclipse of the Sun Wednesday 11th August 1999'.

Boat trips are available further down the road, and a ferry across to Mount Batten; if the Waterfront Walkway is proving to be entertaining, keep walking. The water taxi to Mount Batten runs daily throughout the year, tel: 07930-838614. Don't miss the **Mayflower Steps,** site of several historic comings and goings, including the *Mayflower*. There is easy access to the Tourist Information Centre in the **Barbican.**

The Waterfront Walkway runs around **Sutton Harbour** and its marina, though a lock gate and **swing-bridge** can be crossed to reach the **National Marine Aquarium.** The route around the marina follows Sutton Road, Commercial Road and Clovelly Road, while the route past the aquarium follows a path and Teats Hill Road to reach Clovelly Road. Either way, turn right up **Breakwater Hill** and pass a huge navigation beacon marker for the South West Coast Path.

Walk up and down a tarmac path on a limestone cliff, passing a huge St Christopher medallion, then continue along the industrial **Cattedown Road** past the Cattedown Wharves. The Passage House pub is available on the way to a level crossing, then turn right along **Maxwell Road** and right again at the Float Bench along **Finnigan Road.** Turn right to cross the **New Laira Bridge,** built in 1962 next to an old railway bridge. Billacombe Road leads past The Morley Arms. The road is very busy, but 'The Poem Wall' alongside offers distraction.

Turn right along a footpath and cycleway at the head of **Pomphlett Lake,** with access to Safeways and McDonald's. The Coast Path is signposted up **Oreston Road,** but you could follow a railway path to stay off the road as far as Radford Castle. Walk up and over Oreston Road, then turn right along **Rollis Park Road** and walk down to The Kings Arms for a view across Cattewater.

Walk up **Park Lane** and cross a restored stone stile, then follow a tarmac path, which reaches a road end but

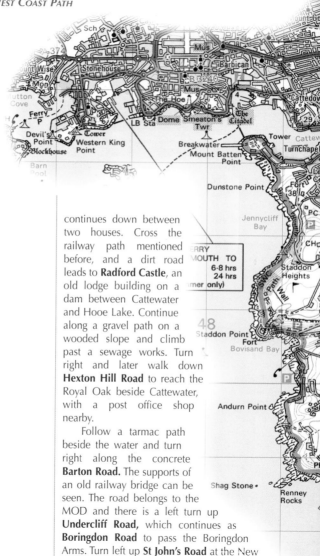

continues down between two houses. Cross the railway path mentioned before, and a dirt road leads to **Radford Castle**, an old lodge building on a dam between Cattewater and Hooe Lake. Continue along a gravel path on a wooded slope and climb past a sewage works. Turn right and later walk down **Hexton Hill Road** to reach the Royal Oak beside Cattewater, with a post office shop nearby.

Follow a tarmac path beside the water and turn right along the concrete **Barton Road.** The supports of an old railway bridge can be seen. The road belongs to the MOD and there is a left turn up **Undercliff Road,** which continues as **Boringdon Road** to pass the Boringdon Arms. Turn left up **St John's Road** at the New

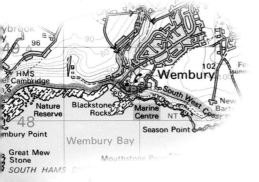

Inn. Keep right at the top to find the marked route going down steps to a marina at **Turnchapel.** Follow the path as marked, avoiding only a small boatyard, to pass the **Mount Batten Centre** and Hotel Mount Batten. The water taxi from the Barbican at Plymouth berths here, and there are toilets just inland.

Walk round to the Breakwater and look out for monuments to RAF Mount Batten and Lawrence of Arabia. There is a bus stop at a turning area by the Cobblers Restaurant. Climb steps up to the **Mount Batten Tower** on a little hill and enjoy the view around The Sound. Walk down and continue along the Coast Path, which leaves the Mount Batten peninsula and climbs gently towards a couple of green spaces at **Jennycliff.**

The second of these spaces has a refreshment hut and toilet. A view indicator contrasts today's view with that of 20,000 years ago, when The Sound was dry land. Climb up to a wooded slope, where the Waterfront Walkway ends and the Coast Path continues. A marker says it is 175.5 miles (283km) to Poole. (I make it 229 miles/368km).

Go down a few steps and up a lot more steps on the wooded slope, then cross a little footbridge over a stream. Emerge from the woods with a fine view of the Plymouth Breakwater, that shelters The Sound from rough weather. Follow an easy cliff path and walk down steps overlooking a small harbour at **Staddon Point.** Cross a large footbridge over a man-made cutting and walk down stone steps to some houses. Turn left to follow a road past a car park and small café, then keep right and follow a path and steps down towards **Bovisand Bay.** Cross a footbridge and climb uphill, then go along the access road through **Bovisand Park,** passing toilets and The Beachcomber Café. There are more toilets towards the end of the road.

Follow the path along the low coast, crossing a couple of little footbridges. Turn round a point at **Renney Rocks** with a fine view of the pyramidal islet called the Great Mew Stone. The path leads to a track running close to the **Heybrook Bay Hotel.** Keep right by road to find two footpaths. One is marked 'Coast Path to Wembury Beach' while the other is the 'Alternative Coast Path' leading up a flight of steps inland. This is because there used to be firing from HMS Cambridge on **Wembury Point.**

The Coast Path is reasonably level and easy, and a footbridge is crossed at **Wembury Beach.** Steps lead up to toilets, the Old Mill Café and Wembury Marine Centre. The village of **Wembury** is just inland; some walkers may wish to continue if they need to use the ferry across the River Yealm, but first check the ferry notices posted at Wembury Beach.

WEMBURY & WEMBURY BEACH

The village is just inland from the beach and facilities include: a few B&Bs; post office; shop; toilets; pub and restaurant. Check the times of the ferry across the River Yealm in advance. Buses can be taken back towards Plymouth to connect with another service to Noss Mayo if you find that the ferry across the Yealm isn't running. Also take note of the tide times for fording the River Erme further along the Coast Path.

DAY 32
Wembury Beach to Bigbury-on-Sea

The Coast Path leaves **Wembury Beach** by climbing up towards the church. Despite the path forking ahead, the separate routes converge again at a **white cottage** where there is a fine view over the mouth of the River Yealm. Follow a track down to the right as indicated for *'Warren Point and Ferry'*. The track leads to a house and steps lead down to the little **ferry pier.** The ferry runs daily from Easter to September, generally from 1000 to 1100 and 1500 to 1600, but check in advance (tel: 01752-880079). An arrow on the pier shows you which way to wave to attract attention.

If you have plenty of time, you could use the ferry to visit **Newton Ferrers,** which has shops, pubs and restaurants; otherwise cross directly to the **Noss Mayo** shore (though you don't actually walk into the village).

Walk up steps from the little pier and turn right along a very narrow road. Keep right to pass **Ferryman's Cottage,** which displays an old scale of ferry charges. Continue through **Passage Wood,** where you can spot woodpeckers and treecreepers. The path eventually leads up to a woodland track, Revelstoke Drive,

At this stage of the walk you should be adept at rigging your walking schedule to fit in with ferry services and the ebb and flow of the tides. Today you need to turn up at a small landing stage at Warren Point and get a seasonal ferry to Noss Mayo. A delightful walk along the coast leads to the tidal River Erme, which you need to wade across at low water. The Coast Path beyond features a series of steep ascents and descents on →

Start:	Wembury Beach (517484)
Finish:	Bigbury-on-Sea (651443)
Distance:	23km (14.25 miles)
Cumulative Distance:	705km (437.75 miles)
Maps:	OS Landrangers 201 & 202, OS Outdoor Leisure 20
Terrain:	Easy to and from the ferry, but a little more difficult on the way to the River Erme. The Erme is tidal and has to be forded with care, so check the time of low water in advance. The final part of the walk is quite difficult, with several ascents and descents, some of which are very steep.
Refreshments:	None. You need to be self-sufficient all day.

← the way to Bigbury-on-Sea, enjoying some of the best cliff scenery on the South Devon coast. Be sure to plan this day's walk carefully.

constructed on the orders of Lord Revelstoke in the 1880s as a carriage drive.

The track winds out of the woods, passing a fine building called **Cellars,** and the old coastguard cottages, then heads back into the woods at **Brakehill Plantation.** The track emerges onto a rugged slope where there are again fine views across the mouth of the Yealm. The gravel surface becomes grassy and offers easy and scenic walking. There are generally fields to the left, and later you pass **Warren Cottage,** which was a lunching stop on the old Revelstoke Drive. Continue along a clear gravel track, which drifts inland later, so cut off down a grassy track as marked, down past a gate.

Walk gently uphill below an old coastguard lookout, then gently downhill and round a corner at an old gate pillar on **Stoke Point.** A gate leads into a wooded area, then there is a car park and an access road for **Revelstoke Park.** There might be a chance to obtain food or drink from this holiday park, but don't rely on it outside peak season. There is a guest house inland at **Rowden.**

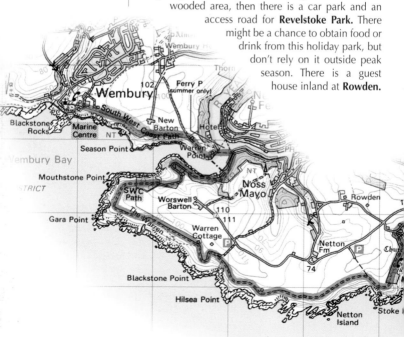

Cross the holiday park access road to continue on the Coast Path.

A gravel track becomes grassy, flanked by hawthorns. Walk along it and pass a couple of gates until there is a left bend inland after a ruined lookout at 100m (330ft) on **Beacon Hill.** At this point, the Coast Path drops steeply down into a grassy hollow and up the other side, though some walkers follow the sheep's example and contour round the top of the hollow. Walk up a track and when a gate is reached on a bend, walk straight onwards as signposted. Continue more or less level until a marker post points downhill to the right. Go steeply downhill, then along a grassy slope, then down through a wooded patch to cross a valley dominated by a rocky tor.

Coast Path walkers follow the easy, grassy Revelstoke Drive

The tor is called **St Anchorite's Rock,** which you pass on the right, crossing distinctive V-notch stiles from field to field. The route has been through fields

continued on
page 198

197

for some time, but now climbs over a cliff and enjoys fine coastal scenery around **Butcher's Cove.** Walk down a slope of gorse and turn round into a valley overlooking a sea full of angular little stacks.

Cross a footbridge over a little stream in the valley, then climb up steps on a slope of gorse. A field path on top gives way to a descent on a wooded slope leading to **Meadowfoot Beach.** Turn left to pass in front of a boathouse and cross the sandy beach to follow the Coast Path over a wooded promontory. Steep steps lead a short way uphill, then simply walk down to a road and onto the Mothecombe Slipway at **Erme Mouth.**

Read the information board about crossing the tidal River Erme. Do not ford the Erme if conditions are against you. Either walk round (11km/7 miles), or arrange for a taxi. Walkers seeking accommodation should bear in mind Windlestraw B&B at Penquite, off-route and inland near Ermington. Mrs Wallis will, by arrangement, help walkers who are struggling to cross the Rivers Yealm, Erme and Avon (tel: 01752-896237).

Most authorities agree that the ford is passable for one hour either side of low water. If gale-force winds are pushing sea water into the river mouth it may not be passable at all; the same applies if the river is carrying floodwater. In calm conditions you may be able to cross three hours before low water and barely wade knee-deep, but never cross if the tide has already pushed over the fording point. The idea is to cross from **Mothecombe Slipway** to **Kingston Slipway** (visible a little further inland on the other side), though it is possible to head for **Wonwell Beach** and cut a corner.

Assuming your landfall is **Kingston Slipway,** walk up to a road-end car park and turn sharp right along a path that runs across a wooded slope. Cross **Wonwell Beach** and follow the path out onto a headland for a fine view back across Erme Mouth. Cross a dip above **Fernycombe Beach,** then climb up onto **Beacon Point,** continuing uphill to 100m (330ft).

Enjoy views inland to the high parts of Dartmoor. Go through a gate in a stout stone wall, then drop into a dip and climb again. Go through another gate and along the path, then cross a valley and climb up onto **Hoist Point,** where there is a stone bench. A steep and rugged

Burgh Island off Bigbury-on-Sea, showing its tidal sand-spit access

path leads down to **Westcombe Beach,** where a foot-bridge spans a stream.

Climb up a steep flight of steps and continue over the clifftop to enjoy extensive views. Walk down to **Ayrmer Cove** and admire its rocky walls, then climb up the other side onto **Toby's Point.** Walk down to **Challaborough Bay** to find a couple of shops and The Regatta Bar, as well as lots of mobile homes. There are also toilets and very occasional buses back to Plymouth. Walk up past a beach café to follow a path to **Bigbury-on-Sea.**

A road runs down towards the shore, where an interesting diversion could be made out to **Burgh Island** by walking across a tidal sandspit. The Pilchard Inn dates from 1336, and a stroll around the island is enjoyable. When the tide covers the sandspit, access may still be available using a curious tall 'sea tractor'.

BIGBURY-ON-SEA

Facilities include: a small range of accommodation, including the hotel on Burgh Island; post office; shops; toilets; pubs and cafés. Buses back to Plymouth or inland to Kingsbridge are very scarce. Check in advance the ferry service across the River Avon for the following morning.

DAY 33
Bigbury-on-Sea to Salcombe

Leave the main car park at **Bigbury-on-Sea** as signposted for the Coast Path and go down a few steps towards the beach. At low water the sandy banks of the River Avon can be followed inland to the Cockleridge. When the tide is in, follow the markers inland instead, over **Folly Hill,** keeping to the left of buildings, then walk up the B3392 road past The Henley Hotel.

Turn right at **Mount Folly Farm** and follow the signpost for the Coast Path. Markers steer a way down a steep slope, where you turn left at the bottom, then look along the **Cockleridge** to find a sign giving information about the ferry. It also gives details of a 12km (7.5-mile) walking route around the **River Avon**.

The ferry generally runs every day except Sundays, early April to early September, 1000 to 1100, 1500 to 1600, tel: 01548-561196 to check. It looks a long way across to Bantham at high water, but yell and wave and jump up and down near the sign to attract attention.

Once across, walk up the slip road from the ferry and turn right to leave **Bantham,** unless you wish to visit the Sloop Inn. The Coast Path follows a road through a

The most important thing to get right today is the initial crossing of the River Avon. The river can be forded at low water, but only by those with a particular understanding of its depth, flow and treacherously soft and uneven bed. As a visitor, don't even think of fording the river; it is too dangerous. There is a ferry at Bantham that will respond to a hearty yell from the Cockleridge, but this is seasonal and does not run on →

Start:	Bigbury-on-Sea (651443)
Finish:	Ferry Inn, Salcombe (742389)
Distance:	21km (13 miles)
Cumulative Distance:	726km (450.75 miles)
Maps:	OS Landranger 202, OS Outdoor Leisure 20
Terrain:	The initial low cliff path has gentle gradients, but the length and steepness of the ascents and descents increases throughout the day.
Refreshments:	There is a pub at Bantham, beach café at South Milton Sands, then a number of pubs and restaurants at Outer Hope. The Port Light Inn is available on Bolberry Down.

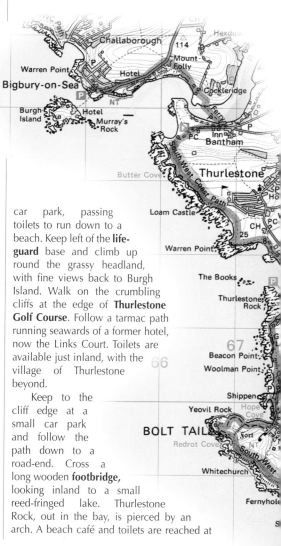

← Sundays. Once across, a reasonably easy Coast Path becomes progressively more difficult, with short ascents and descents on the way to Outer Hope and Inner Hope being followed by rather more rugged slopes between Bolt Tail and Bolt Head. There are some steep and rocky slopes around Starehole Bay before the route reaches Salcombe.

car park, passing toilets to run down to a beach. Keep left of the **lifeguard** base and climb up round the grassy headland, with fine views back to Burgh Island. Walk on the crumbling cliffs at the edge of **Thurlestone Golf Course**. Follow a tarmac path running seawards of a former hotel, now the Links Court. Toilets are available just inland, with the village of Thurlestone beyond.

Keep to the cliff edge at a small car park and follow the path down to a road-end. Cross a long wooden **footbridge**, looking inland to a small reed-fringed lake. Thurlestone Rock, out in the bay, is pierced by an arch. A beach café and toilets are reached at

South Milton Sands, where a dusty dirt road leads out of a car park. Follow the road inland from the Thurlestone Rock Apartments, then turn right as signposted for the Coast Path at a thatched building. The cliff path runs past the **Beacon Point Hotel.** Climb gradually uphill, then descend more steeply to **Hope Cove.**

OUTER HOPE & INNER HOPE

Facilities are concentrated around Outer Hope and include: a small range of accommodation; post office; shops; toilets; pubs and restaurants. Buses run inland to Kingsbridge for further connections.

Follow the road through **Outer Hope** and walk along a tarmac path, seawards of the Cottage Hotel, to reach **Inner Hope** and its thatched houses. Walk up steps and along a woodland path, emerging onto open slopes to continue up to the headland of **Bolt Tail.** Avoid short-cutting; it really is worth walking round the headland. The path along the rest of the cliff coast is initially a little vague in places, but becomes much clearer later. Climb in stages, then on top of **Bolberry Down,** at 120m (395ft), you could detour to the left for the Port Light Inn.

Follow a broad path beyond a small car park and walk along a crest with a view inland to Southdown Farm. The path is rough and stony as it drops down from **Cathole Cliff** into a valley. Cross a footbridge above the rugged **Soar Mill Cove** and climb uphill, intrigued by bizarre spiky rock formations. The path is almost level as it wanders

continued on page 204

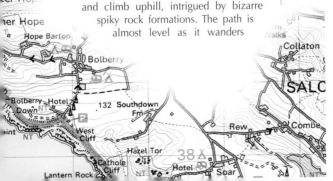

203

through gorse along the tops around **The Warren.** There are options to short-cut, but the Coast Path keeps right to reach **Bolt Head,** with an old concrete lookout. Walk down to the lookout, turn left and continue down a rugged path. Cross a stream at the bottom using a stone slab and go through a gate above **Starehole Bay.**

Climb up a steep slope and follow a flight of stone steps past a fine pinnacle of rock at **Sharp Tor.** Note the 'stare hole' pierced through the tor. Turn around a rocky ledge that has a fence for protection, and enjoy the view towards Salcombe. The path becomes well wooded and widens to become a dirt road. Turn right down a road to pass the **Bolt Head Hotel,** then pass the **South Sands Hotel.** There is a summer ferry service from South Sands to Salcombe, but the Coast Path follows the road. Walk steeply uphill, then down to North Sands, another small beach, then up again and down to **Salcombe.**

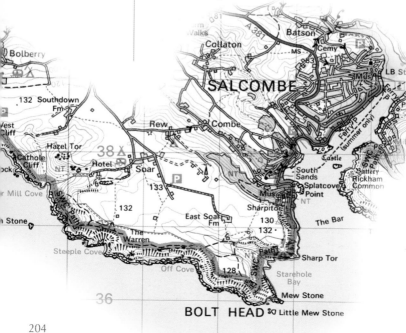

Steep and rugged slopes surround Starehole Bay on the way to Salcombe.

SALCOMBE

Facilities include: plenty of accommodation, including a youth hostel at South Sands and nearby campsites; banks with ATMs; post office; plenty of shops; toilets; several pubs and restaurants. Transport links include buses inland to Kingsbridge, back to Plymouth, and on Sundays direct services to Exeter. There is a museum. Tourist Information Centre, Council Hall, Market Street, Salcombe, Devon TQ8 8DE, tel: 0906-3020180, email: info@salcombeinformation.co.uk

DAY 34
Salcombe to Stoke Fleming

After using the ferry from Salcombe to East Portlemouth, walkers follow a rugged path that quickly develops a series of steep little ascents and descents. Enjoy the cliffs and coves and turn round Prawle Point, the southernmost point in Devon. An easier walk leads towards Start Point, then the route is quite exposed in a couple of places. A long shingle beach stretches away from Hallsands to Beesands and well beyond Torcross. There is an unfortunate move away from the coast beyond Strete Gate, and the route becomes fiddly as it tries to avoid the main road through Strete and Stoke Fleming. There have been attempts over the years to negotiate a coastal path, and these continue apace.

Start at the **Ferry Inn** and get the ferry from **Salcombe** to **East Portlemouth.** This runs daily throughout the year, tel 01548-842364. Come ashore at a little café and turn right as signposted for the Coast Path to Mill Bay. Follow the wooded minor road, which rises and falls to reach **Mill Bay** and toilets. Turn right up a woodland path signposted for Gara Rock, emerging onto an open slope of bracken and gorse. There are two paths available; an upper and lower path; they meet further along. Watch out for a small, whitewashed lookout with a conical thatched roof high on the cliffs. Just behind it is the **Gara Rock Hotel,** which offers food, drink and accommodation for the sake of a short detour.

The path drops into a dip where there is a beach far below the hotel. Cross a little footbridge beside a crumbling **ruin** and climb up and around another slope of bracken and gorse. Walk down to cross a small stone culvert, then up again, using a few steps to cross a rocky little notch and ledge. Follow the path over the back of **Gammon Head** and walk down into a dip overlooking a fine sandy beach in a rocky cove. The cliff path continues round an adjacent cove, then turns a rocky point where a few steps have been cut. Zigzag uphill and pass through a narrow gap between a boulder and a wall, then head for the National Coastwatch Station on **Prawle Point.** This has a small Visitor Centre with information about the local birds, including the rare cirl bunting, gannets, great skuas, cormorants, kittiwakes, herring gulls, black-headed gulls and great black-backed gulls.

Refreshment is available inland at the Pig's Nose pub and café in East Prawle, otherwise head for the nearby old **coastguard cottages** and cross the field below them. Continue though cereal fields close to the coast, with a curious cliff-line set well back from the sea. Looking back to Prawle Point, a rock arch can be seen. When a track heads inland, follow it, but swing back

Start:	Ferry Inn, Salcombe (742389)
Finish:	Stoke Fleming (863484)
Distance:	31km (19.25 miles)
Cumulative Distance:	757km (470 miles)
Maps:	OS Landranger 202, OS Outdoor Leisure 20
Terrain:	Rugged cliff paths with several short and steep ascents and descents at first, becoming easier beyond Prawle Point. There are some exposed steps on Start Point, and more ups and downs on the way to Torcross. The last part is easier, though moves inland.
Refreshments:	The Gara Rock Hotel is beyond East Portlemouth. Food and drink can be obtained at Hallsands, Beesands, Torcross and Strete.

round to the right to continue along the Coast Path. This passes well in front of **Maelcombe House,** then runs through a sparse patch of woodland. The path is rather rough and uneven, though gently graded as it turns round a little point. Head inland a short way, and turn right at a gate to follow a track past a big house. This is mostly a grassy track, passing seawards of another big house, then shifting gently down to **Lannacombe Beach,** where yet another big house sits at a valley mouth.

Danger signs advise you to keep inland of red markers along a crumbling cliff edge at **The Narrows,** but the path is well inland most of the way. Another sign later advises *'Please exercise extreme care when using this section of coast path'* and there is an exposed bit along a rock ledge. Fine rocky views embrace a pinnacled ridge leading to the lighthouse on **Start Point.** The path reaches the ridge well back from the light, joining its narrow access road. A signpost gives the distance back to Minehead as 449 miles (722km) and ahead to Poole as 164 (264km). (I make it 463.5 miles/746km back to Minehead and 167 miles/269km ahead to Poole.) Turn left to reach a car park and information board, then follow a path on the right down a steep, scrubby slope to reach **Hallsands.**

HALLSANDS

Hallsands was once a village of 37 houses in a double row; home to 128 people, protected by a shingle ridge that was part of the one stretching all the way round Start Bay. When the Devonport Docks were being developed near Plymouth, dredgers removed vast amounts of shingle offshore; the beach began to shift, subjecting the village to serious wave damage. The London Inn was destroyed in the winter of 1903–4, and by 1917 what remained of the village was evacuated after a severe winter storm. The residents were compensated, but no one admitted liability. A newspaper reported; 'The beach went to Devonport, the cottages went to the sea'. The remarkable Trout sisters built Trouts Hotel on the clifftop and this is now used as apartments, though there is a café open to the public. Go down to a viewpoint to see the ruins.

Continue walking along the clifftop, up and down steps, to reach toilets and a B&B near a car park. The pebbly beach at **Greenstraight** looks like

PRAWLE POINT

mixed beans and is followed until a path leads up onto **Tinsey Head.** A field path gives way to a path crossing a rugged slope, then heads down to **Beesands.** The Cricket Inn offers food, drink and accommodation, and also operates a tearoom. The stout sea wall protects a long row of cottages, and you follow a road past **St Andrew's Church,** a shell-fish processors and toilets.

The Coast Path is sign-posted along a dirt road from the **village green,** and a small reed-fringed lake can be seen inland. Keep to the left of a white house called

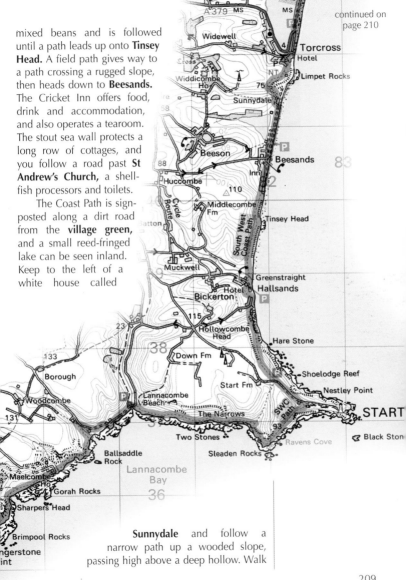

continued on page 210

Sunnydale and follow a narrow path up a wooded slope, passing high above a deep hollow. Walk

209

down through a field and wood, then zigzag carefully downhill as marked, passing **Cliff House** and Cliff Cottage to find stone steps leading down onto the

promenade at **Torcross.** Walk along the promenade to the far end of the village.

TORCROSS

The reed-fringed Lower Ley, inland of Torcross, is the largest natural lake in the West Country. It is reckoned to be 3000 years old and was formed when the sea heaped up the shingle bar around Start Bay. It is protected as the Slapton Ley National

Nature Reserve. Ducks, grebes, swans and herons can be spotted, as well as otters; there is a birdwatching hide. A battered American Sherman tank has been pressed into service as a war memorial, specifically to commemorate the 'Operation Tiger' D-Day practice landings on Slapton Beach.

Facilities include: a small range of accommodation; post office shop; toilets; pubs and restaurants. Buses run back to Kingsbridge and Plymouth, and ahead to Strete, Stoke Fleming and Dartmouth.

Walk through the car park at the far end of **Torcross** and pick up a path that runs along the narrow strip between the reedbeds and the main road. Cross a road near **Slapton Bridge,** where there is access off-route to Slapton village, the Tower Inn, Queens Arms and post office stores. Continue along the path, crossing the main road and following an abandoned stretch of old road now free of traffic. Cross back over the main road onto the path again, then cross back with a little more care on a busy bend to the **Strete Gate picnic site.**

There are toilets here, then a tarmac path runs uphill and narrows, while a wooded cutting opens up to

The village of Torcross, its pebbly beach, and the waters of Slapton Ley

211

Looking across the reedbeds and waters of Slapton Ley from Torcross

become a clear access road leading back up to the main road. Turn right and take care following the main road towards the village of **Strete.** Turn left up **Hynetown Road,** then turn left when **St Michael's Church** is reached.

STRETE

Facilities include: a small amount of accommodation, including a campsite; post office stores; pub; restaurant. There are buses back to Torcross, Kingsbridge and Plymouth, and ahead to Stoke Fleming and Dartmouth.

After turning left up from **St Michael's Church,** turn right as signposted for the Coast Path along a Public Bridleway. Walk straight through a housing estate and keep following blue marker arrows until the main road is reached again beyond the village. Turn sharp left down the main road and walk round a bend past **Landcombe House B&B.** Turn up to the left as signposted for Southwood, and keep straight on and downhill as the road becomes completely grass-grown. Turn right down a road, then left along the main road, with access to **Blackpool Sands** and refreshments if required.

Turn left along a road to pass some thatched cottages, spotting an **old mill** building round a bend. Turn right as signposted for the Coast Path up a Public Bridleway, which can be wet and muddy as it climbs. Turn left along a broader track, then right to walk down a road into **Stoke Fleming.**

STOKE FLEMING

Facilities include: a small range of accommodation, including a campsite; post office; shop; toilets; pub. You may notice that the name 'Bidder' is popular: George Parker Bidder, 'The Calculating Boy' (referred to by the engineer George Stephenson), lived here in the 19th century.

DAY 35
Stoke Fleming to Brixham

Follow the main road through **Stoke Fleming,** but turn left uphill past the Stoke Lodge Hotel, following a minor road, then turn right along **Ravensbourne Lane** to regain the main road. Cross over and follow another narrow minor road away from the village. This runs along, then drops down and makes a loop around **Rockvale.** Walk up the road and down again, then up from **Redlap House** to a junction and car park. Turn right at a National Trust sign for **Little Dartmouth** and walk through fields back to the coast. Look back to Strete Gate from **Warren Point** to Strete Gate to see how much of the coast has been forbidden to walkers.

Turn left to follow the Coast Path across open slopes with good views, then walk round a rocky cove. There are patchy woodlands ahead and the path can be narrow and overgrown; this is followed by a broad path running through mature woodland. Follow a narrow access road up to a house called **Wavenden,** then turn right and right again to follow a path down the wooded slope. Turn right down a zigzag path and steps, almost to a secluded beach, then climb up steps with chains alongside and follow a tarmac path up to a road. Turn

This is quite a difficult stretch, regaining the coast after the detour inland, then working around a rugged series of headlands to reach Dartmouth. There is a regular ferry from Dartmouth to Kingswear, and although these two places are full of historical interest, you should keep an eye on the time. The walk beyond Kingswear, around Froward Point, is quite convoluted and may take longer than you imagine. There are also several long and steep →

Start:	Stoke Fleming (863484)
Finish:	Brixham Harbour (925563)
Distance:	24km (15 miles)
Cumulative Distance:	781km (485 miles)
Maps:	OS Landranger 202, OS Outdoor Leisure 20
Terrain:	Mostly rugged coastal paths, including some long, steep ascents and descents, making this a rather difficult stretch.
Refreshments:	Plenty of places offer food and drink around Dartmouth and Kingswear, but there is nothing on the way to Brixham.

← ascents and descents on the way to Brixham, although short-cutting is possible before Berry Head.

right and walk down steps to reach **Dartmouth Castle.** The castle is made up of the 14th-century Fortalice, 15th-century Gun Tower, 19th-century Victorian Old Battery, while the mid-19th-century Castle Light is now the tearooms.

Walk to nearby **St Petroc's Church** and follow a tarmac path to a road. A seasonal ferry down to the right runs to Dartmouth, while the Coast Path runs parallel to **Castle Road,** perched high above a wall. Follow the road through **Warfleet,** overlooked by the Dartmouth Pottery. Watch for the Coast Path signposted down steps to the right for the ferry, and walk through 16th-century **Bayards Cove Fort.** A cobbled waterfront leads to the ferry, close to **Agincourt House,** dating from 1380. You

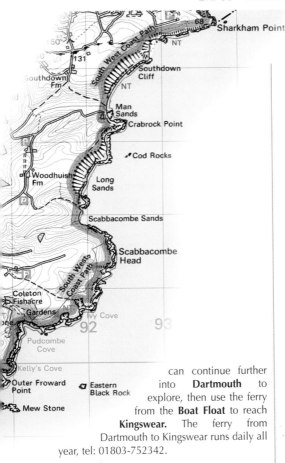

continued on
page 216

can continue further into **Dartmouth** to explore, then use the ferry from the **Boat Float** to reach **Kingswear**. The ferry from Dartmouth to Kingswear runs daily all year, tel: 01803-752342.

DARTMOUTH

Dartmouth, built on a natural deep-water channel, has been favoured as a port since the 12th century. You will notice the huge Royal Navy College, and there was formerly a thriving fishing industry. Fleets of ships used to carry Crusaders to the Holy Land, though today the channel is likely to be filled with pleasure craft.

Facilities include: plenty of accommodation; banks with ATMs; post office; several shops; toilets; many pubs and restaurants. Transport links include buses back to Stoke Fleming, Strete, Torcross, Kingsbridge and Plymouth, and services inland to Totnes to connect with the main line railway. There are boat trips available, and the ferry across the river. There is a museum in The Engine House. Tourist Information Centre, The Engine House, Mayor's Avenue, Dartmouth, Devon TQ6 9YY, tel: 01803-834224, email: enquire@dartmouth-tourism.org.uk

KINGSWEAR

Facilities include: a small range of accommodation; post office; shops; toilets; pub; restaurants. Transport links include the Paignton & Dartmouth Railway, offering steam-hauled services connecting with the regular railway around Torbay. There are also buses to Brixham and Torquay.

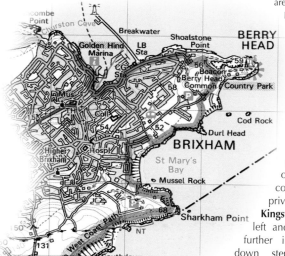

The Coast Path in **Kingswear** runs through an arch beside the post office, then turns left up the **Alma Steps.** Turn right at the top and follow a narrow road out of the village, continuing along a private road towards **Kingswear Court.** Fork left and follow the road further inland. Turn right down steps into **Warren**

Woods and continue down a zigzag path. Cross a stream on a small concrete slab at the bottom, then walk a short way up an access road with a castle-like folly to the right.

Turn left up steps and follow a wooded zigzag path. A broad and easy path continues across wooded slopes and there are fine views back to Dartmouth Castle. Huge pines grow on this slope, then after passing a National Trust sign for **Higher Brownstone,** the path narrows and leads to **Brownstone Battery**, built in 1940 and decommissioned in 1951. There are fine views over **Inner Froward Point.**

A narrow path zigzags down towards the sea, then swings left and later zigzags uphill again. A broader track is followed for a while, then a narrow path runs downhill to **Outer Froward Point,** with views over the guano-spattered Mew Stone. Continue working your

A Coast Path walker trudges up to a marker post above Ivy Cove

way around the cliffs, meandering in and out, up and down, and do the same around the wooded **Pudcombe Cove.** Turn right as signposted for Sharkham Point, and the path leaves the wooded cove and runs more easily across an open slope. The path drops downhill, then contours to the left, before climbing slightly into a valley. Climb out of the valley, then drop down towards the coast and turn left across a slope of bracken. A short, steep drop leads into another valley where there is access to **Scabbacombe Sands.**

Cross a footbridge above at the beach access point and pass a sign for **Woodhuish.** A short, steep climb is followed by a short descent, then comes a longer, steep, grassy ascent. An overgrown, flowery cliff edge is followed by a grassy descent. Keep to the right of a row of small whitewashed cottages to reach **Man Sands.** There is an old limekiln on the beach, and you walk along the top of the storm beach to continue. A steep and grassy climb leads onto **Southdown Cliff,** then the path is flanked by bushes on top. Zigzag down a slope of bushes and bracken and cross a little footbridge. Follow a grassy path out to **Sharkham Point** and stay on the marked path all the way round.

Looking along the roller-coaster cliffs to Sharkham Point and Berry Head

The path is sometimes completely enclosed by bushes as it makes its way round **St Mary's Bay,** and there are plenty of wooden steps to climb. A diversion inland around **St Mary's Holiday Village** avoids a land-slip. Follow the perimeter fence and turn right along **Douglas Avenue** to find a path back onto the coast. The path is easy, crossing polished marble-like stiles made of local Devonian limestone, also used to build thick defensive walled forts on **Berry Head.** The area is managed as a National Nature Reserve and there is an interesting **Visitor Centre**. You can also follow a road into the fort on the end of the headland to find the Guardhouse Tearooms.

If the fort on **Berry Head** isn't to be visited, then swing left along the road beforehand and walk to a set of gates. Step to the left down a gravel path into woods, and walk down steps to the right. Turn right down a road, passing the **Berry Head Hotel** and continue to the Shoalstone Car Park and toilets. A waterfront walk leads towards **Brixham,** though part of the road still has to be followed. A harbourside walk leads from the **Breakwater** to the centre of town. A statue of **William Prince of Orange** stands at the head of the harbour, recording his landing on 5 November 1688.

BRIXHAM

Brixham is essentially a fishing port turning its hand to tourism. Facilities include: plenty of accommodation; banks with ATMs; post office; shops; toilets; several pubs and restaurants. The Brixham Heritage Museum offers a complete grounding in the town's history; a replica of the Golden Hind stands at the head of the harbour. The original was Sir Francis Drake's vessel from 1577–80. Transport links include buses back to Kingswear and ahead to Paignton and Torquay. National Express buses run from Brixham to London and Birmingham. There are summer ferry services between Brixham and Torquay. Tourist Information Centre, The Old Market House, The Quay, Brixham, Devon TQ5 8TB, tel: 09066-801268, email: brixhamtic@torbay.gov.uk

DAY 36
Brixham to Shaldon

Some walkers skip the first half of today's route, believing that the Brixham-to-Torquay stretch must be a dreary and over-populated. In fact, there are fine rocky headlands, dense woodlands, secluded bays and little parks. There are times when the urban sprawl of Torbay is all too apparent, and there are busy promenade walks at Paignton and Torquay, but →

Start from the *Golden Hind* at the head of **Brixham** harbour and walk round the harbourside, passing offers of ferries to Torquay or day cruises to Dartmouth. The Coast Path is signposted between the **Brixham Harbour Office** and the Mission to Deep Sea Fishermen. Pass the AstraZeneca Brixham Environmental Laboratory, then climb up concrete steps into the **Battery Gardens.** The battery dates from 1940 and the Coast Path later diverts inland, up to a road-end at the **Brixham Battery Heritage Centre.**

Turn right up a tarmac path between holiday developments to reach **The Grove**, an ancient semi-natural woodland. Drop downhill and follow the clearest seaward path through the woods. The bedrock is hard Devonian limestone, highly polished by walkers' boots. Cross a small beach at **Churston Cove,** then climb up lots of steps. An easier woodland path leads onwards, though it is rocky in places. There is a golf course to the

Start:	Brixham Harbour (925563)
Finish:	Shaldon (935722)
Distance:	31km (19.25 miles)
Cumulative Distance:	812km (504.25 miles)
Maps:	OS Landranger 202, OS Outdoor Leisure 20, OS Explorer 110
Terrain:	After an early rugged path over little headlands and through woodland, the route becomes quite easy past Goodrington, Paignton and Torquay. Leaving Torquay, the frequently wooded coast has numerous steep ascents and descents.
Refreshments:	Plenty of places offer food and drink through the Torbay resorts. After leaving Torquay, refreshments are available at Babbacombe, Watcombe and Maidencombe.

continued on page 223

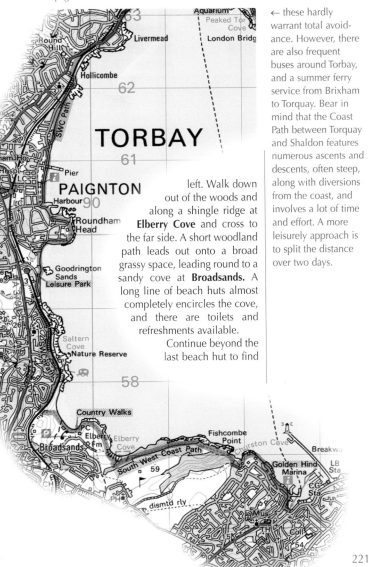

← these hardly warrant total avoidance. However, there are also frequent buses around Torbay, and a summer ferry service from Brixham to Torquay. Bear in mind that the Coast Path between Torquay and Shaldon features numerous ascents and descents, often steep, along with diversions from the coast, and involves a lot of time and effort. A more leisurely approach is to split the distance over two days.

left. Walk down out of the woods and along a shingle ridge at **Elberry Cove** and cross to the far side. A short woodland path leads out onto a broad grassy space, leading round to a sandy cove at **Broadsands.** A long line of beach huts almost completely encircles the cove, and there are toilets and refreshments available.

Continue beyond the last beach hut to find

Replica of Sir Francis Drake's Golden Hind at the head of Brixham Harbour

a tarmac path rising up beneath a **railway viaduct.** Turn right up concrete steps as signposted for the Coast Path to Goodrington. Pass between houses and the railway line, or mobile homes and the line, crossing a dip and climbing again. Walk downhill and eventually under the railway line, then along the promenade at **Goodrington South Sands.** The South Sands Café and toilets are passed, then a shop, amusements, the Waterpark and **Inn on the Quay.**

A short promenade walk leads round **Goodrington North Sands** to another beach café. The lower path seen ahead ends suddenly beyond some beach huts, and there are zigzag paths all over the reddish cliffs of **Roundham Head.** The correct line is marked by South West Coast Path disks set into the ground, but you could simply make your own way up to the top of the headland and continue round the clifftop through **Roundham Gardens.** Turn right along Cliff Road and walk down to the little harbour at **Paignton** to reach a post office store and The Pier Inn.

PAIGNTON

This is essentially a holiday resort, whose facilities include: abundant accommodation; banks with ATMs; post office; shops; toilets; pubs and restaurants. There are buses linking with other Torbay resorts, as well as both the Paignton & Dartmouth Railway and a branch line linking with the main line railway at Newton Abbot. National Express buses run from Paignton to London and Birmingham. Tourist Information Centre, The Esplanade,

Paignton, Devon TQ4 6ED, tel: 0906-6801268, email: paigntontic@ torbay.gov.uk

Walk through a covered gap in the **Harbour Light Restaurant** to reach the **Esplanade**. Paignton's long line of hotels are set back from the sea beyond a fine green space. There is a cinema, **pier** and offers of food and drink. At the end of the Esplanade, if the tide is in, shift inland a little on a busy road, otherwise walk on the beach for a short stretch to reach **Preston Sands**. There are toilets, a café and beach huts. Find a gap in the beach huts before reaching the last ones at

continued on page 224

BABBACOMBE

Mackerel Cove

Blackaller's Cove

BAY

Maidencombe

Sladnor Park Ho

Rock Ho

Bell Rock

Watcombe Head

Watcombe

Petit Tor Point

St Marychurch

Model Village

Oddicombe Beach

Cliff Rly

Field System

TORQUAY

Babbacombe

Watts Hill

Long Quarry Point

Anstey's Cove

Ellacombe

Wellswood

Kents Cavern

Black Head

Leisure Centre

Marina

Corbyn's Head

Aquarium

Kilmorie

SWC Path

Livermead

Peaked Tor Cove

London Bridge

Meadfoot Beach

East Shag

Daddyhole Cove

Thatcher Rock

a sandstone headland, then follow a tarmac path over the clifftop. Turn left to cross a bridge over the railway, then turn right into **Hollicombe Park**, where there are toilets.

Leave through the main gate at **Hollicombe Park** and turn right up the main road. Head down across a railway bridge and into **Torquay** along the coast. There are hotels along the road, as well as toilets on a green space at **Corbyn Head.** Try to avoid the road by walking on the sea wall, or further inland on the grassy spaces around Torre Abbey, but aim to reach the **harbour** and Tourist Information Centre.

TORQUAY

Torquay developed as a resort as a result of the Napoleonic Wars, its scenery being promoted and its architecture remodelled to create the 'English Riviera' to satisfy those who could no longer make the 'Grand Tour' of Europe. By the mid-19th century the town had a railway and improved access. Increased development made Torquay, Paignton and Brixham into a single conurbation, referred to as Torbay. In high summer it can be very crowded.

Facilities include: abundant accommodation; banks with ATMs; post office; shops of all types; toilets; several pubs and restaurants. Transport links include a branch line connecting with the main line railway at Newton Abbot. Frequent buses run to other Torbay resorts, and ahead to Shaldon, Teignmouth and Exeter. National Express buses run from Torquay to London and Birmingham. Tourist Information Centre, Vaughan Parade, Torquay, Devon TQ2 5JG, tel: 0906-6801268, email: torquaytic@torbay.gov.uk

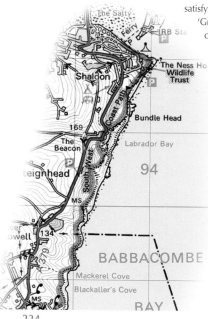

Continue walking from the harbour up **Beacon Hill** to the Imperial Hotel. Turn right as signposted for the Coast Path, following a tarmac path between stone walls. Turn left as marked up steps on a wooded slope to reach a **viewpoint.** Walk down a bit, along, then up more steps. The route passes beneath a castellated summerhouse; this is the **Rock End Walk.** Climb up to a grassy area and car park, looking at a line of rocky stacks like giant stepping stones leading out to sea.

Keep to the edge and walk down steps, then follow a tarmac path down to a road bend. Turn right as marked down more steps to reach toilets and a beach café below **The Osborne Hotel.** Follow the coastal road past **Meadfoot Beach,** a rough and bouldery expanse. Watch for a signpost at a car park, where a path heads uphill to a higher road. Turn right to follow the higher road uphill.

On the right is a Coast Path signpost for **Thatcher Point**; but the path has suffered a landslip and if you go there you must return to the road. Continue uphill by road and later pass another path signposted for **Hope's Nose.** Again, if you go that way, you must return. Use a path climbing parallel to the road, over a rise, then down to land back on the road.

Turn right as signposted for the Coast Path to Ansteys Cove, using the **Bishops Walk,** created around 1840 on the orders of the Bishop of Exeter. Follow the easy path across a wooded slope, forking left at a junction, passing a **shelter** and avoiding steps downhill. Reach a car park on emerging from the woods, then turn right along the **Palace Hotel** road. The Bishop of Exeter once lived in a mansion called Bishopstowe, now the Palace Hotel. There is no access to **Redgate Beach,** following a series of rockfalls that left the area too dangerous.

Turn right up from the Palace Hotel road as signposted *'To Babbicombe & St Marychurch over the downs',* climbing up steps on a wooded slope, then turning right to emerge onto a grassy area on top of the cliffs. There is a tall fence around the cliffs, with barely a peep over to the devastated Redgate Bay, nor much of a view of the amazing jagged rock scenery on **Long Quarry Point.** Continue as marked across the grassy area, then walk down into a wood. Zigzag down steps, and turn down round a road bend, then right down through the woods again. Watch carefully for markers to hit a steep road bend at the Cary Arms well below **Babbacombe.**

Drop down to the beach, toilets and café, continuing along concrete and wooden walkways over rocky outcrops. Climb a few steps and turn right to follow the wooded edge above **Oddicombe Beach.** There is a cliff railway, where the Coast Path climbs inland up the beach access road. Take a path and steps up to the right, climbing alongside the **cliff railway,** then passing beneath it. Follow the path faithfully as marked; it runs downhill, then there are steps uphill. There is also a diversion inland to avoid an unstable edge. Head up to a busy road at **Babbacombe** and turn right. Turn right again along **Petitor Road** to continue along the Coast Path by turning left.

The route is well-wooded, though runs close to the **Torquay Golf Course.** It pursues an undulating course, where you should beware of spurs to the right, as well as those to the left that lead too far inland. Marker posts indicate turns for Watcombe and Maidencombe; follow these to drop down to the **Watcombe** beach access road. If you head down to the beach, you pass toilets and reach a beach café. The Coast Path, however, climbs uphill a little, then heads up steps on the left on a wooded slope, signposted for Maidencombe. Follow the path down into mature woodland, then turn right and climb up steps with a rail alongside. At a signpost, turn left for the *Coast Path*, or right on an *Alternative Route*.

The *Coast Path* heads inland and becomes a decent track, then you turn right at a gate and head downhill to rejoin the Alternative Route. The *Alternative Route* drops down the wooded slope and swings left to climb back up steps to rejoin the Coast Path. Either way, continue along a path that runs more alongside fields than in the woods. It reaches toilets above another beach access road. Follow the road up to the left, then right at a car park. There is a pub in sight called the Thatched Tavern in **Maidencombe.**

Turn right after leaving the car park, but before the pub, along a track marked for Shaldon. Turn left along a path before the last house, then follow paths alongside fields, but occasionally in the woods near the cliff edge. The path undulates, and although descents are reasonably gentle, there are a couple of steep ascents using steps. Tight zigzags lead down onto a wooded slope, then climb uphill, before walking down steps and along a wooded edge to reach a tall fence around a clifftop house. Follow the fence inland and uphill, using steps to reach a road above **Labrador Bay.**

Turn right round a road bend, then walk parallel to the road on a tight path, before turning right into a field as signposted for Shaldon. There is a steep and grassy descent, then go up a few steps and walk alongside a **golf course.** Watch for an exit down steps to the right, then turn right down a deeply entrenched track. A path on the right leads up into **Ness Woodland,** where you walk beside a fence up to a viewpoint, then down to Ness House Hotel & Restaurant. A narrow coastal road runs into the village of **Shaldon.**

The Ness in evening light as seen from Ness House near Shaldon

SHALDON

Facilities include: a small range of accommodation, including a campsite; post office; shops; toilets; pubs and restaurants. There are buses back to Torquay, and ahead to Teignmouth, Dawlish, Dawlish Warren, Starcross and Exeter. If more facilities are needed, is a year-round ferry runs from the Ferryboat Inn at Shaldon over to Teignmouth.

Start with a short ferry journey from Shaldon to Teignmouth. If the ferry isn't running, or you want to make an early start, walking round via Shaldon Bridge will take only a few minutes longer.

The way out of Teignmouth is dependent on the tides, and the route later plays hide-and-seek with the coastal railway. A ferry from Starcross is used to reach Exmouth, the alternatives being rail or bus journeys, or a very long walk inland. →

The day starts with a short ferry journey from in front of the Ferryboat Inn at **Shaldon** over to **Teignmouth,** tel: 01626-873060. The ferry runs all year, and has operated since the 13th century, but if not running for any reason Shaldon Bridge offers quick access to Teignmouth. It first opened as a wooden toll bridge in 1827, the longest in the country, and was replaced by the current structure in 1931.

TEIGNMOUTH

Teignmouth was burnt by the Danes in AD800, burnt again in 1340, yet again in 1690, then damaged by the Germans in World War II! Visit Teignmouth Museum to learn all about the town's chequered past, and its rise as a fashionable 19th-century resort.

Facilities include: a good range of accommodation; banks with ATMs; post office; shops; toilets; several pubs and restaurants. Transport links include main line railway services, including Virgin Trains to and from Scotland and Penzance, as well as Great Western trains to and

Start:	Shaldon (935722)
Finish:	Budleigh Salterton (067818)
Distance:	23km (14.25 miles)
Cumulative Distance:	835km (518.5 miles)
Maps:	OS Landranger 192, OS Explorers 110 & 115
Terrain:	Easy walking along coastal paths, or through nearby fields, using good paths, tracks and roads. Beyond Exmouth, there are fairly gentle cliffs, becoming a bit more rugged towards Budleigh Salterton.
Refreshments:	Plenty of places offer food and drink at Teignmouth, Dawlish, Dawlish Warren, Starcross and Exmouth.

from London Paddington. Buses run back to Shaldon and Torquay, and ahead to Dawlish, Dawlish Warren and Starcross for Exeter. National Express buses run from Teignmouth to London and Birmingham. Tourist Information Centre, The Den, Sea Front, Teignmouth, Devon TQ14 8BE, tel: 01626-215666, email: teigntic@teignbridge.gov.uk

← A fairly easy cliff walk continues from Exmouth to Budleigh Salterton.

Landing at **Teignmouth,** turn left into town, passing the Lifeboat Inn. Head for the promenade and follow it to the **pier,** built in 1865, where the Tourist Information Centre and town centre are easily reached. The grassy area inland is known as **The Den;** once used for horse racing and drying fishing nets, now surrounded by the hotel façades of Den Crescent. Follow the promenade to the **Teign Corinthian Yacht Club,** then consider the tide.

You can continue along the stout **sea wall** beside the railway, heading for a prominent headland with the slender **Shag Rock** offshore. However, there is a problem at high water, as you have to go down steps and walk under the railway, which can be flooded. If the route is passable, it is followed by a walk up **Smugglers Lane** to reach the main road at **Holcombe Cross.**

Deckchairs arranged on the promenade alongside The Den at Teignmouth

The *inland route* from the **yacht club** climbs up a road and crosses a bridge over the railway. The road narrows and there is a **park** to the left. You can walk in the park, or continue along a track and field path further inland. Walk between tall walls, passing houses, to reach a bus stop on the **main road.** Turn right downhill, passing **Holcombe Cross** where the main Coast Path joins from Smugglers Lane.

Walk up the busy main road, then turn right up **Windward Lane** and left as signposted for the Coast Path. This rises and falls alongside a

field, with views ahead to Dawlish and Exmouth. Walk down steps towards the railway line, then uphill and inland to the main road and a bus stop. Veer right along a quieter road, originally the main road, passing **The Toll House.** The road gets narrower and leads back to the main road. Look out for a path rising to the right to a good cliff **viewpoint.** Walk downhill, zigzagging on a tarmac path, then cross a footbridge over the railway to continue along the sea wall to **Dawlish.** There is access to the town from the railway station.

DAWLISH

The black swan has been a symbol of Dawlish for nearly 50 years. Check out the waterfowl on Dawlish Water; an attractive little stream running though town, and visit the Wildfowl Complex. Facilities include: a range of accommodation; banks with ATMs; post office; shops; toilets; pubs and restaurants. There are buses and trains both ways along the coast, and further afield. Tourist Information Centre, The Lawn, Dawlish, Devon EX7 9EL, tel: 01626-215665, email: dawtic@teignbridge.gov.uk

Follow the sea wall onwards from the **station.** Some low sections on the sea wall can be flooded at high water. If they are, stay inland of the railway, until the road veers left towards a **post office,** then take an unmarked path to the right beforehand. If you follow the sea wall, you cross the railway using a **footbridge** (not the one at the old Coastguard cottages, but the one further along) to meet the inland path. Cream teas may be available at a house where the two paths meet.

Continue into a **small park** and climb up wooden steps. The Coast Path runs parallel to the railway, but is flanked by deep bracken so the line is hidden. Walk down through a wood to pass close to the **Langstone Cliff Hotel,** then follow a broad and stony path to **Dawlish Warren.** This is promoted as a 'family beach resort' and has accommodation, food and drink. A signpost reads 'Starcross Ferry 2.5 miles (along roads)'. If you object to that, you can catch a bus or train onwards to the village of Starcross, or all the way around the River Exe to Exmouth.

The road out of **Dawlish Warren** has a footway, but this doesn't extend through **Eastdon,** so beware of the traffic. There is another footway between the road and railway later, but not at **Cockwood,** where the road runs round a little harbour and passes the Anchor Inn. The Ship Inn is a little further inland. After turning right along a busier road, use a footway to reach **Starcross.** Walk to the railway station and cross a footbridge over the line, then double back to gain the large wooden pier for the ferry to **Exmouth.**

continued on page 233

STARCROSS

Facilities include: a little accommodation; post office; a few shops; toilets; pubs and restaurants. The ferry from Starcross to Exmouth runs daily from April to October, generally hourly and times can be checked in advance, tel: 01626-862452. If the ferry isn't running, the railway can be used to reach Exeter, where a change of train leads onwards to Exmouth. The same journey can be done by bus.

DAWLISH

Coryton's Cove

Horse Cove

Holcombe
The Parson and C
Shag Rock

Sprey Point

TEIGNMOUTH

Pier

RB Sta

The Salty

The Ness Ho
Wildlife
Trust

Shaldon

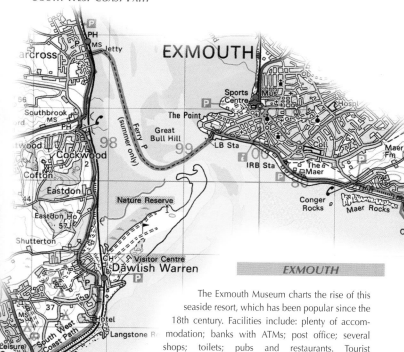

EXMOUTH

The Exmouth Museum charts the rise of this seaside resort, which has been popular since the 18th century. Facilities include: plenty of accommodation; banks with ATMs; post office; several shops; toilets; pubs and restaurants. Tourist Information Centre, Alexandra Terrace, Exmouth, Devon EX8 1NZ, tel: 01395-222299, email: exmouth@btinternet.com

Jurassic Coast World Heritage Site: From now until the end of the South West Coast Path you are walking through the Jurassic Coast World Heritage Site. The coast has an intensely absorbing geology and a range of amazing landforms. The rocks are often →

Leave the ferry and head for the **Esplanade** to walk through **Exmouth.** There are walking and cycling lanes, and a sandy beach. When the beach rears up into dunes, the grassy expanse of **The Maer** is just inland, managed as a local nature reserve. It covers 4ha (just under 10 acres) and boasts 400 species of flowering plants. At the end of the road is a café and toilets at **Foxholes.**

Tucked away round the back of a car park, branching off **Foxholes Hill,** a Coast Path signpost points the way to Sandy Bay and Budleigh Salterton. A tarmac path rises through bushes and continues with views

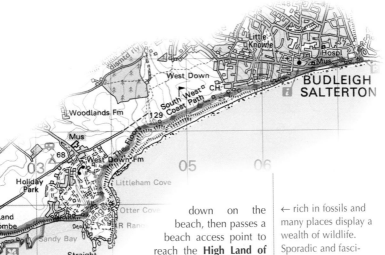

down on the beach, then passes a beach access point to reach the **High Land of Orcombe.** This grassy area leads towards a crumbling cliff-line. Don't go down steps to the beach, but stay high and climb gently uphill. Walk downhill and keep to the seaward edge of a vast mobile home site at **Sandy Bay.**

Pass to the left of the Beachcomber Pub Diner and walk straight through a car park. There is a short, steep ascent between the mobile homes and the Royal Marines Ranges on **Straight Point.** There is no access to the rocky point. Keep to the grassy cliff edge at a higher level, but cut across a dip and climb a little to enjoy splendid views from **Littleham Cove** to Budleigh Salterton, with crumbling red cliffs rearing up impressively.

Leave the mobile homes behind and walk gently along a field path. Steps and a footbridge lead across a little wooded valley, then another field path rises beyond. Beware of the crumbling cliff edge, then climb uphill following a deeply entrenched path onto **Beacon Hill.** There is a trig point at 129m (423ft) among the heather and gorse scrub. The smoother slopes of the **East Devon Golf Course** are further inland. Note how the path is covered in pebbles that have popped out of the

← rich in fossils and many places display a wealth of wildlife. Sporadic and fascinating information panels focus on specific aspects of the coastline.

233

Straight Point is used as a firing range by the Royal Marines

bedrock, where they have been held fast for hundreds of millions of years. They were originally piled up here by a vast river flowing from where Normandy is now located!

Follow the path down a slope of holly and pines, passing into denser woodland. If there is a diversion down to the main road, turn right and right again via **Victoria Place** to get back onto the cliffs. Eventually, a tarmac path runs down alongside the houses at **Budleigh Salterton** to reach the pebbly beach.

BUDLEIGH SALTERTON

Facilities include: a small range of accommodation; banks; post office; shops; toilets; pubs and restaurants. There are buses back to Exmouth and Exeter, and ahead to Sidmouth. Tourist Information Centre, Fore Street, Budleigh Salterton, Devon EX9 6NG, tel: 01395-445275. No email available (2002).

DAY 38
Budleigh Salterton to Seaton

Walk along the sea front at **Budleigh Salterton,** the Marine Parade. The pebbly beach is cluttered with small boats, and a tarmac path runs alongside a line of beach huts, passing toilets to reach a car park. It looks as though you could follow a pebble ridge to a cliff, but the River Otter cuts a deep channel unseen from this perspective, so turn inland from the car park. A path runs inland through the **Otter Estuary Nature Reserve.** The marsh was once more extensive, but during the Napoleonic Wars French prisoners built an embankment and some of the land was reclaimed. There are a couple of observation platforms. Turn right to follow a road across the **River Otter,** noting that ships once used to sail inland as far as Otterton.

Turn right again as signposted for the Coast Path. Walk between a field and a wooded slope, where tall pine trees dominate. There is access to a **bird hide** on the right, otherwise keep straight on for a view back across

An easy initial walk becomes more difficult on the way to Sidmouth. Beyond Sidmouth a series of valleys cut into the cliff coast, leading to a succession of ascents and descents. Some of these are quite steep and arduous, but some of the clifftop walking is fairly level and easy. After passing Branscombe Mouth, there is an interesting and scenic path through the →

Start:	Budleigh Salterton (067818)
Finish:	Seaton (245899)
Distance:	28km (17.5 miles)
Cumulative Distance:	863km (536 miles)
Maps:	OS Landranger 192, OS Explorers 115 & 116
Terrain:	Easy start to the day, becoming progressively more difficult. A series of valleys is crossed, sometimes with steep ascents and descents. Later parts of the walk can be particularly arduous, but the end is fairly easy.
Refreshments:	There is a pub at Ladram Bay. There are plenty of places to eat and drink around Sidmouth. Food and drink are available at Branscombe Mouth and in the village of Beer.

← 'undercliff' on Beer Head. A few minor undulations around Beer finally takes the route into Seaton. Some walkers might like to break this day into unequal halves at Sidmouth and cover the distance over two days.

the river mouth. The path climbs easily up the red sandstone cliffs, undulating gently and passing a derelict building. The cliff breaks into a series of attractive red stacks at **Ladram Bay,** where you walk through the Ladram Bay Holiday Centre. Swing inland a little to cross the beach access road, and climb up from the **Three Rocks Inn** to continue along the cliffs.

A field path gives way to a steep climb up the wooded slopes of **High Peak,** but the route heads off to the left and omits the summit, which reaches 157m (515ft). Follow a broad path until it runs downhill, then turn right. Cross a dip in the

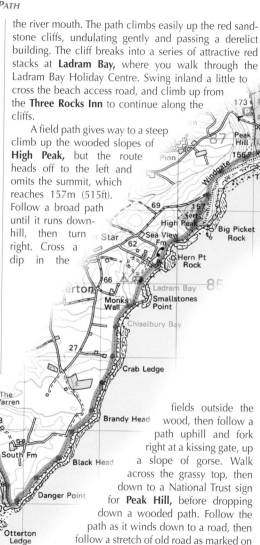

fields outside the wood, then follow a path uphill and fork right at a kissing gate, up a slope of gorse. Walk across the grassy top, then down to a National Trust sign for **Peak Hill,** before dropping down a wooded path. Follow the path as it winds down to a road, then follow a stretch of old road as marked on the right. A generous grassy slope is available

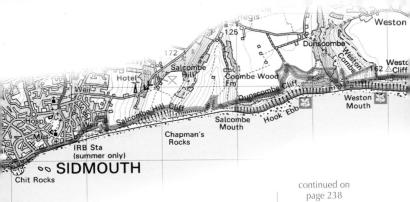

continued on
page 238

between the cliffs and the road dropping to Sidmouth. The **Clock Tower Café** and
Jacob's Ladder are prominent features ahead. Walk
down towards the sea and use a low-level path at the
foot of the cliffs to reach **Sidmouth.**

SIDMOUTH

Facilities include: a range of accommodation; banks with
ATMs; post office; several shops; toilets; plenty of pubs
and restaurants. Transport links include buses back to
Budleigh Salterton, Exmouth and Exeter, and ahead to
Branscombe, Beer, Seaton and Lyme Regis. The Sidmouth
Heritage Centre could be visited. Tourist Information
Centre, Ham Lane, Sidmouth, Devon EX10 8XR, tel:
01395-515441, email: sidmouthtic@eclipse.co.uk

Walk along the **Esplanade** to pass **Sidmouth,** with easy
access to facilities. Cross **Alma Bridge** over the River Sid.
The old steps and cliff path are closed, so climb up a
convoluted tarmac path on a steep, wooded slope. Walk
up **Cliff Road** and **Laskeys Lane,** swinging back towards
the cliffs. Follow a path beside a field up towards
wooded **Salcombe Hill.** Steps lead up through the
woods, emerging with open views. There are benches
and a view indicator, though little chance of seeing
Normandy or Brittany as marked! The altitude is around
160m (525ft).

237

Continue as signposted for the Coast Path, passing a stone commemorating the fact that **South Combe Farm** was presented as an open space in 1937. Walk along the top fields, then steeply downhill on steps. Walk down through the fields, but not to the beach at **Salcombe Mouth.** Head inland a little as marked and cross a **footbridge** over a wooded stream. Head up across a field to reach the cliff again. Cross a stile and zigzag up a path with steps, to reach the top of **Higher Dunscombe Cliff.**

Walk across the level clifftop; look down to Weston Mouth, but don't walk down there yet. Turn left inland on a grassy ribbon of a path, turning round the head of a valley in a wooded patch. Continue along the path, through a kissing gate, then there is a view over a flinty cliff edge. Walk down into woods, zigzagging as marked, and continue down steps to the beach at **Weston Mouth.** Turn left, passing an area where a stream usually forms a pool behind a shingle ridge.

Zigzag up steps, then climb across a field towards the cliffs. Climb up a steep, rugged, scrubby slope with zigzags and steps to ease the gradient. The top of **Weston Cliff** is almost level. Pass the **Weston Wild Flower Meadow,** where nearly 100 species of grass and flowers have been established, as well as insects, butterflies and a variety of birds.

Watch for markers as the Coast Path heads inland, crossing a little valley just inland from **Coxe's Cliff** to avoid difficulties later. Turn right as signposted and work a way around field edges, then cross a grassy clifftop with views down wooded slopes. There are little

dwellings tucked out of sight on the slopes, while the clifftop bears the rumpled earthworks of an **ancient fort.**

Turn left inland, down a wooded slope and further inland along a track. Turn right and follow the track as it undulates across a wooded slope. There is one open stretch with a view of the village of **Branscombe.** Continue along a woodland path and descend closer to the cliff edge. The way is steep and has steps in places. Walk down through a couple of fields to reach the pebbly beach at **Branscombe Mouth,** the Sea Shanty Restaurant and toilets.

Cross a river at a footbridge below the restaurant, then turn right up the Coast Path and climb onto **East Cliff.** Head towards the cliff edge, crossing a cattle grid to enter the **Sea Shanty Caravan Park.** (Note that you could use the path over **Hooken Cliffs** to reach Beer, but you would miss the undercliff.) Fork left after entering the site, then walk as marked for Beer, turning right along the Coast Path through the

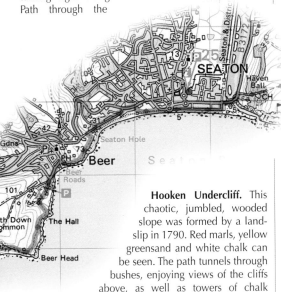

Hooken Undercliff. This chaotic, jumbled, wooded slope was formed by a landslip in 1790. Red marls, yellow greensand and white chalk can be seen. The path tunnels through bushes, enjoying views of the cliffs above, as well as towers of chalk

239

ahead. Zigzag to the top of the cliff and turn right for **Beer Head.**

There are fine views around **Seaton Bay** as the Coast Path wanders through fields and down past a camp and caravan site. Turn right along a tarmac path, **Little Lane,** then right down **Common Lane** into the village of **Beer.** A vigorous little stream runs alongside **Fore Street.** Food and drink are available in pubs, and there is a little accommodation, including a youth hostel.

Cross the beach access road to reach the toilets, then the Coast Path runs up a flight of steps and off to the right, before zigzagging up more steps from a **shelter.**

Coast Path walkers collapse on the pebbly beach at Weston Mouth

There is an *alternative route* that avoids using so many steps, meeting the main route only a couple of minutes later. Follow a tarmac path round the wooded slopes of the **Jubilee Memorial Grounds,** enjoy a view over Seaton Bay and drop down to a road. Turn right down **Beer Hill** to reach the **Cliffside Cabin,** with refreshments and toilets.

If the tide allows, go down to the rugged beach at **Seaton Hole** and turn left, coming up onto the Coast Path later. At high water, you should follow the **Old Beer Road,** then link with the Coast Path as it follows a generous grassy strip overlooking **Seaton.** Either way, come down to a roundabout for immediate access to the town and its services.

SEATON

Facilities include: a range of accommodation, including a nearby campsite; banks with ATMs; post office; shops; toilets; pubs and restaurants. There are buses back to Sidmouth and ahead to Lyme Regis. Tourist Information Centre, The Underfleet, Seaton, Devon EX12 2TB, tel: 01297-21660, email: info@seatontic.freeserve.co.uk

DAY 39
Seaton to Seatown

Extensive woodlands are rare along the South West Coast Path, but walking through the Undercliff between Seaton and Lyme Regis is like being in a jungle. A series of landslips has left the slopes beneath the cliffs in a jumbled state, colonized by trees and bushy scrub that limit seaward views considerably. The Undercliff is protected as a National Nature Reserve and is a world unto itself. On entering Dorset, →

Follow the promenade to leave **Seaton** and turn left inland along the edge of a boatyard to reach the main road. Turn right to cross the **River Axe** by using the old **Axmouth Bridge** (pedestrians only) then follow the main road for a short while. Turn right up the steep access road for **Axe Cliff Golf Club,** signposted as the Coast Path to Lyme Regis. Walk up to the club house and continue straight up across the golf course as marked, watching out for flying golf balls. Follow a track away from the golf course and turn right at a Coast Path signpost. A sign warns that the path can be arduous and may take up to 4 hours to reach Lyme Regis.

The path steps from field to field, then runs along the top of the wooded landslip slopes, then eventually takes the plunge down into the wooded scrub. Pass an English Nature National Nature Reserve sign. **The Undercliff** covers 324ha (800 acres) of wild, unspoilt terrain. On Christmas Eve 1839, some 8 million tons of soil and rock slid seawards and opened up a huge chasm. The separated block became known as **Goat Island,** yet local farmers still managed to wrest a crop of

Start:	Seaton (245899)
Finish:	Seatown (420917)
Distance:	21km (13 miles)
Cumulative Distance:	884km (549 miles)
Maps:	OS Landranger 193, OS Explorer 116
Terrain:	The first half of the day is through the rugged, wooded 'undercliff' to Lyme Regis. A series of landslips beyond require diversions inland, and a series of ascents and descents can be steep at times.
Refreshments:	Plenty of places offer food and drink around Lyme Regis and Charmouth.

wheat from it the following summer! The problem with landslips is traced to the unstable Gault Clay, which deforms, destabilising the harder foxmould, chert and chalk above it. Ash, field maple and hazel grow on the Undercliff; ivy creeps over boulders and trees, while ferns sprout exotically in damp hollows.

The path is initially narrow and uneven and proves tough underfoot. However, it enters mature woodland,

← Lyme Regis is a busy resort with a rocky shore that is regularly beaten and chipped by geologists, along with Charmouth famous for yielding a wealth of fine fossils from the Jurassic period. The nature of the geology is such that landslips are common and have resulted in a series of diversions from the coast. Always look out for changes to the route, though the high point of Golden Cap remains on the Coast Path before the descent to Seatown.

A narrow path runs through the Undercliff from Seaton to Lyme Regis

243

broadens and is more gently graded. It becomes a little more difficult, then when rhododendron and yews are noticed, a good track is joined at another English Nature sign. Walk downhill a few paces, then swing left inland, and take a right turn as signposted for the Coast Path. (The former **Allhallows College** is just inland, but there is no access.) Steps lead up and down, then uphill again; the path is fairly rugged and well-wooded throughout. Pass a manhole cover and the path broadens, running downhill with a pipeline alongside to reach the **Pinhay Springs & Pumping Station** and more English Nature information boards.

Turn left at the pumping station and follow a narrow, battered access road uphill, then down a little. Turn right at a fork among tall **beech trees.** One part of the path can be wet and muddy and it continues across the rugged slopes, with green pools of water hidden in wooded hollows. Steps lead uphill; the path broadens at another English Nature sign to join an access road near **Underhill Farm.** Follow the road onwards.

Turn right along a path, passing a National Trust sign for **Ware Cliffs.** Turn right again, walk down a grassy swathe with woods on either side, and enjoy views to the distant Isle of Portland. Cross a stream and fork right, entering a wood at a signpost for the Coast Path and The Cobb. Walk down steps on the wooded slope and continue past a few mobile homes to reach the harbour.

The Cobb was a small harbour

constructed in the 13th century, rebuilt in Portland stone in the 19th century.

Turn left to walk along the seafront through **Lyme Regis**, with toilets and places to eat and drink. Keep walking all the way to Rock Point Inn and the end of the promenade. The stout sea wall that supports the promenade is used to store a vast reservoir of sewage for release into the sea at appropriate intervals.

LYME REGIS

Lyme Regis received its Royal Charter in 1284. There are some splendid old buildings, plus a number of shops selling fossils. The Lyme Regis Museum has plenty of background about the town, plus more fossils. There are boat trips available, and guided fossil walks. In fact, you see fossils everywhere! Spiral ammonites and bullet-like belemnites are common, but the rocks also yield ichthyosaur bones.

Facilities include: a good range of accommodation; banks with ATMs; post office; several shops; toilets; pubs and restaurants. Transport links include buses back to Seaton and Sidmouth, and ahead to Charmouth, Bridport and

continued on page 246

245

West Bay. Tourist Information Centre, Guildhall Cottage, Church Street, Lyme Regis, Dorset DT7 3BS, tel: 01297-442138, email: e-mail@lymeregistourism.co.uk

Once past the **Rock Point Inn** the sea wall and promenade soon come to an end. The route diverts a long way inland and doesn't regain the coast until well beyond Charmouth. *When the tide is out* (providing you keep clear of the base of the cliffs in case of rockfalls) it is possible to walk to Charmouth and avoid the detour inland. Check the tide times if choosing this option.

To walk inland, follow a zigzag route up ramps and steps from the end of the sea wall. You can pass through the **churchyard** before the main road is followed uphill. Pass a big car park and toilets, then the Coast Path is signposted on the right. It runs diagonally up through a field, then crosses a couple more fields to reach a wooded area on **Timber Hill.** Turn left along a track, then right along a woodland path. This climbs up steps, then is diverted down to the left to a road. Turn right up the road, passing the entrance to the **Lyme**

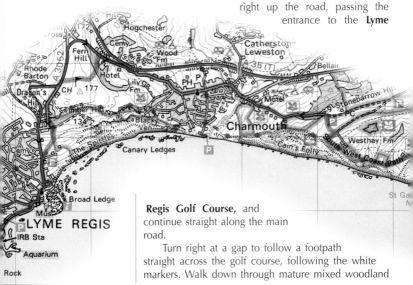

Regis Golf Course, and continue straight along the main road.

Turn right at a gap to follow a footpath straight across the golf course, following the white markers. Walk down through mature mixed woodland

to reach the main road again beside the **Fernhill Hotel.**
Turn right and walk down beside the road. Keep right at
a roundabout to follow the road to **Charmouth.**
Although you can follow a couple of roads to the right
to reach the beach, the diverted Coast Path is signposted
all the way through the village along **The Street.**

CHARMOUTH

Facilities include: a small range of accommodation,
including campsites; post office; shops; toilets; pubs and
restaurants. Buses run back to Lyme Regis and ahead to
Bridport and West Bay. It is worth going down to the
beach, where the Charmouth Heritage Coast Centre is
full of fossils, and there is a beach café and toilets.
Hopefully, a true coastal footpath will one day be re-
established, but unfortunately the cliffs are very
unstable.

The Street crosses **County Bridge,** followed by another
bridge; turn right up **Stonebarrow Lane.** Follow this
narrow road all the way to a car park on top of
Stonebarrow Hill. Turn right to pick up the Coast Path,
pasing the point where the original route comes down
steps on a hillside. Continue down into a valley and
cross a footbridge over a stream well below **Westhay
Farm.** Climb up the other side of the valley and head
inland, then walk down to cross another footbridge over a wooded stream.

Climb uphill again and drift further inland around a wooded landslip, then walk down through fields to cross another footbridge over a wooded stream above **St Gabriel's Mouth.** Climb up steps and walk along a crumbling edge, then zigzag up a gravel path with steps and a rope handrail. The higher part of the slope is covered in bracken and gorse, but the top of **Golden Cap** is grassy with clumps of broom and heather. This is the highest point on the south coast, bearing a monument and a trig point at 191m (627ft). Enjoy extensive views back along the coast and ahead to the Isle of Portland.

The path descends inland and seems almost to double back on itself, but swings round and is signposted to the right from a wooded patch below the summit. Walk down through fields, then note a diversion inland to the left, into a small wood. Cross a footbridge and walk through a field, then turn right down a road through the tiny settlement of **Seatown.** There is a shop at a holiday park and campsite, as well as the **Anchor Inn,** another little shop and toilets by the beach. The inn provides accommodation, and there are a few more places to stay 1km (.5 mile) inland at Chideock.

DAY 40
Seatown to Abbotsbury

Leave **Seatown** by crossing a footbridge and walking through a car park to pick up the Coast Path. Walk uphill along **Ridge Cliff,** following the path over a grassy bump, a dip, then steeply up onto the next bump and gently across a dip. **Thorncombe Beacon** is the last bump, bearing a beacon post at 155m (509ft) and offering wonderful views ahead along Chesil Bank. The Coast Path drops steeply down across a dip and climbs a little; some walkers may be drawn along an easier path to Down House Farm, which promises cream teas. The rest of the descent is grassy and easy, though a bit steeper on the final stretch down to the beach at **Eype's Mouth.** There is a shop and café at Eype House Caravan Park; Eype's Mouth Hotel is a little further up the road.

Cross a footbridge or stone slabs across a small stream near the pebbly beach, then walk straight uphill, signposted for West Bay and Abbotsbury. Beware of the crumbling edge of **West Cliff**. The path later moves inland a bit while passing a campsite. Walk down to land on the promenade at **West Bay.** Follow the quay-side path inland a little to get round the **harbour.**

The cliff coast gradually dwindles, though there are still some short, steep ascents and descents around Eype's Mouth and Bridport. After passing Burton Beach, the cliffs give way to the long pebbly beach of Chesil Bank. The origins of this remarkable landform are still a matter for debate. The beach stretches in a graceful arc from Bridport to the Isle of Portland. The cobbles on the Isle of Portland are potato-sized, →

Start:	Seatown (420917)
Finish:	Abbotsbury Swannery entrance (577846)
Distance:	20km (12.5 miles)
Cumulative Distance:	904km (561.5 miles)
Maps:	OS Landrangers 193 & 194, OS Explorer 116, OS Outdoor Leisure 15
Terrain:	The first part of the walk includes cliffs with some short and steep ascents and descents. The rest of the walk is either along a beach or just inland along field paths and tracks that are mostly level and easy.
Refreshments:	Food and drink available at Eype's Mouth, West Bay, Burton Beach and West Bexington.

Looking back towards Golden Cap from the cliffs above Eype's Mouth

← while the ones at Bridport are bean-sized, and the change in size is gradual along the length of the beach. You can ponder over this natural phenomenon while walking to Abbotsbury, where the route detours inland around the West Fleet. There is also an 'Inland Coast Path' that follows the crest of the downs from West Bexington to Osmington Mills (details at the end of the book).

WEST BAY

This was Bridport's harbour, but lost a lot of trade when the railway reached the town in 1884. Facilities include: a small amount of accommodation; post office; a few shops; toilets; pubs and restaurants. There is easy access inland to Bridport for a fuller range of services. Buses run to Bridport, back to Charmouth and Lyme Regis, and ahead to Abbotsbury.

Follow the road away from the harbour to a pub, the **West Bay,** where the Coast Path crosses a car park to return to the cliffs. A very steep climb rises from the shingle beach. **East Cliff** overhangs in places: don't walk too near the edge. A level and easy walk along the clifftop, with a **golf course** alongside, leads to a steep descent to cross a dip and a short, steep climb up the other side. Walk along again, then drop down to an extensive mobile home park and continue along an **embankment.**

It may be possible to cross the mouth of the **River Bride** without getting wet feet. The Coast Path actually wanders upstream alongside the river, crossing a footbridge at a campsite halfway to **Burton Bradstock,** then heading back towards the river mouth. A short climb leads onto **Burton Cliff** and a level clifftop walk runs onwards. Drop down to the beach at **Burton Hive,** with the Hive Beach Café. The next ascent is gentle, passing close to the Bronze Age burial mound of **Bind Barrow.** Pass seawards of another caravan site, then a National Trust sign for **Cogden.**

Walk down onto the beach, where the tiny pebbles prove to be a drag underfoot. Fortunately, the route shifts onto a track at the back of **Chesil Bank.** There is a further diversion inland to pass a narrow reedbed at **Burton Mere.** As Chesil Bank blocks a view of the sea, all you see are the fields, though the path is pleasant, level and grassy. One wooded patch can be wet and there is a wooden boardwalk. Keep to the marked path which is eventually signposted onto the back of Chesil Bank again. Turn left to continue, passing a little pool and a log seat. Note the rubbery sea kale and other specialised

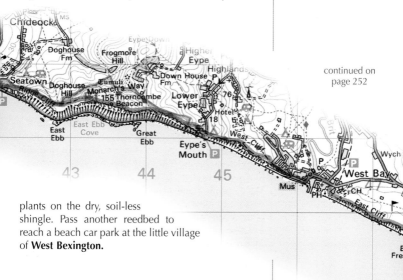

continued on page 252

plants on the dry, soil-less shingle. Pass another reedbed to reach a beach car park at the little village of **West Bexington.**

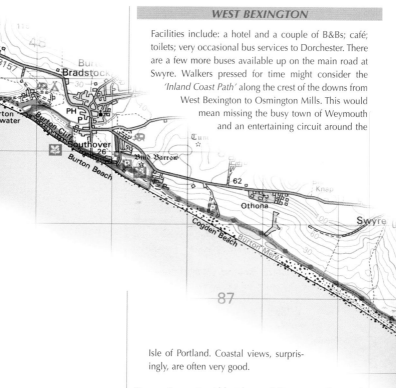

Facilities include: a hotel and a couple of B&Bs; café; toilets; very occasional bus services to Dorchester. There are a few more buses available up on the main road at Swyre. Walkers pressed for time might consider the *'Inland Coast Path'* along the crest of the downs from West Bexington to Osmington Mills. This would mean missing the busy town of Weymouth and an entertaining circuit around the

Isle of Portland. Coastal views, surprisingly, are often very good.

To continue to Abbotsbury, follow a rather soft shingle track that becomes firmer and eventually passes old **coastguard cottages** in a walled garden. Continue along a narrow coastal road and eventually pass **Castle Hill Cottages.** The road turns inland at a refreshment hut, toilets and car park. Not far inland, and worth a detour, are the **Abbotsbury Sub Tropical Gardens.** Founded in 1765 as a kitchen garden for the Countess of Ilchester, these gradually evolved into an exotic display of unusual plants.

The Coast Path continues along the back of Chesil Bank from the car park, entering the **Chesil Bank and**

The 14th-century St Catherine's Church on a hilltop above Abbotsbury

The Fleet Nature Reserve. Walk along the shingle, but turn inland when reedbeds are reached. Turn right at a junction of paths, following the route signposted for the Swannery, though you could keep

straight on ahead for Abbotsbury. The Coast Path crosses a hillside, heading well inland, passing above two wartime pillboxes. Walk down to reach a track near a restaurant at the entrance to **Abbotsbury Swannery.** If you wish to visit the village of **Abbotsbury** or seek accommodation, turn left up the road.

ABBOTSBURY

The village is well worth a visit. Only a fragment of its old abbey remains, dating from around 1400. Visit the Church of St Nicholas and prepare to be surprised by the thatched Smuggler's Barn, formerly the tithe barn and now something of a theme park. St Catherine's Church is a remarkable hilltop chapel, probably 14th century, and perfect for an evening stroll. The chief attraction is the Abbotsbury Swannery, where hundreds of mute swans have been pampered on the West Fleet since 1393.

Facilities include: a small range of accommodation; post office; a few shops; toilets, pubs and restaurants. Buses run back to West Bay, Bridport, Charmouth and Lyme Regis, and ahead to Weymouth.

DAY 41
Abbotsbury to Ferrybridge

Start:	Abbotsbury Swannery entrance (577846)
Finish:	Ferrybridge, Weymouth (666762)
Distance:	18km (11.25 miles)
Cumulative Distance:	922km (572.75 miles)
Maps:	OS Landranger 194, OS Outdoor Leisure 15
Terrain:	Easy walking along fields paths and gentle coastal paths.
Refreshments:	Moonfleet Manor Hotel & Restaurant and Lynch Cove.

If you spend the night in **Abbotsbury,** follow the road back down to the restaurant at the entrance to **Abbotsbury Swannery** to pick up the Coast Path. Pass the restaurant and toilets and follow the road until it starts climbing. Cross a stile on the left, walk a short way up to a corner of a field, then cross another stile on the left. The path wriggles uphill and passes marker posts that show the way onwards along a downland crest and across a slope. Pass above **Clayhanger Farm** and take all the stiles as they come until a rough vegetated slope is reached. Cross a stone stile and walk downhill

This stretch seems rather distant from the coast, working its way over rolling hills, through fields and past woodlands. When salt water is reached, it is the shallow West Fleet and East Fleet, not the open sea. From time to time there are good views of Chesil Bank stretching into the distance, and some walkers must →

continued on page 256

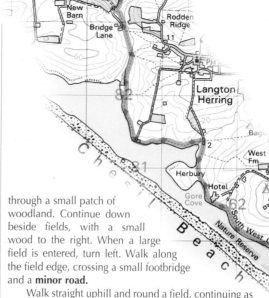

← wonder why they aren't crunching along the pebbles. A firing range at Tidmoor overshoots Chesil Bank, affecting access to one stretch. Also, terns nest on the bank, laying eggs that look deceptively like pebbles, so during the breeding season you shouldn't walk along the beach. At Ferrybridge you can either walk out onto the Isle of Portland, or head straight for Weymouth.

through a small patch of woodland. Continue down beside fields, with a small wood to the right. When a large field is entered, turn left. Walk along the field edge, crossing a small footbridge and a **minor road.**

Walk straight uphill and round a field, continuing as marked turning left and right round a wood, then walk downhill. The sea glitters in the distance and the Coast Path meanders alongside fields to reach it. Keep looking for signposts and crossing stiles as necessary to reach the shore. **West Fleet** may look like Swan Lake if there are flocks of swans around.

The Coast Path follows the gentle shores of the West Fleet lagoon

Turn left along the shore and walk beside big cereal fields, crossing a road-end near some huts and boats. The village of **Langtree Herring** is out of sight inland, but boasts a pub. Continue round a bay and cross a footbridge at its head. Cut across the little peninsula at **Herbury,** following a drystone wall through fields. Walk from Gore Cove to the **Moonfleet Manor Hotel & Restaurant,** with boats moored nearby. Cross a boardwalk in a small wooded patch and continue along the shore of the **East Fleet,** passing cereal fields. Watch out for horseriders using gallops alongside one field. Pass a campsite, then pass another little huddle of huts and boats. Walk round a bay to reach **Tidmouth Army Rifle Ranges.**

A map board shows both the Coast Path and an inland diversion, both of which are signposted. If there is firing, take the inland route to the left. The Coast Path runs round the end of the point, past masses of gorse, to reach **Lynch Cove** and a holiday centre where there is a campsite. The path rises up a bushy slope, then heads inland around the tall fence bounding the **Wyke Regis Training Area Headquarters.** Head back down to the coast as signposted and continue along a low grassy clifftop. Cross a little beach at **Pirate's Cove** and follow the

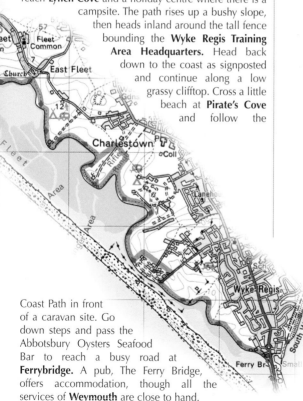

Coast Path in front of a caravan site. Go down steps and pass the Abbotsbury Oysters Seafood Bar to reach a busy road at **Ferrybridge.** A pub, The Ferry Bridge, offers accommodation, though all the services of **Weymouth** are close to hand.

DAY 42
Isle of Portland Circuit

The Isle of Portland is essentially a tilted block of Upper Jurassic limestone. It is still referred to as the Manor of Portland and the production of famous Portland stone continues apace. Old quarry tracks are followed round the cliffs of the island, and other roads, tracks and paths have been sign-posted to create a circular route. If you book into a place for two nights, you can leave most of your gear behind and enjoy a leisurely, lightweight walk round the island.

The traditional approach was by ferry from Wyke Regis, but the Ferry Bridge now means that traffic can hurtle back and forth. Access on foot in the past meant walking to Abbotsbury, then crunching along Chesil Bank!

Follow the busy Portland Beach Road across the **Ferry Bridge** and consider your options. There is a footway beside the road all the way to the Isle of Portland, but this is also a cycleway. You could use the rugged trackbed of a disused railway line to the left of the road. Another option is to walk to the Chesil Beach and Nature Reserve **Information Centre,** where there is a snack bar and toilets, then crunch along the shingle ridge, listening to the sea raking thousands of pebbles back and forth. The **Mere Tank Farm** is an oil storage depot and is a poor introduction to the **Isle of Portland.**

Chunky pebbles on Chesil Bank lead the eye towards the Isle of Portland

Start/Finish:	Ferrybridge, Weymouth (666762)
Distance:	25km (15.5 miles)
Cumulative Distance:	947km (588.25 miles)
Maps:	OS Landranger 194, OS Outdoor Leisure 15
Terrain:	After a walk beside a busy road, a steep climb leads up to a fine cliff path. Most of the circuit is easy, though there are some short, steep ascents and descents.
Refreshments:	Food and drink can be obtained at Fortuneswell and Portland Bill, or by detouring off-route**.**

Walk to **Victoria Square** and pass The Little Ship pub, then head right for the **Cove House Inn.** Walk along a stout sea wall, but not all the way to the end. Climb up a tarmac path marked as the *'Round the Island Path'.* A narrower path continues more steeply uphill at **West Weare** and a flight of steps leads even higher, with a fine view back along the length of Chesil Bank. A sculpture showing a fisherman and a quarryman to the left is titled 'The Spirit of Portland'. The Coast Path, however, is off to the right along the clifftops.

The path runs close to **Tout Quarry,** which has ceased production and is now an SSSI, and home to over 40 imaginative sculptures. Stay on the broad path, however, passing huge stacks of stone that were quarried but never removed. Pass through a Cyclopean **arch** made of such blocks, then squeeze past a concrete structure on its seaward side. (Note that a diversion may be signposted before this point, in which case follow the marked route).

The aspect of the scenery changes. The cliffs remain splendid, but inland reveals a housing estate, and the broad, grassy path passes the **Southwell Business Park.** Pass between an old lighthouse and the National Coastwatch Station. Continue down a gentle grassy slope and aim to the right of the red-and-white lighthouse at **Portland Bill.** Pick a way through jumbled quarried stone to find **Pulpit Rock** and a fine rock platform battered by the sea. Explore very carefully around here, or not at all in heavy seas.

You could visit the **Lighthouse Centre,** or take a break at the nearby café, and there are toilets. Summer bus services run to and from Weymouth. Continue along the coast past several little **beach huts** and note the signs that announce you are

on the Crown Estate. A more open coastline features fine quarried cliffs. The **Cave Hole** is close to an old hand crane. Another **hand crane** stands on a more obviously quarried slope further along.

Follow quarry tracks closest to the cliffs until diverted uphill to the road. Turn right as signposted for the Coast Path, walking along a broad grassy strip beside the road. Everything is dusty as there is a working quarry across the road. Pass a viewpoint at **Cheyne Weares,** then further along the road a Coast Path sign shows the way down to the right. A zigzag path with steps crosses a rocky slope and markers show the way down to

The curious Pulpit Rock stands off a rock platform at Portland Bill

Church Ope Cove. There are beach huts here, and toilets if you go all the way down to the beach, otherwise start climbing a long flight of steps. The ruins of the 13th-century church of **St Andrew** are signposted, while high above the cove is 15th-century **Rufus Castle.** Keep climbing the steps to reach a viewpoint.

Turn right up a few gentle steps to follow the Coast Path onwards, then turn right along a track. After a short way, turn left up a path, then right along a grassy clifftop path marked as the Coast Path. This runs past a **working quarry,** then a narrow and enclosed cliff path leads to a road. Continue seawards of a towering prison wall: the Young Offenders Institution at **The Grove.** A footpath sign points along a road marked as private, still running alongside the prison wall. Later, veer away from the wall as marked, and the route uses a track leading onto **MOD property.** Keep right at junctions as marked and follow a tarmac road to reach a deep moat and tunnel mouth. The tunnel leads through a massive embankment to the **Verne Citadel**, once a fortress for 1000 troops and now a medium security prison.

The Coast Path turns left away from the tunnel mouth and passes the entrance to the **High Angle Battery,** built in 1892 and worth an exploratory detour. Follow the road down to a junction and turn right down **Verne Hill Road.** Head off to the right and contour round the grassy banks of **The Verne,** dropping down to the left to a road bend. Follow **Verne Common Road** down to the main road, then cut through **Victoria Gardens** to reach **Victoria Square** and follow the main road back to **Ferrybridge.**

ISLE OF PORTLAND

Facilities include: a small range of accommodation, including a youth hostel; post office; shops; toilets; pubs and restaurants. There are fast and frequent buses to and from Weymouth, which has a much greater range of services, and where further connections can be made with buses and trains.

DAY 43
Ferrybridge to Lulworth Cove

Leave **Ferrybridge** in the direction given by the Coast Path signpost for Weymouth. Follow a tarmac footpath and cycleway at first. This is the **Rodwell Trail** and it can be followed to the centre of Weymouth. However, keep to the right at a cutting to follow the true line of the Coast Path, and drop down from the old trackbed to the coast, then follow a road inland. A small park on the right has access to the ruins of 16th-century **Sandsfoot Castle** and there are toilets nearby. A footpath on the right used to lead to the **Western Ledges,** but has been closed due to a landslip. Continue along the road, turn right and keep right to pick up a path at a **coastguard station.**

Walk round a grassy area on the clifftop, then cross a concrete footbridge over a road and continue into **Nothe Gardens.** A variety of paths can be used to approach **Nothe Fort** on the end of the point, where you swing round to the left towards **Weymouth.** Again, a variety of paths can be used, but go down stone steps to the quayside where there is a short ferry service across

The day starts with a walk through Weymouth. The Coast Path is a rather patchy affair and is diverted around a landslip on the Western Ledges. There is a short ferry available across the River Wey; walking round via the Town Bridge takes only a few minutes longer. The Rodwell Trail offers a rapid alternative route from Ferrybridge to the centre of Weymouth, along an old railway trackbed converted →

Start:	Ferrybridge, Weymouth (666762)
Finish:	Lulworth Cove (823800)
Distance:	23km (14.25 miles)
Cumulative Distance:	970km (602.5 miles)
Maps:	OS Landranger 194, OS Outdoor Leisure 15
Terrain:	Easy walking through Weymouth and Bowleaze Cove, progressively more difficult to Osmington Mills and beyond, with some very steep ascents and descents towards the end.
Refreshments:	Plenty of places offer food and drink through Weymouth. There are also pubs or cafés at Bowleaze Bay, Osmington Mills and Ringstead Bay, with the chance of an ice cream van at Durdle Door.

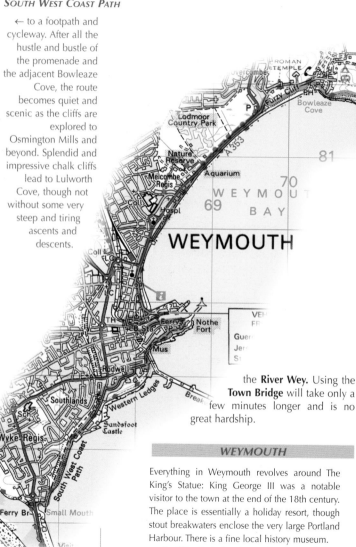

← to a footpath and cycleway. After all the hustle and bustle of the promenade and the adjacent Bowleaze Cove, the route becomes quiet and scenic as the cliffs are explored to Osmington Mills and beyond. Splendid and impressive chalk cliffs lead to Lulworth Cove, though not without some very steep and tiring ascents and descents.

the **River Wey.** Using the **Town Bridge** will take only a few minutes longer and is no great hardship.

WEYMOUTH

Everything in Weymouth revolves around The King's Statue: King George III was a notable visitor to the town at the end of the 18th century. The place is essentially a holiday resort, though stout breakwaters enclose the very large Portland Harbour. There is a fine local history museum.

Facilities include: plenty of accommodation,

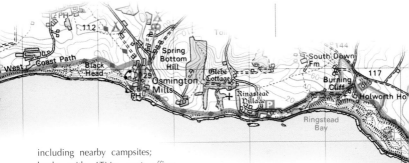

including nearby campsites;
banks with ATMs; post office;
several shops; toilets; lots of pubs and restaurants.
Transport links include a railway, with South West Trains
to London Waterloo and Wessex Trains to Bristol. There
are buses back to Abbotsbury and Bridport, and ahead to
Osmington Mills and Lulworth Cove. Buses run
frequently between Weymouth and the Isle of Portland,
forever streaming through Ferrybridge. National Express
buses run to London, Birmingham and Liverpool. Tourist
Information Centre, The King's Statue, The Esplanade,
Weymouth, Dorset DT4 7AN, tel: 01305-785747,
email: tourism@weymouth.gov.uk

continued on
page 266

Walk past **The King's Statue** and Tourist Information
Centre, then along **The Esplanade.** At first there is a busy
road alongside, then a quieter one, then it continues as
a sea wall with the **Lodmoor Country Park** inland. There
is one last café on the sea wall, then the route runs up a
road and passes the **Spyglass Inn.** Turn right onto a
grassy slope above the crumbling **Furzy Cliff,** rising a bit
before descending to **Bowleaze Cove.** Keep inland a
little to work a way through the holiday development,
cross the **River Jordan,** then pick up the Coast Path as it
passes seawards of the **Riviera Hotel.**

The crumbling cliffs are a problem and the Coast
Path keeps shifting inland after each landslip. Walk
round **Redcliff Point** and pass below an adventure
centre. Follow the perimeter fence uphill and inland,
then continue along the path as marked, quite a step

back from the cliffs, running through fields and contin-uing into woodland on **Black Head.** There are some wet areas crossed using boardwalks. When the route returns to the cliffs, it immediately heads

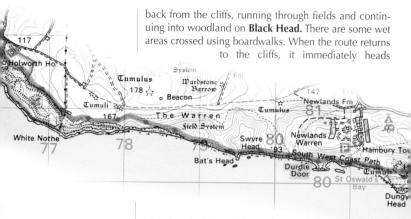

inland to the left and drops down to a wooded area beside a campsite. The *'Inland Coast Path'* rejoins the main route here. Land on a road and turn right down to **Osmington Mills.**

OSMINGTON MILLS

Facilities include: limited B&B accommodation and campsite; toilets; 13th-century Smugglers Inn and a clifftop café. There are occasional buses back to Weymouth and ahead to Lulworth. Some buses go from a shop and holiday park up the road, while others need to be joined at Osmington village.

To leave **Osmington Mills,** walk down to the Smugglers Inn and round the left-hand side of the building. The Coast Path climbs back to the cliffs and tunnels through bushes on top. A gradual descent leads into wooded patches to reach a coastal track at some houses on **Ringstead Bay.** Follow the track and it suddenly turns left inland to toilets, a shop and a **café** at a car park.

Turn right just before all these and continue as marked for the Coast Path to White Nothe. The gravel track becomes grassy, then rises through woods. Keep right as marked and follow a path up out of the woods

DAY 43 – FERRYBRIDGE TO LULWORTH COVE

onto the edge of **Burning Cliff.** A band of oil shale in the cliff burst into flames in 1826. Keep climbing onto a battered, narrow road, passing tiny **St Catherine's Chapel**, essentially a wooden hut, though a slightly larger and more imaginative structure may be built.

Turn right above the chapel, along a woodland path, crossing the **Holworth House** access road. Continue uphill through a field to the top of a cliff, where there is a fine view back round Ringstead Bay. The chalk cliff leads to the headland of **White Nothe,** where you veer inland a bit, passing seawards of old Coastguard cottages at 167m (548ft). The walk is easy along the clifftop, then there is a gradual descent into a big grassy hollow at **The Warren.** A monstrous roller-coaster route follows.

Climb steeply uphill beside a sheer, crumbling chalk cliff. There is a brief respite on top, followed by a gentle descent to **Bat's Head.** Make a detour out onto the narrow headland for the best views along the coast. A steep descent leads to a gap

The celebrated rock arch at Durdle Door is an icon for the Dorset coast

Lulworth Cove and a view along the coast to the distant St Aldhelm's Head

overlooking a spiky chalk stack, then there is another steep climb uphill at **Swyre Head.** Drop steeply downhill again, then enjoy increasingly good views of the rock arch of **Durdle Door** on the next ascent. When you reach steps giving access to a beach, you could go down to inspect the arch at closer quarters, but the Coast Path is uphill instead.

Follow a clear track, and there may be an ice cream van parked alongside. The track runs up to a campsite, but the Coast Path follows a narrower path off to the right. Climb up a long flight of steps above **St Oswald's Bay** and enjoy the view down to the lovely cliff-backed curve of **Lulworth Cove.** A broad, stone-paved path leads down to the village and on to the cove. There is also a spur path leading to the smaller rocky inlet of **Stair Hole,** which makes a fine evening stroll.

LULWORTH COVE & WEST LULWORTH

Facilities include: a range of accommodation, including a youth hostel and nearby campsites; post office; shops; toilets; pubs and restaurants. There is a Heritage Centre and the interesting Dolls House, which illustrates life in a Victorian fisherman's home. Transport links include buses back to Osmington and Weymouth, and inland to Wareham and Poole for further bus and rail connections.

DAY 44
Lulworth Cove to Swanage

Follow the road almost to the shore of **Lulworth Cove** and turn left up steps beside The Beach Café, as marked for Bindon Hill and the Range Walks. Climb up the wooded slope and emerge on a grassy slope, turning right to follow a fence round the top of the cove. Turn right and follow a flight of stone steps steeply downhill, then turn left away from a beach at the bottom. Walk through bushes and emerge on the grassy crest of **Pepler's Point** to enjoy views back across Lulworth Cove.

Enter the **Lulworth Ranges** at the Fossil Forest Gate; maybe detour to the right to spot bulbous shapes on a rock ledge near the sea. These are the imprints of gymnosperms, or early conifers, preserved in palaeosols, or their original ancient soils. They are 135 million years old and their closest living relatives are in Australia.

Immediately beyond Lulworth Cove lies the Royal Armoured Corps Gunnery School, on the Lulworth Ranges. This tank range extends along the coast to Kimmeridge, as well as inland. There is no access when the range is in use. However, the 'Range Walks' are normally open around Easter, May Bank Holiday, →

Start:	Lulworth Cove (823800)
Finish:	Swanage (032787)
Distance:	33km (20.5 miles)
Cumulative Distance:	1003km (623 miles)
Maps:	OS Landrangers 195 & 195, OS Outdoor Leisure 15
Terrain:	A particularly long, tough stretch. Although there are some easy parts, there is also a series of steep ascents and descents. Most of the walk is remote from habitation, accommodation, food and drink, so pay careful attention to inland escape routes in case they are needed later in the day.
Refreshments:	There may be nothing along the way until the bar and restaurant are reached at Durlston Castle on the outskirts of Swanage. An ice cream van may appear at Gaulter Gap. Diversions inland to Kimmeridge or Worth Matravers can be made if food and drink are needed.

← Spring Bank Holiday, most of the summer and the Christmas/New Year period. Many weekends throughout the year are also available. The ranges cover some of the best coast in Dorset and it is a great shame to miss it.

When putting your Coast Path schedule together, time your arrival so that you can enjoy this stretch.

Check the open periods well in advance, tel: 01929-404819. This is also a long and hard day, which you might wish to split at some point. However, accommodation is both scarce and off-route, and refreshment is almost entirely lacking, so carry supplies with you.

There is no need to go down the steps to see them as several specimens can be viewed from further along the Coast Path.

Keep to the grassy path and walk between the **yellow marker posts.** It goes without saying that you should stick to the path and never tamper with anything metal on the ranges. Enjoy the view around **Mupe Bay,** where rock stacks look like giant stepping stones stretching to Worbarrow. Walk round Mupe Bay and climb steeply uphill using steps, avoiding a big rockfall on the chalk cliffs of **Bindon Hill.** Continue along the clifftops overlooking a tank range, then descend steeply to a beach at **Arish Mell.** Climb steeply up the other side, drifting well inland from the cliffs, levelling out before climbing again, then cross a stile by a gate. Go up through the grassy ramparts of an Iron Age fort called **Flower's Barrow.**

There is a picnic site in the ancient fort, and two gaps in the ramparts. Go through the gap on the right and walk steeply downhill to **Worbarrow Bay.** The path drops almost to the shingle beach, crossing a footbridge, then heads inland a few paces up a track. Watch for a few steps on the right leading up to a viewpoint overlooking the bay and **Worbarrow Tout.** The track, incidentally, leads inland to the deserted village of **Tyneham,** which was commandeered by the Army as a 'temporary' training area in the 1940s. Descendants of the villagers would like the Army to give it back!

Continue climbing between yellow posts as usual, and walk along the top of **Gad Cliff,** eventually reaching a stone seat at a junction of paths. You can detour left onto a grassy hill called **Tyneham Cap** at 167m (548ft), or simply keep right for the Coast Path down to **Hobarrow Bay.** Walk along the cliffs and note the rocky, tidal ledges below. A level walk along a good track continues round **Kimmeridge Bay** to leave the Lulworth Ranges at a BP installation famous for its 'nodding donkey' oil pump. An information board explains how oil has been pumped from an anticline trap since 1959.

Follow the track to a road and keep right to take a path seawards of a row of cottages at **Gaulter Gap.** Cross a footbridge and walk up steps to a car park, where an ice cream van may be stationed. (The village of **Kimmeridge** is inland, offering a chance to obtain food and drink.) Walk round to another car park and toilets, then down a narrow road towards the **Fine Foundation Marine Centre,** where you can learn about the Purbeck Marine Wildlife Reserve. Turn left before the centre to follow the Coast Path.

Steep steps climb up a wooded and open slope to reach the **Clavell Tower**, a dangerously crumbling structure dating from 1830. Walk gently downhill, and uphill, and continue in that fashion, crossing little foot-bridges in some of the dips. The roller-coaster route becomes more difficult on the approach to **Houns-tout Cliff,** crossing a dip above a little waterfall, then climbing steps up a wooded slope to reach a stone seat on top, around 150m (490ft) above sea level.

Climbing steeply from Arish Mell to the ancient hillfort of Flower's Barrow

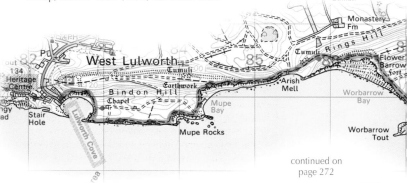

continued on page 272

A steep flight of stone steps run down the other side, then you turn left inland. Cross a field to a gate, then cross an embankment and turn right along a narrow road. Turn left along a track to reach a gate at a couple of houses at **Hillbottom.** Turn right down a battered road, then right again at a gate. Turn left up a grassy track, then right as marked up a grassy path. This leads back onto the cliffs, and all the junctions are marked for St Aldhelm's Head. Walk along the clifftop, then steeply downhill, then up a steep

flight of stone steps. **St Aldhelm's Chapel** is off to the left, a square structure with a fine, vaulted stone roof supported by a stout pillar. The nearby National Coastwatch Station prefers the name **St Alban's Head.** The altitude is over 100m (330ft) and there is an interesting radar memorial on the headland.

Continue along the Coast Path, which is now rather easier. Detour inland around a **quarried area** and go down a bit to cross a valley where there are a couple of houses. If food, drink or accommodation are needed, turn left up a track to walk off-route to the village of **Worth Matravers.** If not, then turn right down the track, then left to pick up the Coast Path and avoid the quarries. Looking along the coast beyond **Winspit,** you can see how the cliffs have been quarried in a series of caves and ledges in pursuit of prized Purbeck marble. A track leads inland before **Seacombe Cliff**, passing quarried blocks, then a sharp right turn leads back towards the cliffs.

Cross a stile where a National Trust sign for **Easington** gives way to another National Trust sign for **Spyway Farm**. The path crosses more rugged slopes on the way above **Dancing Ledge**, passing daymark pylons before entering **Durlston Country Park**. Keep seawards of the lighthouse and walk down to the square-cut holes of **Tilly Whim Caves**. Climb up steps and pass more daymark pylons and follow a good path onwards. This passes the former entrance to Tilly Whim Caves, which were originally quarried, then opened as an attraction in 1887. They were closed in 1976 due to rockfalls.

Interesting commentaries and verses are carved on large tablets of stone. A

continued on page 274

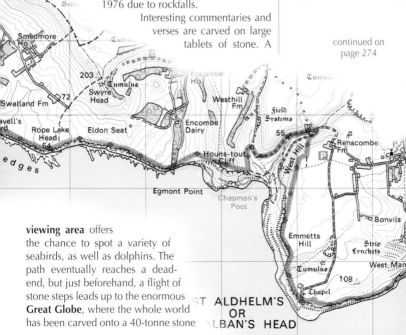

viewing area offers the chance to spot a variety of seabirds, as well as dolphins. The path eventually reaches a dead-end, but just beforehand, a flight of stone steps leads up to the enormous **Great Globe**, where the whole world has been carved onto a 40-tonne stone sphere. As you have covered about 1000km (620 miles) at this stage, you might like to plot your route on the Great Globe, only to see it pale into insignificance on the world stage!

Walk up to **Durlston Castle,** which has a bar and restaurant. Allow extra time, or pay a return visit in the morning, if you want to check out the **Visitor Centre** nearby. The Coast Path runs along a broad track through mature woodland, away from the castle entrance. A left turn leads out onto a road, where you turn right uphill, then right again along **Belle Vue Road.** When the road bends sharply left, exit to the right into a grassy space and walk gently down to the end of **Peveril Point,** with a National Coastwatch Station and toilets. Fine views extend back round Durlston Bay and ahead round Swanage Bay to Old Harry Rocks, Bournemouth and the Isle of Wight.

Find and follow a **concrete walkway** beside the cobbly shore, but give this a miss if heavy seas are swilling across it. A minor road can be used instead. Detour inland a little to pass the **Swanage Sailing Club,** then follow the promenade into town.

SWANAGE

The fortunes of Swanage used to be linked with the Purbeck marble quarries around the coast. These ran into a decline, but the arrival of a railway meant that the town could develop as a tourist resort. The closure of the railway (or at least its conversion into a short steam-hauled line) has done nothing to diminish tourism, and the town can sometimes be very busy.

Facilities include: abundant accommodation, including a youth hostel and nearby campsites; banks with ATMs; several shops; toilets; plenty of pubs and restaurants. Transport links include buses back to Worth Matravers and inland to Wareham and Poole, and buses ahead to Studland, South Haven Point and Bournemouth. National Express buses run from Swanage to London. The Swanage Heritage Centre is worth a visit. Tourist Information Centre, The White House, Shore Road, Swanage, Dorset BH19 1LB, tel: 01929-423636, email: mail@swanage.gov.uk

DAY 45
Swanage to South Haven Point

The last day's walk is also the shortest. Leaving Swanage, the route makes its way out onto a sheer-sided chalk point for a fine view of Old Harry Rocks. Bournemouth and the Isle of Wight can be seen across Poole Bay, places that aren't part of the South West Coast Path. An easy beach walk, or an alternative route through heathery dunes, leads finally to South Haven Point. It is the end of the walk; another journey completed. There is hardly time to think back along →

Walk along the promenade to leave **Swanage**. If the tide allows, pick a way along the shore until you can climb up onto the low cliff. The Coast Path heads inland from the promenade, along **Ulwell Road** and to the right of All Saints Church to reach a post office store at a road junction. Turn right along **Ballard Way,** then enter the **Ballard private estate** and follow footpath signs. These lead to a private green on the clifftop, where you turn left. Walk down steps, across a **footbridge,** then up more steps to follow the Coast Path as marked for **Ballard Down.**

On the ascent, turn right through a **gate** and pass gorse and brambles to reach an open grassy, flowery slope beyond. Follow a clear grassy path and maybe look over the cliff edge from time to time to see splendid chalk pinnacles. Note how **The Foreland** is pierced by arches, which enlarge, then collapse, leaving pinnacles and stacks such as **Old Harry Rocks.** In the far distant past, the chalk ridge stretched all the way from the Foreland and Old Harry Rocks to the distant Needles and the Isle of Wight.

Turn round the end of the point and follow a broad, grassy path onwards. Watch out for a stone marked for the Coast Path to Studland, and bear right. You can then

Start:	Swanage (032787)
Finish:	South Haven Point (036867)
Distance:	12km (7.5 miles)
Cumulative Distance:	1015km (630.5 miles)
Maps:	OS Landranger 195, OS Outdoor Leisure 15
Terrain:	A promenade walk, a final steep ascent, a gentle descent, ending with a choice of a beach walk or a heathery dune walk.
Refreshments:	There are a couple of pubs, restaurants and beach cafés around Studland.

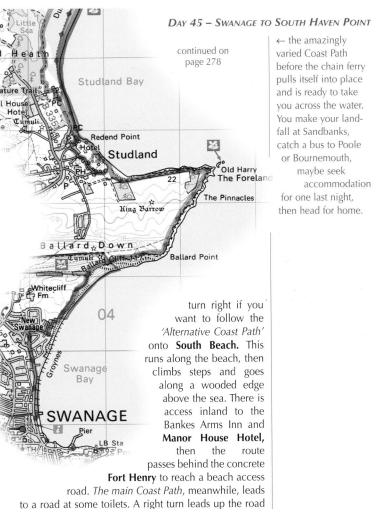

continued on
page 278

← the amazingly varied Coast Path before the chain ferry pulls itself into place and is ready to take you across the water. You make your land-fall at Sandbanks, catch a bus to Poole or Bournemouth, maybe seek accommodation for one last night, then head for home.

turn right if you want to follow the *'Alternative Coast Path'* onto **South Beach.** This runs along the beach, then climbs steps and goes along a wooded edge above the sea. There is access inland to the Bankes Arms Inn and **Manor House Hotel,** then the route passes behind the concrete **Fort Henry** to reach a beach access road. *The main Coast Path*, meanwhile, leads to a road at some toilets. A right turn leads up the road to pass the Bankes Arms Inn and **Manor House Hotel,** and by keeping right you will be led down to the beach access in company with the alternative route.

There are toilets and a beach café at the road-end, then another choice of routes. The Coast Path simply follows the **sandy beach.** Sometimes this can be very crowded, though the crowds thin out further along. An *'Alternative Coast Path'* passes the café and toilets, and picks a way along sandy trails past beach huts. Pass the **Middle Beach Shop** and work past more beach huts. Pass toilets and a **National Trust shop,** which offers food and drink, then pass through a barbecue area. Drift inland along a sandy track marked by yellow posts. It can be heavy going through soft sand. The path is flanked by masses of heather and is called the **Heather Walk.**

Turn left inland, then right along a narrower **sandy path** through the heather. The route is still marked by yellow posts, with **wet woodland** to the left and masses of bog myrtle among the heather. Eventually the alternative route meets the main Coast Path at **Shell Bay.** A short walk along the sandy beach leads to the road-end at **South Haven Point.** Before you have time to realise it, your long, long walk along the South West Coast Path is over.

THE JOURNEY HOME

In practical terms, you have to wait for the chain ferry to arrive, then cross to Sandbanks. This is a regular, year-round vehicle ferry, tel: 01929-450203. There is a South West Coast Path signpost pointing back the way you came, but your walk is now over. If you have any time to spare at Sandbanks, there is food and drink available, as well as accommodation. Catch one of the regular buses to Poole or Bournemouth to link with other bus or rail services. Virgin Trains *Wessex Scot* runs through the Midlands and Northern England to Scotland. South West Trains run to London Waterloo. National Express buses leave the area for London, Birmingham and Liverpool. Sit back and relax, and you'll soon be home!

Looking at The Pinnacles on the way out to the end of The Foreland

Sunset over Poole Harbour, seen on completing the South West Coast Path

INLAND COAST PATH
West Bexington to Osmington Mills

Start at the beach car park and café at **West Bexington.** Follow the road uphill and inland through the village. Pass **The Manor Hotel,** then when the road turns left, continue straight uphill as signposted for the Hardy Monument and Osmington Mills. Follow a track uphill and fork right at a junction to reach the B3157 road. Almost immediately, switch to the fields to the right of the road, walking roughly parallel to it, passing a National Trust sign for **Limekiln Hill.** Actually, keep more to the bushy edge drifting further away from the road. The path later goes through the bushes and through a small gate, then a vague path continues onwards and gently up to the road again.

Keep walking as signposted and eventually cross the road at **Tulk's Hill,** following a distinct ridgeway path to a trig point on top of a **hillfort.** There are fine views of Chesil Bank, the Isle of Portland, Weymouth and the Hardy Monument, as well as the rolling Dorset downs. The path runs through gorse scrub and further along the crest of the downs, crossing a narrow road. Keep to the grassy crest beyond, and note a handful of low tumuli dotted about **Weares Hill** later.

It may seem like a contradiction to call any route an 'Inland Coast Path', but that is what the signposts say. Walkers who are happy to plod along the coast to Weymouth need take no notice of the route, but those who are running out of time and would like to skip a couple of days might be interested. Regardless of the fact that it runs inland, it is a fine route in its own right, wandering along the crest of the downs with splendid →

Start:	West Bexington (531864)
Finish:	Smugglers Inn, Osmington Mills (735816)
Distance:	27km (16.75 miles)
Maps:	OS Landranger 194, OS Outdoor Leisure 15
Terrain:	Mostly along good paths and tracks, with some short road walks, over gentle downs. Some paths can be vague and there are a couple of steep slopes. The route is marked as the *Inland Coast Path.*
Refreshments:	None apart from at the start and finish, though an ice cream van may occasionally park near the Hardy Monument.

← views across Dorset. It is completely lacking in facilities, apart from what is available at West Bexington, Osmington and Osmington Mills. Using the route cuts 67km (41.75 miles) off the Coast Path, decreasing the total distance of your walk along the South West Coast Path by 40km (25 miles).

Go through a gate and walk around a gentle grassy edge overlooking the village of **Abbotsbury.** When two gateways are reached later, go through the one on the left. At another gate, enter a big field and follow vague, grassy wheel-marks straight up through it on **White Hill.** Turn left at another gate and walk down to a road, then look ahead to spot a signpost pointing to the right for the Hardy Monument. Bear left at a **stone marker** and walk up a few steps, then continue along field boundaries to reach a gate marked 'Evershot Farm Hampton Dairy'. Just to the right of the gate is a small **stone circle.** Follow a clear track to a road on **Portesham Hill** and turn left.

Almost immediately, turn right off the road and follow a fence across a field. Continue alongside a walk through the next field, and note the access up to the right for the **Hell Stone,** which is worth a detour. Continue alongside the fields and into the bottom corner of a mixed woodland. Turn left to follow a woodland track uphill. Fork right and emerge from the wood to follow a path up a heathery slope to reach the towering **Hardy Monument**, erected in memory of Lord Nelson's flag captain, Sir Thomas Masterman Hardy, who lived at nearby Portesham. If you are lucky, there may be an ice cream van parked here, but don't rely on it.

Look down to a road below the monument to spot a signpost, 'Inland Route Avoiding Road'. This reveals a narrow path leading into a forest on **Black Down,** joining the road again further downhill. Turn left along the road, then right, as signposted for the 'Inland Coast Path to Osmington'. The path is enclosed by scrubby hedgerows, then runs along the crest of **Bronkham Hill.** Note the many grassy tumuli along the way. Go through a gate as marked by a blue arrow and walk along a gorse-covered crest. Emerge on a grassy crest beside a couple of storage tanks, then head downhill alongside fields to pass beneath pylons on **Corton Down.**

The path runs very gently uphill and there are still plenty of **tumuli** arranged alongside, like little wilderness hillocks surrounded by cereal crops. The route is mostly signposted for Bincombe and it is a simple matter of following a grassy track onwards, passing a small **communication mast.** Walk gently down to the **B3159 road** and cross over it.

Follow a broad and clear gravel track onwards, almost to the brutally busy A345 road on **Ridgeway Hill.** Turn right down a track before reaching it, then watch very carefully to spot a narrow stile hidden in the hedgerow on the left. Cross a strip of a field, then with great care cross the A345 road. Go through a gate and walk up an overgrown track that gets much better. It seems to lead to a **radio mast,** but you turn right beforehand and go through a gate as marked. Cross a track and continue across a field to reach a road.

Turn right along the road, walking alongside the **Came Down Golf Course.** Turn right again at a road junction, walking along a track signposted for

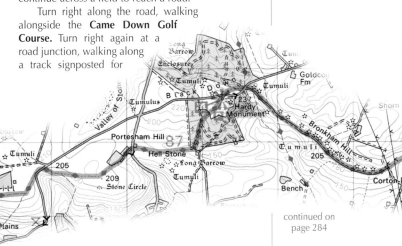

continued on
page 284

Bincombe. When you reach the tiny village, turn left down a road, then left again along a track passing a church. Keep left as signposted for Osmington and follow a track gently uphill across the steep grassy slopes of the combe. Pass under a **pylon line** at the top and go down through a small gate. Swing left and walk down to a road. Turn left and pass a building, then turn right at a

Inland: A gentle, winding track climbs up across steep grassy slopes from Bincombe

road junction for **Sutton Poyntz.**

Turn left as signposted for Osmington and follow another grassy ridgeway path uphill and along the crest of the downs. Turn right along a track after a ruin, and note the **tumuli** dotted around in the fields. Follow the track over **Whitehorse Hill,** where it is possible to divert to the right to see the **White Horse,** ridden by George III, carved on the hillside. Otherwise, continue onwards to find a signpost pointing downhill to the right for Osmington and Lulworth. Walk down the chalk track, flanked by trees at the bottom. Follow a road up into the village of **Osmington,** with lots of thatched houses. Turn left at a crossroads, then right, and reach the main A353 road at **The Sunray** pub. The village has a couple of B&Bs and bus services to Weymouth, Lulworth and Wareham if required.

Turn left along the main road and cross over with care at Craig's Farm Dairy to continue along the footway. Turn right as signposted for Osmington Mills, crossing a small footbridge, then following a field path uphill. Yellow bin lids help you to spot the little stiles on the ascent. Walk down through fields, alongside a campsite, then down through a wooded patch to a road in company with the main Coast Path. Turn right down to Osmington Mills.

OSMINGTON MILLS

Facilities include: limited B&B accommodation and campsite; toilets; 13th-century Smugglers Inn and clifftop café. If buses are needed, there are occasional services back to Weymouth and

ahead to Lulworth. Some buses go from a shop and holiday park up the road, while others need to be joined at Osmington village.

LISTING OF CICERONE GUIDES

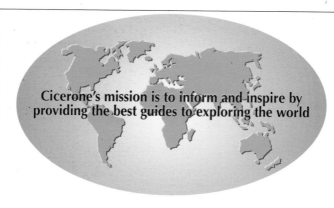

Cicerone's mission is to inform and inspire by providing the best guides to exploring the world

Since its foundation over 30 years ago, Cicerone has specialised in publishing guidebooks and has built a reputation for quality and reliability. It now publishes nearly 300 guides to the major destinations for outdoor enthusiasts, including Europe, UK and the rest of the world.

Written by leading and committed specialists, Cicerone guides are recognised as the most authoritative. They are full of information, maps and illustrations so that the user can plan and complete a successful and safe trip or expedition – be it a long face climb, a walk over Lakeland fells, an alpine traverse, a Himalayan trek or a ramble in the countryside.

With a thorough introduction to assist planning, clear diagrams, maps and colour photographs to illustrate the terrain and route, and accurate and detailed text, Cicerone guides are designed for ease of use and access to the information.

If the facts on the ground change, or there is any aspect of a guide that you think we can improve, we are always delighted to hear from you.

Cicerone Press
2 Police Square Milnthorpe Cumbria LA7 7PY
Tel:01539 562 069   Fax:01539 563 417
e-mail:info@cicerone.co.uk   web:www.cicerone.co.uk